D1590594

LOREN EISELEY

E. Fred Carlisle

LOREN EISELEY
The Development of a Writer

UNIVERSITY OF ILLINOIS PRESS

Urbana Chicago London

Library of Congress Cataloging in Publication Data

Carlisle, E. Fred (Ervin Fred), 1935-
  Loren Eisely—the development of a writer.

  Bibliography: p.
  Includes index.
  1. Eiseley, Loren C, 1907-1977.   2. Authors, American—
20th century—Biography.   3. Anthropologists—United
States—Biography.   I. Title.
  PS3555.178Z6   1983   818'.5409 [B]   82-8459
  ISBN 0-252-00987-8

Grateful acknowledgment is made for permission to use excerpts from the following
copyrighted material:

Loren Eiseley, *All the Strange Hours* (New York: Charles Scribner's Sons, 1975).
Copyright ©1975 by Loren Eiseley. Reprinted with the permission of Charles
Scribner's Sons.

Loren Eiseley, *The Immense Journey* (New York: Random House, 1975). Copyright
© 1946, 1950, 1951, 1953, 1955, 1956, 1957 by Loren Eiseley. Reprinted with the
permission of Random House, Inc.

Loren Eiseley, *The Innocent Assassins* (New York: Charles Scribner's Sons, 1973).
Copyright © 1973 by Loren Eiseley. Reprinted with the permission of Charles
Scribner's Sons.

Loren Eiseley, *The Night Country* (New York: Charles Scribner's Sons, 1971).
Copyright © 1975 by Loren Eiseley. Reprinted with the permission of Charles
Scribner's Sons.

Loren Eiseley, *Notes of an Alchemist* (New York: Charles Scribner's Sons, 1972).
Copyright © 1972 by Loren Eiseley. Reprinted with the permission of Charles
Scribner's Sons.

Loren Eiseley, *The Unexpected Universe* (New York: Harcourt, Brace, and World,
1969). Copyright © 1964, 1966, 1968, 1969 by Loren Eiseley. Reprinted with the
permission of Harcourt Brace Jovanovich, Inc.

For

BARBARA CARLISLE

My best reader

Contents

Preface   ix

1   The Face of the Lion   1

2   An American of the Middle Border   11

3   Death, Drifting, and Depression   21

4   The *Prairie Schooner*   40

5   The Young Poet   57

6   Excavations in a Timeless Land   78

7   The Turn toward Science   94

8   The Writer as Scientist   116

9   The Obituary of a Bone Hunter   138

10   *The Immense Journey*   150

11   The New Idiom   181

Checklist   188

Index   195

Preface

When I began planning this book, I had intended to write some kind of critical biography of Loren Eiseley, but after a series of conversations and a modest correspondence with him, it became clear that my original plan would have to change—more than once. The book that I have finally written draws on all of the literary and biographical sources available to me; through them, it tries to explain Eiseley's development as the writer of a number of eloquent and profound books. I have done research in Nebraska (his home state), Philadelphia (his home for the last thirty years of his life), and New York City. I met with him a number of times to discuss his life and work. In many instances, I have more information than his autobiography provides. But my book is not a biography in the strict sense, nor is it an authorized biography in any sense. Eiseley did not want one written, nor does his widow, Mabel Langdon Eiseley.

My relationship with Loren Eiseley was a curious one. It began in 1973 when I wrote him about his work, expressed my interest in writing about him, and asked to meet him. He replied very cordially, and we arranged a meeting on September 21, 1973. Several months later, Eiseley wrote me that outside the pages of his books, he did not wish to say very much about his personal or private life. It was not altogether clear, however, just what he meant to exclude, because in the same letter he said, ". . . with the above restrictions understood I am willing to help, but only as much as a timid fox whose ears are already badly chewed" (Mar. 23, 1974).

Later, in September, we had a very good conversation in which he talked about many things, some of them personal, and he indicated that at some point I might be able to look at his journals, although he was not very definite. But then in November, 1974, he pretty much withdrew from his offer to help at all. Apparently he was hard at work on his autobiography and did not wish to discuss the parts of his life that he was then writing about. He recalled for me a remark he had made in an earlier letter (Mar. 23, 1974): "Think of me . . . as a dead vagrant in a morgue whose life, if you persist in reporting it, can only be made out by a few bits of impersonal paper in his pocket." And then he said, "The detective story is yours." At that point, I initiated a good deal of additional research, independent of Eiseley.

When I saw him in February, 1975, we had another friendly (and to me encouraging) conversation. He offered to provide me with galleys or page proofs of his autobiography, which he had virtually finished (it was in fact published in October, 1975); he expressed his willingness to expand areas he had touched only lightly in the book; he reminisced a little about the 1930s; and he did say that he trusted me. He also said that I could quote him about his offer to expand on certain parts of his life. In June, my wife and I had dinner with the Eiseleys in Philadelphia, and in September, he sent a long, handwritten letter answering a number of questions I had asked about his poetry and some of the people he knew. Several months later, however, he changed his mind and suggested that we "terminate" the project—presumably, his limited collaboration with me. He added that he did not wish his decision to seem unfriendly or to reflect displeasure on the two essays that I had already written about him, and he ended his letter, "As for hearing about myself or stirring any more deep buried memories, I think it unwise to subject either myself or Mrs. Eiseley to any further excavations" (Jan. 28, 1976).

I made one (at least) tactical error along the way that may have produced the sudden change. I sent a letter to one of Eiseley's former colleagues (someone he had identified in *All the Strange Hours*) asking generally about Eiseley's years at the University of Kansas (1937-44). I wrote without securing Eiseley's permission, and evidently this distressed him a great deal. At that point, he telephoned a number of his friends and asked them not to talk with me about him. Whether I simply made a mistake, violated his privacy, or acted improperly is still not clear to me. My intention was to maintain the integrity of my own work and at the same time write an accurate and fair book. My real error occurred when I assumed that Loren Eiseley *would* at some time reveal things about his life that he did not carefully control or stage. I made an equally significant mistake when I assumed that he was dealing with me in some kind of personal or special way. He was a very private person who had a powerful sense of the public image he wanted to present. And even though I came to care about the man I sensed was there, as well as the author, I could never break through.

Later that year, in August, I believe, I visited him once again, and shortly thereafter he wrote, "It was good to see you and Mrs. Carlisle recently and I will most certainly be happy to be of any help I can and will look forward to hearing from you." Once more I felt encouraged, but by this time he was about to enter the hospital for the first in a series of operations—"surgical exploration," as he called it. I suspected then that he might be dying. I had only one more letter from him.

Three months before his death (he died July 8, 1977), he wrote to tell me of his decision to have his personal papers destroyed. In the same letter, he rejected the possibility of any further conversation or correspondence: "I am adamant in my decision to answer no more questions from anyone." Eiseley assured me that his decision was neither personal nor the product of momentary illness. Nevertheless, he must have been suffering mentally and physically from his operations, his illness, and the prospect of dying. In November, 1977, when I was in Nebraska to speak at the Loren Eiseley Memorial Convocation, I learned through a casual, but pointed, remark by Bertrand Schultz—one of Eiseley's oldest friends—that the papers had in fact ("of course" was what Schultz said) been "incinerated."

As it turns out, not all of Eiseley's papers have been destroyed. There is a substantial collection in the archives at the University of Pennsylvania, as well as the Loren Eiseley Conference Room there containing his library and a collection of his own books. The collection is equally notable for what is missing—notebooks, personal or private correspondence, and so on. It is difficult to tell exactly what has happened—especially now that a few excerpts from the so-called *Lost Nature Notebooks of Loren Eiseley* are being published with Mrs. Eiseley's permission (see the June, 1982, issue of *Omni*).

But I do know what I have done: I have tried to combine literary, scientific, biographical, autobiographical, and historical material with the techniques of literary criticism and scholarship in order to explain how Eiseley came to be the writer and anthropologist he was. In doing so, I have drawn on certain psychological concepts, mainly those of Erik Erikson and Heinz Lichtenstein. Rather than apply these systematically, however, I have used them thematically, letting them inform some of my interpretations but not dominate them. I have also drawn on some of Kenneth Burke's notions about the symbolic nature of language. Through these, I try to show that, to an unusual extent, Eiseley was a man-of-words, a person created and sustained largely through language. In doing all this, I have attempted to make my interpretations accessible to all serious Eiseley readers, rather than just to other critics, scholars, and professors.

Chapters 1 and 2, "The Face of the Lion" and "An American of the Middle Border," explore the way childhood experiences, family history, place, and regional history helped shape Eiseley's personality. Out of that background came a profound sense of place and two strong impulses—escape and survival. Chapter 3, "Death, Drifting, and Depression," continues to explore the relations between personal experience, public events, and Eiseley's home territory by recounting a major identity crisis for Eiseley and his life as a drifter. The fourth and fifth chapters, "The *Prairie Schooner*" and "The Young Poet," explain his literary background and its role in his personal and artistic development. Chapters 6 and 7 take up Eiseley's scientific background and show how his turn to science was a natural psychological and intellectual development. Chapter 8 discusses Eiseley's transition from a writer of rather straightforward scientific papers to the author of more personal and comprehensive essays. The ninth chapter, "The Obituary of a Bone Hunter," focuses on the critical events that marked his transformation into the author of *The Immense Journey*. The tenth chapter discusses *The Immense Journey* at some length. I speak briefly about its publication and reception, but mainly show how Eiseley drew on all of his experience and knowledge to create this re-

markable book. In the last chapter, "The New Idiom," I summarize
the features of his unique style and the essential role of language in
his life.

In his final letter to me, Loren Eiseley left me with this ad-
monition: "I sincerely hope that if you are a friend of mine you will
understand my motivation and try, if you must write a critique, to
leave the author out of it." He was dead within three months. I
have thought a great deal about what he said, and to this day I am
not sure how I could have complied. I have written about Eiseley,
but I have not left the author out. He did not, so how could I? He
put himself in his books over and over and more and more as the
years passed, until it just does not seem possible to read Loren
Eiseley's books without in fact reading Loren Eiseley. *Am* I his
friend or not? I would like to believe that in some larger sense I am.
But the answer may be important only to me.

I would like to acknowledge the quarterlies and reviews in which
the poetry and prose by Loren Eiseley that I have used first
appeared: *Prairie Schooner*, the *Midland, Voices, Poetry,* and the
American Mercury. I am also grateful to Charles Scribner's Sons,
Harcourt Brace Jovanovich, Inc., and Random House, Inc., for
allowing me to quote from their books by Eiseley.

Joseph G. Svoboda, University Archivist, University of Nebraska—Lincoln, kindly granted me permission to quote from Eiseley's
letters in the Lowry C. Wimberly Collection. For making certain
other library and museum materials available to me, I would like to
thank Francis James Dallett, Hamilton Y. Elliot, Jr., and Maryellen
Cook Kaminsky of the University of Pennsylvania Archives; Robert
Boyce, formerly of the University of Nebraska Library; Lloyd
Tanner and the staff of the Nebraska State Museum; Anne K.
Reinert and James E. Potter of the Nebraska Historical Society;
Harold Helfrich, Director of the News Bureau, University of Penn-
sylvania; and Jean Adelman of the University of Pennsylvania
Museum Library.

I would like to thank C. Bertrand Schultz for a day of conversation and a fascinating tour of the Nebraska State Museum
holdings, where we were joined by Mylan Stout. I am indebted, as

well, to many other acquaintances and friends of Loren Eiseley, many of whom are acknowledged in the notes.

For invaluable assistance early in my research, I wish to thank James H. Pickering. Jana L. Carlisle assisted at several points. Roger K. Meiners, James McClintock, and Douglas L. Peterson provided helpful early readings of the manuscript. For close and very helpful criticism, I also thank Miles Richardson and Gale H. Carrithers, Jr.

Shirley Kirkland provided invaluable typing and editing assistance. I am grateful to Judith McCulloh, Senior Editor of the University of Illinois Press. She indeed kept the faith and made sure that I did. Her editorial support and advice have been excellent.

My wife, Barbara Carlisle, has provided intelligence, insight, and support from the beginning.

Loren Eiseley

The Face of the Lion

How does one choose one's life?

In "The Face of the Lion," a poem published in 1972, Loren Eiseley journeys far back into his past to recover a few fragments of his childhood. As he digs into those depths, the days and hours of over sixty years fade away before a series of painful images. The poem speaks of frequent quarrels between his parents and the home "where little kindness was." It describes the way Eiseley lay crying in the darkness of his room, clutching his stuffed lion in fear. He lay silent and sleepless, waiting for light—for morning or for something to change. But "no light ever came," and so he and his lion fell asleep, only to awaken once more to loneliness. Silent, fearful, frustrated, the child had no way to speak his distress, no way to stop the quarrels, and no way to bring love into his family or peace and security to himself.

Eiseley can barely go back to those experiences, as he says in the poem:

> I cannot practice
> the terrible archaeology of the brain
> nor plumb
> one simple childhood thought. I want no light to shine
> into those depths forever. . . .[1]

But he does, with difficulty, and accompanied only by the lion—an image of the resources that enabled him to survive.

Eiseley seems to have written the poem and his autobiography at about the same time, and even though he does plumb those depths at some length in the autobiography, he does so hesitantly, painfully, and selectively. The parts about his childhood and his years at the University of Nebraska were especially difficult for him to write. The times were very far away, and only remnants remained; yet those fragments had a powerful emotional presence. As much as he might have wished to ignore his childhood and youth, he could not.

Sometimes he did not even wish to avoid that period and longed, instead, to return. In "The Mist of the Mountain,"[2] Eiseley speaks about the warmth and security of his childhood home and appeals to his parents to take him back, "even though life was harsh." Once again, he is years away as he speaks. This time he is standing outside "a drab house at the edge of town" looking in at himself, sitting at the kitchen table with his father and mother. It is warm and safe there; at least it appears so to a man who, for the moment, longs to turn away from the complexities of age and the nearness of death:

> I have rushed like a moth through time
> > toward the light in the kitchen.
> I am safe now. I never grew up.
> I am no longer lost in the mist of the mountain.

Although at the end he imagines he has returned, the poem, in fact, reveals the radical separation of the aging man from the five-year-old boy. The past haunts him, but time has cut him off from it forever. Ironically, the poet may be doubly deprived. Not only is he unable to return; the harmony he imagines may never have existed. In a sense, Eiseley longs for two impossibilities: the suspension and even reversal of time and the restoration of nonexistent peace and harmony.

From these late poems, we can sense something of the emotional content of Loren Eiseley's childhood. Very early in his life he started running mentally, trying to escape. Lonely, anxious, and impoverished, he kept hoping for love, and that desire turned into a lifelong search for his real home and his true identity.

Eiseley remembers his parents' marriage as simply "unfortunate."[3] Not only were there frightening quarrels; there was no kindness or tenderness, only the "fierce" love they somehow shared: "I never learned what had attracted my father to her. I never learned by what fantastic chance I had come to exist at all."[4] Eiseley recalls only that once she had been very beautiful, and somehow that must explain it. The same account speaks of his mother's deafness and describes her "harsh, discordant, jangling" voice. Elsewhere, he writes about "her gift to make others suffer."[5] He speaks of her "petulant violence,"[6] her quarrelsomeness, arbitrariness, hysteria; he describes her as a witch.[7] It takes little effort to imagine the effect of that voice and personality—itself harsh and jangling—or to hear Eiseley's anger and resentment toward his mother and affection for his father. Had it not been for her extreme oddness, her derangement and irrationality, perhaps their family would not have been so isolated, so rejected, and the child himself so alone and deprived.

His own conscious memory of his mother and his parents' marriage goes back to an incident like the one he describes in "The Face of the Lion." He recalls his parents' endless pacing and quarreling late at night while he lay in bed trying to hear what they were saying. Once he asked them to stop. "A small toddler, I climbed from bed and seized their hands, pleading wordlessly for sleep, for peace, peace. And surprisingly they relented, even my unfortunate mother."[8]

Elsewhere in *All the Strange Hours* and *The Night Country*, he reveals other troubling experiences with his mother. Recalling the time a neighborhood bully had beaten his face bloody, Eiseley explains that after his own rage and frantic blows had actually chased the other boy away, he turned homeward, "but not for succor." When he got there, his mother saw his face and became hysterical. He turned away, as he "always" did. His mother could give no comfort or kindness, and he was learning not to ask for any.[9] One day, when Eiseley was still a young boy, ten at the most, his father warned him not to mistreat her. "'Your mother is not responsible, son. Do not cross her. Do you understand?'"[10] The boy's promise could not last forever, and he remembers breaking it shortly thereafter by cruelly defying her in front of a gang of boys he was playing with. She commanded him to come home, and he refused:

> Slowly I turned and looked at my companions. Their faces could not be read. They simply waited, doubtless waited for me to break the apron strings that rested lightly and tolerably upon themselves. And so in the end I broke my father's injunction; I ran, and with me

ran my childish companions, over fences, tumbling down haystacks, chuckling, with the witch, her hair flying, her clothing disarrayed, stumbling after. Escape, escape, the first stirring of the running man. Miles of escape.

Of course she gave up. Of course she never caught us. Walking home alone in the twilight I was bitterly ashamed. Ashamed for the violation of my promise to my father. Ashamed at what I had done to my savage and stone-deaf mother who could not grasp the fact that I had to make my way in a world unknown to her. Ashamed for the story that would penetrate the neighborhood. Ashamed for my own weakness. Ashamed, ashamed.[11]

Such defiance is quite normal for a ten-year-old, but Eiseley's great need to escape and Daisy Eiseley's handicap and severe neurosis make this conflict—indeed, his whole relationship with her—particularly intense and telling. His mother loved him in her strange and fierce way, but in truth, she did not know how to love him. Young Eiseley's defiance speaks as much about her fundamental rejection and betrayal of him as about his desire to escape her control.

By his early twenties, Eiseley understood that his mother "was paranoid, neurotic, and unstable."[12] His final judgment of her, expressed when he recounted her death (Daisy Corey Eiseley died in a nursing home in Lincoln on November 27, 1959), seems even harsher: "Her whole paranoid existence from the time of my childhood had been spent in the deliberate distortion and exploitation of the world about her."[13] He thinks of her as a "center of violence and contention" whose influence, even at her death, was "still spreading toward infinity even in the lives of those who had never known her in life."[14]

After his mother died, Eiseley went to Lincoln to claim memorabilia and objects that were his, but he found only a few things, among them a picture of his mother, at age six, and her sister taken in Dyersville, Iowa, his mother's birthplace. "Here on this faded porch it had begun," he reflects, "the long crucifixion of life"[15]— hers as well as his. Eiseley claims that he was no longer bitter—what good would it do?—and he is not entirely without sympathy or sensitivity to her pain. He admires her courage, and he recognizes how agonizing life had been for her. Yet he lost her without ever having had her, and his own pain and the scars from their relationship possessed him until the end of his life. She had deprived him of language, or at least of normal language development. She had produced profound fears and then deprived him of warmth, tenderness, peace—of a mother's love. He blamed her even for his own childlessness. Small wonder that Eiseley felt she had betrayed him.

By contrast, his father gave him far more. Clyde Eiseley had a "great genius for love"[16] and a beautiful voice that brought sound, words, and poetry into the silence of the boy's life. Rich as that relationship must have been, Eiseley experienced another form of poverty through his father. Clyde was an economic failure, and throughout Loren's childhood the family was very poor.

When Eiseley describes his parents' marriage as unfortunate, he is thinking of his father. It was unfortunate for *him*, and he could, Eiseley believes, "easily have fled, leaving me inarticulate."[17] But he did not. The patience, love, and commitment he demonstrated suggest the elder Eiseley's stability in emotional and human matters. Eiseley remembers his father as kind, thoughtful, courteous, and mild—a powerful stabilizing and enriching influence.

Eiseley wrote less about his father than about his mother, but the man's presence and Eiseley's love and respect for him permeate his books and were reflected in his conversations with me. He could not speak about his father without being visibly moved. When Eiseley was five years old, in 1912, there was a prison break in Nebraska. Three prisoners killed the warden and his deputy, blew open the gates with nitroglycerin, and escaped into a winter blizzard. Their freedom did not last long, but the details are less important than Eiseley's memory of how his father reacted. Clyde Eiseley regretted that the escapees would not make it and seemed, somehow, to be "out there in the snow" with them. The paper naturally reported them as wrongdoers, and the boy mentioned this to his father. "'But papa, . . . the papers say they are bad men. They killed the warden.'" "'Yes, son,' he said heavily. Then he paused, censoring his words carefully. 'There are also bad prisons and bad wardens.'"[18] Trapped in the prisonhouse of a terrible marriage, as Eiseley believed, his father must have identified deeply with the prisoners' desire to be free. Eventually, that 1912 prison break became an important symbol for the son, and in his autobiography he, too, identifies with Tom Murray, the leader—but that is another and later part of the story.

The elder Eiseley may once have been an actor; at least the son accounts for his father's remarkable voice and talent for language that way. He describes him as "a strolling itinerant actor in his younger years." Unclear as that is and suggestive even of a kind of unsettledness, the power of his voice and the worlds his words opened for Loren are very clear: "He could still declaim long rolling Elizabethan passages that caused shivers to run up my back."[19] Although they had few books (at one point Eiseley says they "owned no books"), his father gave him the excitement of language and probably the desire to find words for himself; and when he could, his father gave him books and encouraged him to read. Years later, Eiseley recalled with more warmth than usual the way books softened the pain of those years:

> One thing which touches me deeply in my memories of my parents is that, although we were poor, I was allowed a little library of my own and that there entered into our household a warmth from the ownership of books such as each of us should cherish and grow old with. With all due recognition of the great libraries which served me through the years, nothing has strengthened the love of books in my heart so much as the little handful of personally owned volumes which first opened to me the doorways of the world.[20]

For all his father's positive influence, however, it is not possible to overlook his problems. Eiseley himself called his father a failure: "I will merely say he had had a great genius for love and that his luck was very bad."[21] As a young adult, Clyde had lost a wife he loved very much and then, later, married an afflicted woman. His other misfortune was in Nebraska "under the yellow cloud," doing work for which he was not suited—selling hardware. In Lincoln he clerked in two hardware stores, F. C. Lahr's and H. C. Wittman's, and at other times, apparently, he traveled.[22]

Perhaps bad luck is the simple explanation, or there may have been something in the father's character to make him a worldly failure. The family moved fairly often when Eiseley was young— Lincoln, Fremont, Aurora. Wherever they lived, they seemed to be outsiders—not only poor, but considered odd and rejected as well. His mother's emotional instability, and thus the family's, and the economic instability that plagued his father, and so the family, placed an incredible burden on the child. It is not surprising that he often wondered how he survived.

Then there is his fathers' death—the most painful loss of Eiseley's conscious life. Unbearable as it was, even after almost fifty years, he did write about it, and he would talk, but reluctantly, briefly, and sadly. In 1956, writing about it for the first time, he describes his distress and the way his grandmother helped salvage his sanity.[23] He was drawn back to that death again in *The Unexpected Universe*, where he describes watching the last moments his father lived.[24] Then, in *All the Strange Hours*, he writes at comparative length about his father's acute suffering as he "died by inches" and about his own sense of helplessness, wondering afterward if he should have tried to quicken his father's death and end the suffering. The pain of that experience and Eiseley's lifelong sense of loss speak for both his love and his gratitude.

Still, in this relationship, Eiseley felt that he did not fully belong. There was a half brother, Leo, fourteen years his senior, the first son, born of a youthful and happy first marriage. Loren was the second, late son, of a second and troubled marriage. Even at Clyde Eiseley's deathbed, Leo took precedence, for it was to recognize him that the elder Eiseley struggled back from the edge of death. "Slowly, to my boundless surprise, the dying man's eyes, indifferent to me for many hours, opened. There was an instant of recognition between the two of them, from which I was excluded. My father had come back an infinite distance for that meeting. It was wordless"[25]

Two worlds seem to be emerging from this account. In Eiseley's words, "one was dark, hidden, and self-examining, though in its own way not without compensations. The other world in which I somehow also managed to exist was external, boisterous, and what I suppose the average parent would call normal or extroverted."[26] He was driven into the first, a world of "utter and profound loneliness,"[27] partly by his mother's affliction and the extreme solitude of his childhood; sometimes he would go out into a Great Plains blizzard so that no one could find him just thirty feet away.[28] He was given the inner, contemplative part of that world by the words, books, and thoughts of his father. His mother also drove him into the second; he had to escape and once in a while directly

defy her. And his father gave him another part of that second
world as well by his example: he was a failure only in the worldly
sense, "not . . . as a man."[29]

Besides his parents, there were a few others in his life, but even
his friendships seemed to underscore his solitariness. Eiseley writes
at more length about "the Rat" than anyone. He met this friend,
just after the Eiseleys moved to Aurora, Nebraska. In Loren the
Rat must have recognized a fellow loner, for he spoke to Eiseley on
the day he moved in and then invited him to join "their gang of
cavemen." For one of the first times in his life, Eiseley felt that he
"belonged to something at last." As "cavemen," they inhabited
Aurora's underground sewers, and while there must have been
several boys, Eiseley talks only about himself and the Rat—two
solitaries who explored the silent and empty underground of their
town. "That was the world we lived in. We never told Mother, and
we avoided Father. We scrounged our own candles; we dragged
food into those abysses. We scratched tribal symbols on the big
tiles by candlelight, as the Rat directed. We raided other bands and
retreated through the sewer network."[30] Within a few months after
they met, the Rat died, leaving Eiseley alone once more.

Most of the other autobiographical incidents he relates simply
reflect isolation and loneliness. When he was very young, for
example, he played by himself in the sand and gravel at a construction site near his home. "No other child on the block," he
observes, "wasted his time like that."[31] Later, during elementary
school, he found a book about home aquariums at the Lincoln City
Library and from it learned how to construct his own. He spent
many hours building, populating, and caring for his aquariums,
and he kept them for many years. Not once does he mention that
others were involved with him.[32] As a nine- or ten-year-old boy,
Eiseley spent hours wandering through the University of Nebraska
museum. Impressed with the drawings of skulls, depicting the
evolution of man, Eiseley molded and baked clay heads in the
kitchen stove at home in imitation of those in the museum: "Practically everything I made was slope-browed and primitive."[33] They
had "that Darwin look," as his grandmother said. In a nearby
unused barn, Eiseley set up his own "museum." He climbed into
the loft and placed his heads along crossbeams up under the roof.
But again, except for his grandmother, who rather distrusted the

museum and the heads, no one else was involved; no one else knew.

For all these difficulties, a few things did enrich his early life, and they were decisive. His father gave him language, and language helped establish his autonomy. It enabled him to ask about many things; it provided a way to expand his imagination and conceive of real futures; and it gave him the possibility of reaching other people. Ultimately, words would help him constitute his mature identity as a writer and scientist. Clyde Eiseley also gave him love at a critical point. This enabled Eiseley to offset, to some extent, the psychological effects of his relationship with his mother. He was not so mistrustful, depressive, disabled in personal relations, or estranged as he might otherwise have been. Even the solitude of his young life—one of its "disadvantages"—contributed in the end to his productive and very successful career as an anthropologist and a man of language.

NOTES

1. Loren Eiseley, *Notes of an Alchemist* (New York: Charles Scribner's Sons, 1972), p. 23.
2. Loren Eiseley, *The Innocent Assassins* (New York: Charles Scribner's Sons, 1973), p. 113.
3. Loren Eiseley, *The Night Country* (New York: Charles Scribner's Sons, 1971), p. 199.
4. Ibid., p. 197.
5. Loren Eiseley, *All the Strange Hours* (New York: Charles Scribner's Sons, 1975), p. 24.
6. Ibid., p. 5.
7. Ibid., pp. 226-30.
8. Ibid., p. 26.
9. Ibid., p. 32.
10. Ibid.
11. Ibid., p. 34.
12. Ibid., p. 24.
13. Ibid., p. 229.
14. Ibid.
15. Loren Eiseley, *The Unexpected Universe* (New York: Harcourt, Brace and World, 1969), p. 86.
16. *Night Country*, p. 199.
17. Ibid., p. 199.

18. *All the Strange Hours*, p. 174.
19. *Night Country*, p. 198.
20. Interviews Box, Loren Corey Eiseley Papers (UPT 50 E36), University of Pennsylvania Archives (cited hereafter as Penn Archives).
21. *Night Country*, p. 199.
22. Lincoln, Neb., city directories, 1916-28.
23. "One Night's Dying," *Night Country*, pp. 169-78. Published originally as "Endure the Night," *Atlantic Monthly*, 211, no. 6 (June, 1963), 75-78.
24. "The Innocent Fox," *Unexpected Universe*, pp. 194-212.
25. *All the Strange Hours*, p. 15.
26. *Night Country*, p. 195.
27. Ibid, p. 196.
28. *All the Strange Hours*, p. 145.
29. *Night Country*, p. 199.
30. Ibid., p. 21.
31. *All the Strange Hours*, p. 29.
32. Ibid., pp. 168-69.
33. *Night Country*, p. 95.

2

An American of the Middle Border

> We were Americans of the middle border
> where the East was forgotten and the
> one great western road no longer
> crawled with wagons.

Sometimes, when Loren Eiseley thought about his family's history, and not just his own home life, he wondered about his survival and especially how he could "have absorbed a code by which to live."[1] His ancestors were pioneers and settlers in the Nebraska Territory. They were wanderers, and like others who had left their homes, they were seeking something different. Their lives necessarily retained some of this unsettled and rootless quality, even after they established new homes. On homestead farms and in small towns alike, the new territory promised little but hard work, high risks, and frequent hardship. Many homesteaders failed and had to return eventually to their original homes, go further west, or resettle in the towns. Those in town risked a great deal, too, for their livelihoods often depended on the prosperity of the farms or on the future of new but marginal communities. Like many farms, not every town survived.

On the farms, people led lonely and solitary lives with only occasional social contacts. In town, because of the uncertainties, they did not always have a strong sense of community either. The traditions the early Nebraskans had to rely on were those they brought with them—their ethnic, religious, folk, and linguistic traditions. But in an unsettled territory, these displaced traditions could not provide quite the same order, meaning, and security as they had originally.

This past is part of Loren Eiseley's family and regional heritage, and it is also the history of American frontier and pioneering life. When Eiseley describes himself as an American of the middle border, he doubtless has this in mind, and he also may be thinking of the home this history in fact gave him. His ancestors *did* settle, thereby giving Eiseley a place, a personal territory that he would explore first as a boy, then as a poet, later as an anthropologist, and finally as a prose writer and a poet once more. That place is the pond where he gathered specimens for his aquariums; it is the small towns and fields of eastern Nebraska, an agricultural territory where life has been hard, the historical habitat of extinct bison; it is a record of man's past; it is, in short, the world. As he explored, he found the land both hostile and homely. Like nature itself, the plains were harsh, and they tried to overpower him and everyone else; but they were also home—the place that bore and sustained him, the land that helped shape his sense of the physical and natural world and, over time, his very identity. He came to have almost a mythical sense of his origins: "I was a child of the early century, American man, if the term may still be tolerated. A creature molded of plains' dust and the seed of those who came west with the wagons."[2]

Charles Frederick Eiseley, the grandfather of Loren Eiseley, emigrated from Germany in 1853 and arrived in the Nebraska Territory in 1858. After the 1848 political upheavals in Germany, many Germans had come to America. They made up the first large group of immigrants to settle in Nebraska. Eiseley's grandfather homesteaded in the territory, and in less than twenty years built a substantial farm. In 1874 he moved to Hooper and started a hardware and implement business that apparently prospered. An important town citizen, he served in both territorial and state legislatures.[3]

At that time Nebraska was a new territory, and the people who went there were indeed pioneers. Before 1860, only the eastern edge, along the Missouri River, had been settled, and very little of the land had been broken for farming. According to Willa Cather, the towns were mere settlements—"straggling groups of log houses, hidden away along the wooded river banks," and "Lincoln . . . was open prairie."[4] Evidently Eiseley's ancestor arrived almost with the first. Even by the mid-1880s, the center of the state was mostly prairie, "raw prairie. The cultivated fields and broken land seemed mere scratches in the brown, running steppe that never stopped until it broke against the foothills of the Rockies. The dugouts and sod farmhouses were three or four miles apart, and the only means of communication was the heavy farm wagon, drawn by heavy work horses."[5] To the end of the century, there were still lands to settle, and even in the first decade of Loren Eiseley's life, a new homestead act was passed to encourage the agricultural development of northwest Nebraska.[6]

During the 1870s, the state's population more than doubled, as many took land under the original homestead act and started to farm. For the most part, they extended conventional, humid-region farming methods westward, often into marginal and sub-marginal land. The farming was relatively large scale, and that required money and machines and thus forced farmers deep into debt. Although optimism grew as new farms and towns appeared, many homesteaders were vulnerable—exposed by debt and then gradually defeated by drought and depression. The Panic of 1873 swept across the region, and agricultural prices fell. Rainfall diminished to below normal amounts. And then in the mid-1870s, the prairies were overrun by hordes of grasshoppers that ate virtually everything: "Where they alighted they covered the ground like a heavy crawling carpet. Growing crops disappeared in a single day. Trees were stripped of leaves. Potatoes, turnips, and onions were pursued into the earth. Clothing and harness were cut into shreds if left exposed. Wheat and oats were mostly in the shock, but the grasshoppers covered the shocks, cut the bands, and gnawed the grain."[7]

Many farmers became destitute and either sold or gave away their claims and returned east. The situation became so bad that the governor formed a citizens' group to establish a relief agency. But before the problems could be solved, circumstances changed: the grasshoppers disappeared, the state entered a wet cycle, and the national economy improved. Agricultural production in Nebraska increased, and immigration, which had virtually stopped, began once more. The farmers' relative economic situation, however, continued to worsen, even through a period of relative prosperity. One could trace a continuing cycle, of boom and growth through the first half of the 1880s, and then another sharp decline and severe depression in the 1890s. The point is simply that homesteaders often led marginal and uncertain lives, depending on uncontrollable cycles of prosperity and depression and rain and drought. Many could not survive.

Faced with building homes in a territory without conventional materials, they covered wooden inner frames with bricks cut from tough prairie sod. Some dwellings were no more than caves; others were more conventional one- or even two-story houses. The severe winters created a serious fuel problem. With practically no wood and only very expensive coal, settlers were forced to scrounge for other burnables. It was not easy to obtain a good supply of water, either. Sometimes it could be found only by drilling very deep and very expensive wells. The difficulties of day-to-day living were great enough, not to speak of the problems of farming. But the most taxing feature of that life was the loneliness—severe enough for the men, virtually unbearable for the women.[8]

Although many homesteaders failed, some did not. Those who stayed and succeeded, like Loren Eiseley's paternal grandfather, must have been sturdy and tenacious—as well as lucky. They were rugged, proud, and willing to make the best of their hard lives. "I have always the hope," Willa Cather stated, "that something went into the ground with those pioneers that will one day come out again, something that will come out not only in sturdy traits of character, but in elasticity of mind, in an honest attitude toward the realities of life, in certain qualities of feeling and imagination."[9] They settled, overcame, and eventually farmed the land successfully.

Although Loren Eiseley says virtually nothing about his own family's early history—where his grandfather homesteaded, when he moved to town to open his business, what happened to the property and the money, how his own father ended up poor—it is difficult to imagine such a sensitive, solitary, thoughtful child growing up in Nebraska without absorbing a strong sense of the land and its history. He did in fact recall stories about how tough the country was, recounting, for example, that "in his young years, my own father had carried a gun and remembered the gamblers at the green tables in the cow towns."[10] He may have heard about the farms, too. Since that history was fairly recent, Eiseley absorbed it in other ways as well. As part of Nebraska's physical and psychological topology in the first two decades of the twentieth century, it slipped into his mind almost unknowingly, mysteriously becoming part of his dreams: "I dream inexplicably at times of a gathering of wagons, of women in sunbonnets and blackgarbed, bewhiskered men. Then I wake and the scene dissolves."[11]

But family and regional history alone did not shape Eiseley's consciousness and imagination. His own early years in Lincoln and in the small towns and fields of eastern Nebraska gave him his first concrete and immediate sense of place. When he spent hours sifting through sand and gravel at construction sites on his street, he was, in effect, touching and collecting the physical things around him and feeding a curiosity about the earth. When he gathered specimens for his aquariums, he went to streams and ponds he knew well. In those days, "the countryside was open,"[12] and there were wide spaces where he could roam. In Aurora, with his friend the Rat and his "comrades of the fields,"[13] he not only learned the intricate maze of the sewers in town, but he and his friends also dug caves and ranged over the surrounding farmland. Once Eiseley made a small cemetery where he buried dead birds and then placed small gold crosses over them, thus in his own way participating in their life and death. None of these boyhood adventures is insignificant. Besides the special impact each may have had, they were establishing within him a sense of what places are like; they were also crucially shaping his sense of himself, for identity, body, and inhabited space cannot be easily divided.

While experiences below ground in the dark and out in the fields and along streams gave him the solitude and protection he needed, those boyhood places were not altogether friendly. The sewers were dangerous, and violence lurked outside of town or on the way home from school. In his own small world, Eiseley was continuing to discover both a friendly and a hostile territory, just as he did in his childhood encounters with other persons and at home.

Eiseley spent most of his childhood and youth in Lincoln, where he was born, grew up, attended school, and went to college, and so it became the most important place in his life. After rapid economic and cultural growth in the 1890s, the city had become a relatively dynamic and lively state capital by 1920, one of the major cities in the state. It had grown to 55,000 people; its economy was prosperous, and it continued to expand and build. The Eiseleys probably did not benefit from very much of this, but Lincoln could provide a child with many escapes and new experiences that a primarily rural or small-town environment might not. Loren seemed especially to benefit from the university, which had developed into a considerable midwestern school, and the Nebraska State Museum.

Since the beginning of the century, the museum had been developing extensive collections of fossils and natural history exhibits. Most of the objects had been found in Nebraska, which was an especially rich source for North American natural history.[14] The museum began to focus and inform Eiseley's fascination with the natural world and give it a historical dimension. Although it probably served at first mainly as an escape, the museum also gave him an image of a possible future—one, obviously, that he later chose.

Living in Lincoln with such ready access to the countryside, Eiseley would have had the experience of both the country—the fields and solitude he came to value—and a midwestern city—a comparatively active and intellectually exciting place. He internalized the landscape outside Lincoln, along with the psychic patterns he developed in relationship to it. I am speaking, for example, of the relationship between solitude and loneliness and spaces where there are few, if any, other people; of the correlation between needs to escape and hide and spaces where one can conceal himself; of the relationship between a pervasive sense of loss and deprivation and spaces that are either harsh and barren or dark and close, where he might find peace; and of the connection between Eiseley's early desires for freedom and the open, fairly unbroken space around Lincoln.

By contrast, just as Lincoln enriched the physical and intellectual landscape of Nebraska, the city filled some of the barren spaces of Eiseley's childhood and youth. Although Lincoln probably also provided space for escape and freedom, and thus functioned psychically in ways similar to the countryside, by enriching Eiseley's impoverished world it became more a complement to the fields and prairies. Lincoln shaped Eiseley's inner city space and determined to some extent the way he would be in city situations.

He internalized, however, a specific Nebraska city and not just the idea of "city" or even of "university town." It is critical, for example, that Lincoln was a comparatively small place, as cities go—simple, conservative, relatively quiet, and part of the prairie— with that particular museum and university; and it is equally important that those open spaces were nearby. These two dimensions of Eiseley's landscape—the prairie and the town—express something of his ambivalence toward places and people. He longed for intimacy and friends; yet he required solitude and privacy to survive. He grew up in a family and a city and longed to escape their confinement; yet he required some society and status to live.

Even after living in Philadelphia for thirty years, he did not feel at home and remained suspicious of the East and its people. There were no prairies, no big sky, no *spaces*. He never completely recovered from the shock of his first move to Philadelphia: "Suddenly the noise, the cacophony of horns, became nerve-shattering." He had, it is true, just "spent a long summer in the silences of vanished geological eras," and so the immediate contrast did disorient him: "The urban world was, for the moment, unendurable to me."[15] But he had also spent a long childhood in silences broken only by the harshness of his mother's voice and then by the sound of his father's voice. Other sounds—of the prairie and its sleepy towns and a relatively quiet city—came later. In Philadelphia that autumn, hearing initially only the harsh sounds, he became understandably anxious. His tolerance for city noise increased, but only in terms of the inner space he carried with him from Nebraska.

As late as 1900, northwestern Nebraska was still undeveloped. With the passage in 1904 of a new homestead act (the Kinkaid Act, which provided for larger homesteads than the original law), the northwest opened to a new surge of settlers, and by 1920 the population had about doubled in the thirty-seven counties involved.[16] The expansion occurred mainly in the first decade and a half of Eiseley's life. The experiences of the Kinkaiders, as they were called, largely repeated the failures and successes of the pioneers in central Nebraska during the 1870s and 1880s. Many who tried to raise cattle discovered that even the larger tracts provided by law were inadequate. Those who tried general farming soon realized that the land was submarginal, and many of them failed. Daily life was equally as difficult in tar-paper shacks and sod houses there as it had been in the center of the state. Some succeeded (those able to dry farm or obtain enough additional land for grazing), or at least they survived; but their lives were still very hard.

Even as Eiseley grew up, pioneer history was repeating itself not far west from him, not far from the spaces of his consciousness. And then, a few years later, something else happened to reinforce

his sense of prairie life. For many years, agriculture had had a
cyclical history of hard times and prosperity; the pioneer experience in northwest Nebraska fit the pattern. But even where farming
had become more developed or advanced, the cycles continued,
and the only consistent trend through them was the steady erosion
of the farmer's economic position.

During World War I agriculture enjoyed a temporary prosperity,
but in the early 1920s the good times suddenly collapsed. While
prices improved somewhat later in the decade, the twenties were
basically depression years for Nebraska farmers. "When the crash
inevitably followed in the early twenties," a state guide observed,
"it was not only the shiftless farmers who were trapped by fore-
closure or crushing indebtedness. Some of the steadiest of conservative, hard-working farmers are still [1939] struggling against
hopelessly large mortgages."[17] The crash occurred when Loren
Eiseley was in his midteens and in high school, and it affected his
family directly. Clyde Eiseley had difficulty keeping a job because
of the severe economic decline everywhere in the state.

By his early twenties, Loren Eiseley was writing poems like "The
Deserted Homestead" (see chap. 5) that reflected his sensitivity to
the hardships of farm life and the harshness of the land. At the
same time, he expressed a strong sense of attachment to the prairie
in poems like "Coyote Country" (see chap. 5). He did not find these
feelings and attitudes just when he started college. Their roots were
formed in early childhood and developed throughout his youth.

In Eiseley's home, natural conflicts, normal differences between
parents, and childhood feelings of ambivalence were intensified by
his mother's pathology and his extreme isolation. His home was in
fact more threatening than inviting, and the longing, fear, and
revulsion this seemed to inspire forced Eiseley to start running for
survival. When he did, he sought refuge in other places, but most of
these turned out to be threatening as well as inviting. While they
offered refuge and freedom, they were often also hard, difficult,
and lonely.

When his experiences of place widened, he found that on the
land people cringed and struggled to survive, just as he had at
home. For them the land *was* home, and so they became deeply
attached to it, just as Eiseley was always attached to both his home

and the region. But it was a hard land, and it defeated many people. Each new place became for Eiseley both a new experience and a repetition of old ones. In each he found the extreme contrasts of his home, the radical polarities of his childhood, and many of his feelings of ambivalence.

Heinz Lichtenstein proposes that identity establishment and maintenance are basic biological principles, and he argues that identity maintenance takes priority over any other human behavior. For once identity breaks down, nothing is possible for an individual; he is simply failing to survive as a human being.[18] Without other clear explanations for why Eiseley made it through, and flourished, this one helps considerably. He lived for many years in a relatively marginal situation where identity maintenance was his primary task. As he struggled, his desire to survive became stronger and more tenacious.

Historically, certain organisms have demonstrated a greater than normal capacity for biological survival. Though marked and scarred, they somehow wriggle through hostile environments and eventually grow and even initiate new species. Loren Eiseley must have possessed such a greater than normal capacity; surely some others would not have survived, at least not so remarkably. During his childhood and youth, however, survival was problematic, as it was for some time thereafter.

Eiseley captures that sense of the future in a story about an abandoned house where another Eiseley family, unknown to him, had apparently lived in the 1890s. He doubts that anyone will believe the story (and one does wonder if it is not more symbolic than actual), but he found there a pair of dice and began rolling them. "I did not know how adults played. I merely cast and cast again, making up my own game as I played." He sensed that he was playing for some kind of stakes, but he wasn't sure. "I played, and here memory fails me. I think I played against the universe as the universe was represented by the wind, stirring papers on the plaster strewn floor. I played against time . . . I played for adventure and escape. Then clutching the dice . . . I fled frantically down the leaf-sodden unused road, never to return."[19] The solitary boy played dice in the midst of a ruined farmhouse—an image perhaps of his family's history and, at the same time, of his own possible future. He played alone against family, history, and place, and then he fled, not knowing how the game would turn out. That lonely game and frantic flight are Eiseley's early life.

NOTES

1. *All the Strange Hours*, p. 26.
2. Ibid., p. 25.
3. *History of Nebraska* (Chicago, 1882), p. 669.
4. Willa Cather, *Roundup: A Nebraska Reader* (Lincoln: University of Nebraska Press, 1957), pp. 1-2.
5. Ibid., p. 4.
6. The historical details in this chapter are based on Neale Copple, *Tower on the Plains: Lincoln's Centennial History, 1859-1959* (Lincoln, Nebr.: Lincoln Centennial Commission Publishers, 1959); Federal Writers' Project, *Nebraska: A Guide to the Cornhusker State* (New York: Viking, 1939); and James C. Olson, *History of Nebraska* (Lincoln: University of Nebraska Press, 1955).
7. Olson, *History of Nebraska*, p. 181.
8. Ibid., p. 214.
9. Cather, *Roundup*, p. 6.
10. *All the Strange Hours*, p. 26.
11. Ibid., pp. 26-27.
12. Ibid., p. 169.
13. Ibid., p. 33.
14. Erwin H. Barbour, "A New Rhinocerous Mount," *Bulletin of the University of Nebraska State Museum*, 1 (1924), p. 38.
15. *All the Strange Hours*, p. 87.
16. Olson, *History of Nebraska*, pp. 268-69.
17. *Nebraska: A Guide*, p. 78
18. Heinz Lichtenstein, *The Dilemma of Human Identity* (New York: Aaronson, 1977).
19. *All the Strange Hours*, pp. 30-31.

3

Death, Drifting, and Depression

I was lost . . . waiting to find a role
for myself.

Loren Eiseley was in California when he received word that his
father was dying. He had fled some months before from his family,
school, and territory and had been riding the trains and drifting,
trying to overcome his growing anxiety and confusion. For as long
as he could remember, he had been running and hiding mentally.
When he grew old enough and the pressures became unbearable, he
began to run farther and longer. Eiseley had dropped out of high
school at least once, but he graduated more or less on time. Then
he enrolled at the University of Nebraska, but he was so unsettled
that he could not remain either in school or in Lincoln, and so he
left—and returned and left again, on several occasions. This state
of mind—in effect, his first major flight—initiated eight years of
crisis, "eight years that might as well have been a prison."[1] The
letter that reached him in San Francisco called him back to witness
the death of virtually the only source of love and kindness in his
childhood and to experience one more critical loss and betrayal.

He arrived home before his father died, and so he saw him and
was even able to give some assistance and comfort during Clyde
Eiseley's last weeks. But Loren also watched and heard his father
suffer, and only then die. By the time he got home, the cancer had
advanced so far that his father could no longer eat; his body had
become shriveled, shrunken, and jaundiced. He lay helpless on a
couch with a "black exudate of blood"[2] seeping from his mouth.
An ugly growth protruded from his side. There were few drugs to
relieve his torture or silence the cries of agony. "He died slowly in
severe bodily torture,"[3] . . . "by inches,"[4] while Loren could only
stand by and suffer his own pain.[5] Clyde Eiseley's death in the

afternoon of March 30, 1928,[6] so distressed his son that for a time
Eiseley's very sanity was threatened.

When the trauma of those weeks ended, the young man realized
that his sleep patterns had become seriously disrupted. First the
ticking of his alarm clock became unbearable. When he tried to
smother it with a blanket, "the ticking persisted as though it came
from [his] own head."[7] He lay for hours "staring into the dark of
the sleeping house, feeling the loneliness that only the sleepless
know."[8] When he became desperate, he stopped trying to sleep and
attempted to read, but he could not concentrate. His grandmother
Corey realized his trouble and started to sit up with him through
those long sleepless nights. She did nothing to alleviate his insomnia or to relieve his larger distress, but at that moment, she
reconnected him "to the living world"[9] and thus saved his sanity.
Clyde Eiseley's death had a deep and long-lasting effect, but
through his grandmother's love, Loren survived the immediate
impact.

As far back as childhood, Eiseley had experienced some sleep
disturbance. He wrote more than once about the nights he lay
sleepless and frightened in his bed, listening to his parents' violent
quarrels. He longed then for peace, and he would wait anxiously
for morning and an end to the nighttime arguments. But neither
peace nor light came, and he would fall asleep, when he could,
without being released from his fear and anxiety.

During his youth, several events besides his father's death may
also have disturbed his sleep patterns. When he was wandering and
riding the trains, for so many years, sleep must have been irregular
and difficult—sometimes even dangerous. Eiseley suggests that his
trouble may have been "augmented"[10] when he took a job as a
nightwatchman in a hatchery shortly after his father's death. He
had to set an alarm clock every hour to wake himself, so that he
could make his rounds. One night he awoke just in time to discover
a small fire that, unnoticed, would have consumed the entire
hatchery and killed him within a few minutes. Naturally, he wonders if his sleeplessness might not express some residual fear of the
fire. Although it is difficult as well as unrealistic to locate the cause
of Eiseley's sleeplessness in any single event, his insomnia did
become acute with his father's death.

When Clyde Eiseley died, Loren lost not only the father he

loved; he also lost his primary guide for living and the last remnant of his home. His estrangement from his mother was so great that she could not possibly represent home for him. And so he became utterly homeless. He had been drifting, but now he was *cast* adrift as well.

His father's death caused him, really, a double loss. When Eiseley saw his father briefly recover consciousness and recognize Leo, his half brother, he realized, perhaps clearly for the first time, that even though he was loved, he was nevertheless a changeling, an orphan. It would be natural for him to feel resentment, but he expresses none. He expresses no sense of betrayal or anger, either. Perhaps, as so often before, he suppressed his feelings and turned away, becoming, it seems, even more confused, desperate, and depressed.

Fortunately, two crucial events helped save his sanity for the moment. His grandmother's kind intervention made a difference. But before that, about a week after the funeral, Eiseley discovered his aunt burning some letters his father had left. On one partially burned page, he saw the single sentence "Remember, the boy is a genius, but moody."[11] At the time, that was enough to give him the sense that his "father had recognized [him] after all."[12] These are the autobiographer's words; it is possible that the youth felt no such clear reassurance. Whatever he felt and understood, the words gave him momentary relief.

Eiseley did not immediately leave again. He says that he tried once more to make progress on his "long-lost degree," but in fact he took only one hour at the university that second semester. Later, in the summer, he enrolled for six, and in the fall of 1928 he was back in school almost full time.[13] He managed to find the night security job in the hatchery, where the work went well, at first, except for the fire. He also worked at other jobs in the hatchery, and at one he had a minor accident with a solution of lye, leaving him with a numb spot on his leg, still there when he wrote his autobiography. Then he moved to lifting heavy feed sacks from trucks into a storeroom. That labor started to build his muscles and strengthen his body until inexplicably he started to weaken and could no longer do the work. When he finally went to the university dispensary for a checkup, his illness was diagnosed as advanced glandular tuberculosis. According to the examining physicians, Eiseley had very little chance of survival. He was shocked and frightened, of course: "I was young [only twenty]. I wasn't interested in dying."[14] And he was already under considerable psychological pressure. He tried to follow the diet and physical regimen for tubercular patients, but his weight kept dropping and his temperature followed the expected pattern. For several years, he had been waiting for something to happen in his life, and now it seemed as if he were simply waiting to die. Even his family expected it.

Fortunately, his uncle was able to help with the expense of a private physician, and that examination turned out differently. It was tuberculosis, all right, but not glandular. Although the virtual certainty of death lessened, Eiseley was not by any means out of danger. He still had a potentially fatal disease that would require over a year of therapy. Two of his uncle's brothers had died from it, and his uncle himself "had had a well-nigh miraculous recovery."[15] Death from TB was hardly an abstraction for him. For the first few months he did not improve, and so his physician recommended that he spend the rest of the summer in Colorado. It was now 1929. He went, accompanied by his aunt, and stayed until his money ran out in the fall. Since his mother had refused to draw on the small sum of insurance money left by his father, Eiseley had to use the very small amount left to him directly. Once more, his mother had rejected him. When he left for the summer, his family apparently treated him as if he were going away to die, and surely Eiseley himself sometimes believed it and always feared it. But he also seemed determined to survive. After he came back from Colorado, his physician found that he was "holding . . . just holding,"[16] and recommended that he go west. With the help of a professor at the university, he found a place in the Mojave Desert where he could stay for a year and finally recover.

He came back from the desert in October, 1930. For over five years, since his high school graduation in 1925, Eiseley's life had been continually disrupted. He attempted unsuccessfully to stay in college; he dropped out and headed west, wandering and drifting; he returned to witness his father's agonizing death; he struggled again with school; and then he spent over a year recovering from tuberculosis. For almost three of these years, Eiseley lived close to death, first his father's and then his own. No wonder he developed a strong sense of the fragility of his own life and an almost morbid fear of dying.

The death of Loren Eiseley's father was not simply another event. It was the crucial event of his adolescence, and it ended his youth and propelled him deeper into confusion. The next two and a half years, roughly, of part-time employment and enrollment in college and of an extended recovery from TB settled nothing. They simply increased Eiseley's discontent and forced him toward another flight. "A yearlong immobility, even my enforced wary care of myself in the Mohave, had left me savage, restless, at odds with my environment. I tried, through university extension courses, to overcome deficiencies and graduate. All failed. I prowled about like an animal. Suddenly, I vanished again."[17] He had become desperate and almost panicky. This time he was running and drifting with thousands and thousands of others. It was the early 1930s.

Even though Eiseley did not intend his autobiography as a carefully dated and accurate chronological account, he did provide enough personal history to dramatize the quality of his actual experience. *All the Strange Hours*, for example, describes three different periods between 1925 and 1933 when Eiseley dropped or was forced out of college. He left the university, first, before his degree was half completed and headed west, drifting all the way to California where he received word that his father was dying. Then his physical illness forced him to leave again, although he seemed to make only spasmodic progress on his degree even while he was in Lincoln. After his cure, he returned to Lincoln again, in the fall of 1930, and for a while he did make real progress; he was enrolled full time during both the 1930-31 and 1931-32 school years. But then at some point he vanished, fleeing on the trains. The autobiography purposely makes the date and duration of this disappearance unclear. It gives the impression that he left Lincoln a few months after he returned from New Mexico in October, 1930; but he was, in fact, enrolled in school for the next two years, although he need not have been *in* Lincoln all that time. According to *All the Strange Hours*, he was going home, heading "east to college,"[18] in "the third year of the Great Depression in the railroad yards of Kansas City"[19] before he changed directions and drifted away once more. This may have been 1932, for he was apparently not in school that autumn at all. In the autobiography, he claims not to remember the day, the month, or the year of his last day as a drifter—"the most perfect day in the world." But he did return, finish his last eight hours, and graduate from the University of Nebraska in June, 1933.

It seems unlikely that Eiseley stayed away for long periods or that he was away only three times. These years may have been even more unsettled and he may have fled and returned, re-enrolled, and dropped out of school more often than even his autobiography suggests. (He completed only three hours in the fall of 1926, for example, and he was not in school at all in the winter and spring of 1927. The autobiography does not make this clear.) In it, Eiseley narrates representative experiences that show what his life was like and thereby reveal his inner turmoil. He often chooses particularly expressive moments or incidents that dramatize an entire phase of his life or state of his mind. So I read the three chapters that recount his "days of a drifter"—"The Trap," "Toads and Men," and "The Most Perfect Day in the World"—as an extended metaphor or a coherent narrative expressing, without exactly identifying, his irregular and unpredictable wanderings. His official record at the university helps clarify this period, but only a little.

During those years, especially after 1927, Loren Eiseley was not only riding trains and going to school. He may have been inwardly drifting the whole time, but he was active in other ways. He was writing poetry and helping edit a new literary magazine, the *Prairie Schooner*. In October, 1927, the first piece Eiseley ever published appeared in the *Prairie Schooner*; titled "Autumn—A Memory," it is a prose meditation about some Aztec ruins. He was just twenty. A year later, the *Schooner* published an early poem, "The Last Gold Penny," a conventional sonnet that speaks of the "hard bargains" "death drives." In 1928, he joined the editorial staff of the journal, and for over a decade after, he contributed poems, narratives, and reviews, edited a regular section of the magazine, and in the early years helped prepare the issues for publication. By the time he graduated from college, Eiseley had published over thirty poems in *Poetry, Voices,* and the *Midland* as well as in the *Prairie Schooner*. But as the poems reveal, he was still drifting. He was also becoming more and more interested in science, and in the summer of 1931, he started working in western Nebraska with the

"South Party," an archaeological-paleontological field party dispatched by the Nebraska State Museum. He worked with them in 1932 and 1933 as well.

Among his *Prairie Schooner* publications were two narratives about riding the rails. The first, "Riding the Peddlers,"[20] appeared in 1933, and the *Schooner* published the second, "The Mop to K. C.,"[21] in 1935. The second piece is particularly revealing of what it was like for him to face life as a "stiff." It describes an encounter between two bums who meet on a freight bound for Kansas City. The narrator seems to be a strong and confident stiff, who has been on the road for some time and who knows the trains and the ways of survival. The other person is a lonely, homeless kid who is dying, probably from tuberculosis, and is desperately searching for a friend or a home to comfort him. Both figures could be Loren Eiseley. The kid could be the victim and orphan Eiseley sometimes felt he was (not to speak of the youth threatened with tubercular death), and the other might be the survivor Eiseley wanted and needed to be. As the two talk, we discover that the boy is in fact an orphan. He grew up in an institution and never knew his parents. When he left "the Home" at thirteen, he just started wandering. Occasionally, he stops somewhere and tries to make or find a home, but every one of his efforts is doomed. Not only is he inept; he is misused and victimized by others. At one point he tells the narrator about the home he almost had in Muncie. "I lived in a big box in Muncie for a week. . . . I ain't never had a home. . . . But I pretty near did in Muncie. This box was on the ends of town, and I was gonna borrow a saw and fix real windows in it." Such a feeble attempt is sad enough, but then, he explains, "some bums broke it up for kindling wood."[22] Another time his homelessness is exploited by a homosexual. "Once outside of Sacramento a guy gave me a real cabin. Anyhow he said I could come and live with him. But the other guys didn't like him. A fellow beat him up, and I ran away."[23] Then he relates an incredibly pathetic experience that shows how his loneliness and illness have affected his mind.

An' once in K.C.—you know the yards in K.C.?—I slept for three days in a corn-shock out by Argentine. I was getting to like it. It was pretty, and quiet-like around there and nobody'd found me out. The next night a mouse scared me and I crawled out, but it was so cold I crawled back in again. I was going to Cal., but I stayed there three

days with the mice. The last day I gave them some crumbs from a
handout. They was gettin' to know me. Mice ain't so bad when you
get to know them. Mostly, I'm afraid of them, though. I guess I was
lonesome.[24]

Lonely, dying, and unstable, the boy is desperate for companionship, and so he clings to the narrator until their paths separate. The
boy gets off at Leavenworth because he thinks he knew someone
there once—but he is really getting off to die. The narrator rides on
toward Kansas City with no apparent destination or aim. As he
says, "I had a thousand miles to go."

Even though the narrator seems confident and able to handle life
on the road, he is by no means free of the loneliness and sense of
futility of the drifter. He is moved by the kid's plight, but at the
same time he feels very uneasy. The narrator does not want to be
affected; he doesn't want the burden of a companion, especially
such a dependent one. "I don't know why I didn't give him the air.
But there was something in his eyes. I couldn't do it. And he looked
so damned miserable sitting there and shaking."[25] So he stays with
the kid for a while and listens to his misery.

He had snudged over until he was against me. Then he went on
more steadily. "I wasn't gonna die in one of those places—all cold
and shiny where you're a number or something."

I wanted to get out of that car. I patted his shoulder and said:
"Listen, Bud, you shouldn't of done that. They might 'a fixed you
up. You shouldn't be doin' that. Do you know somebody at Leavenworth? Shall I take you to a hospital?"

Oh, it was swell, all right, sitting there in the dark, getting colder
and colder, with that voice like a sick girl's going on and on in the
darkness. And the wheels going faster and faster and that damned
hoghead hooting away off over the river like he wanted a clear track
to hell.

I hardly knew what he was saying, at first. I just kept wailing
inside, "Don't let him cry, for Christ's sake, don't let him cry." You
can't keep a tension like that. You'd go mad. There wasn't anything I
could do. It was all in the cards. I said that to myself and eased down
and tried to listen to him.

He didn't cry, either. He just kept leaning against me and babbling.
It was doing him good. He kept talking about a long string of places
he'd been, and at first I couldn't figure it out. Every bum knows

towns from New York to Frisco, but why talk about that? There's
the same bulls and the same people in all of them.[26]

It is not just the boy's feelings that trouble the narrator. He seems
to recognize something of himself in the boy—the lonely, homeless,
frightened man who is running and running. And this is the real
source of his uneasiness.

After the kid has exhausted himself talking, he starts to fall
asleep.

> He drew a long breath, and I stood up in the dark and took the
> overcoat off and tossed it over him as he lay shivering.
> "You sleep now," I said. "I'll tell you when we get to Leaven-
> worth." I'd have given him my shirt to get him quiet.
> "Ya won't leave, will ya Jack?" he asked me under the coat.
> "No," I said.
> "Jack—"
> "Yeah?"
> "I was ridin' the passengers 'cause I was lonesome and they went
> fast." I waited awhile and pretty soon he said again, half asleep,
> "Cause they went fast."
> Poor devil—running from himself, I suppose. I walked up and
> down in the other end of the car to keep warm. It was quiet except
> for the steady roar of the wheels. We were running alongside the
> Missouri. The driftwood in the moonlight looked sometimes like
> bodies floating.[27]

Both seem to be waiting for nothing. The kid is waiting to die, and
the narrator is waiting for the next thousand miles to pass.

Although "The Mop to K. C." is not explicitly autobiographical,
it nevertheless speaks about Eiseley's experience. The story dramatizes the circumstances and internal conflicts that several times had
forced Eiseley to flee. In the kid, he has concentrated his own
feelings of homelessness and victimization and his fears of dying or
disappearing. In the narrator, he has placed his own strength and
worldly wisdom, also his own pain and confusion and helplessness
as he watches someone die. The story says less about the conditions
themselves, but they are there, briefly mentioned or implied. The
police might run you out; other bums might steal from you; homo-
sexuals might prey on your poverty and hunger; the cold nights
make you shiver and sleep fitfully; and irregular and inadequate
eating make the life not only difficult but unhealthy. In his other

story, "Riding the Peddlers," Eiseley alludes also to the class hatred and class struggle that erupted during the Depression.

All the Strange Hours gives a somewhat more detailed and forceful account of the hardships, dangers, and violence of those years. In "The Trap," Eiseley summarizes:

> It was a time. Leave it at that. The young, the middle-aged, the old[,] even a few case-hardened women. We lay like windrows of leaves on sandbars beside the Union Pacific, the Rock Island, the Santa Fe, the Katy. At night our fires winked like the bivouacs of armies. We rode the empty fruit trains coming through Needles into the sand hell of the Mohave. Railroad detectives blackjacked us or turned aside in fear of numbers. We gathered like descending birds in spite of all obstacles. Like birds, some of us died because we were old, and we perished, unnoticed, of cold in the high Sierras or we slipped under the wheels of freights in moments of exhaustion. If found, what remained was buried in nameless graves along the track. Cheap liquor killed us; occasionally we died by the gun and so did the railroad detectives, pushing their luck too far with sullen unknown men in the night on swaying car tops.
>
> It was a time of violence, a time of hate, a time of sharing, a time of hunger.[28]

On his way back from California to his father's bedside, Eiseley was almost killed by a brakeman who tried to force him off a train going sixty miles an hour. Eiseley was riding the second blind on a night mail train when the brakeman suddenly stepped out of the following car. "'Get the hell off,' he demanded. 'Jump, you bastard.'"[29] When Eiseley hesitated, the man hit him and tried to push him off. "He was making a mistake," Eiseley tells us. "I was in my late teens but I was all bones and rawhide, and murder was licking like flame along the edges of my mind."[30] Fortunately, the train started to slow for a stop, so both were saved from the consequences of their own violence. Afterward, Eiseley understood the hatred and hostility behind the brakeman's attack. "This man was not a cop, he was a worker out of my father's time. He was trying to kill me for no reason but the sheer pleasure of it." Eiseley also recognized the savagery that erupted within himself. "There was no mercy on that rocking, speeding mail train, none in my mind. I could have killed him. I could kill him now after all these years. It is thus one learns the depths of hatred."[31]

After he left the train and escaped the area, Eiseley met a man in a hobo camp who asked about his bruises. This man, who had obviously been around, suggested that the youth travel with him for a while. Before they split up several days later, the older man explained what had happened on that train—what was happening, really, all across America. "'Remember this,' he said suddenly . . . 'The capitalists beat men into line. Okay? The communists beat men into line. Right again?' . . . He pointed gently at my swollen face. 'Men beat men, that's all. That's all there is. Remember it, kid.'"[32] Eiseley never saw him again, but he obviously did not forget his message. Men beat men. In times of stress, the savagery erupts that men have carried in them "from some dark tree in a vanished forest." The savagery may sometimes kill; in hostile environments, it also makes survival possible.

Besides the violence and hatred, there were moments of kindness and sharing. The man's grizzled generosity and advice were gestures of concern, or at least as close to concern as the time permitted. Remember the narrator in "The Mop," who could afford only so much sympathy, or else go mad with the tension; but he did let the kid affect him, and he offered the boy a few hours of companionship. Eiseley also remembered a time several years later when another brakeman had made a desert crossing bearable. He helped Eiseley and several others avoid a railroad detective at the front of the train, then showed them an open refrigerator car where a large slab of ice quenched their thirst and kept them cool.[33] These were exceptional moments, however; more often, the drifters encountered contempt and hostility in the towns, brutality from the police, violence and danger on the road, and hunger, cold, and loneliness everywhere. They, too, were cringing and struggling to survive.

During these years, Eiseley saw many signs that in one way or another read: "Jobless men keep going. We can't take care of our own."[34] No town welcomed the thousands who were on the road; many were openly hostile. Sometimes the drifters were hustled out of town right away; sometimes they were given a night and then required to leave early the next morning. And there were always enough police and strong-arms to enforce a town's rules. In one incident described by Thomas Minehan in *Boy and Girl Tramps of America*, a local sheriff and nine or ten men armed with pick handles meet a large group of young people just as they are leaving the railroad yard. The sheriff arrests them but promises not to hold them beyond morning if they go to jail quietly. He wants no panhandling in his town, and so he offers them a deal: "The last freight has just pulled out of here. There ain't another one along until eight o'clock tomorrow morning. I got a offer to make you. How would you like to get a nice supper, a good warm bed, a nice breakfast and be out of here in time to catch that morning train?"[35]

They have no choice, of course, and one who does try to escape is beaten back into line with pick handles. The night in jail is no deal. The group is herded like "monkeys in a zoo" into a large bullpen with no furniture. They are fed slop for dinner: "one cup of cold tomatoes, mostly juice, one cold boiled potato with the scabrous jacket still on, one slice of muggy bread." When one of them asks for something to drink, a deputy answers, "Shut up, you goddam ungrateful bum, you. . . . Don't you appreciate what you're getting for nothing?" They are forced to sleep on a steel floor with no pads or blankets. In the morning, they are given (the fifty or sixty of them) three wash basins, newspapers for towels, and a bar of caustic soap. There is only cold water. Breakfast consists of watery cornmeal mush and a slice of dry, sour bread. As he promised, the sheriff does release them and then marches them through town to the morning freight, waiting with his deputies until the train leaves for Chicago.[36]

The police, sheriffs, and railroad detectives not only enforced a town's vagrancy laws, or a railroad's orders to keep the trains clear; they also "officially" expressed the hostility and fear felt by the townspeople. Given their power and authority, they were able to convert those feelings into violence, and they often did. Sometimes a threat was enough. It was enough to keep in line the fifty or sixty kids who were arrested. And it was enough to control the hungry drifters in the small desert town that Loren Eiseley describes: "The place was a trap. The railroad ran through a concavity in the desert which contained the town. The police watched the two ends of the bottleneck." They waited for the strangers to leave or to steal. In either case, their presence threatened violence. And if the stiffs did get out of town, they might run into a particularly ruthless railroad detective "who was capable of occasional killings just inside an easily stretchable law of trespass."[37]

Sometimes the drifters were so hungry, sleepy, or desperate that they did do something to evoke a response, often an unnecessarily violent one. But more often, they did nothing but exist and try to survive, and that also evoked violence. Tom Kromer, in *Waiting for Nothing*, narrates a number of incidents in which he and others were the victims of such violence. On one especially cold and rainy night, when they had no place to go, Kromer and a companion found an empty building where a number of others were sleeping for the night, "good enough for a couple of drowned rats hunting a hole." Warm and dry there, Kromer fell asleep.

> I do not know how long I am asleep. I awake with a jerk. All around me are lights. They flash back and forth. It seems as though there are a thousand lights that flash through the dark. I hear a rat squeal and scurry across the floor. What the hell? I am half asleep, but I know that there is something wrong. My heart pounds. It chokes me. I am afraid. I hear heavy shoes thudding on the floor. I hear stiffs running back and forth and yelling at the top of their voices. A light flashes into my eyes and blinds me.
>
> "Get up out of there," says a voice. "Get up out of there before I kick the living hell out of you."
>
> I know what it is now. It is the bulls. Jesus Christ, can't they ever let a man alone? A man can't even sleep. You can't crawl into an empty rat-hole, for the bulls. This bull grabs me by the throat and yanks me to my feet. I reach over and bundle my clothes up in my arms. He thinks maybe I am reaching for a gat or a club. I feel his fist smash into my mouth. I feel the blood that oozes from my lips. I dress as they shove us outside. There are a bunch of cops out here. There are a bunch of stiffs herded between them. They are red-eyed and sleepy.[38]

Men do beat men.

Kromer expresses the anger and frustration of the hundreds of thousands who in those years were on the road because of hard times and bad luck. Many had either no home to return to or no way to go back to a home that might still be there. And so they drifted, lonely, forlorn, and desperate, filled with the rage and despair of the victimized outcast.

Riding trains presented other dangers as well—"the bloody God-damned accidents" that Eiseley talks about. It was so easy to fall from a moving train, if a person were at all careless; and if a tramp tried to jump one and missed, he could easily be killed. When

Eiseley was following one of his impulses to return to school, he
made the serious mistake of riding an express all night, hanging on
"in the most dangerous spot in the world,"[39] on the iron ladder
behind the tender.

> How many hours, how many miles, how much sleep loss can a
> man take? What mania had possessed me to outride relays of riders
> in the most dangerous, muscle-jerking spot on a locomotive? I was
> fully awake now, but too weak even to crawl over the tender on to
> the coal, or back to the safety of the blind. I shook my head,
> tightened my cramped fingers, and waited for the next stop. It
> wouldn't happen again, it wouldn't, it wouldn't. I had seen one death
> of this kind. I didn't intend to make a second. We flashed over a
> bridge I thought I dimly recognized. We slowed for a station. I
> waited till we stopped. Never mind the cops. They could have me. I
> descended and stood silently beside the tender. Only a tired switch-
> man appeared as the fireman high on the tender took on water.[40]

Carelessness, recklessness, inexperience, bad judgment, an accident, a brutal detective—anything could do it. Although death and
injury were not commonplace, they were all too familiar. For
example, in 1929 the Missouri Pacific Railroad "took official
notice" of some 13,745 transients on their trains—trespassers, as
the railroad called them. They also "noticed" that there were 259
accidents among these transients: 103 were killed and 156 injured.[41]
This report involved one railroad only, the year before the great
hordes of drifters took to the road, and only those transients who
happened to be counted. There must have been many, many more.
The men and women on the road led pretty basic and primitive
lives. They spent most of their time looking for food and shelter or
trying to fend off boredom and loneliness. Ordinarily, when it was
warm, they slept outside or on trains. Although conditions were
not comfortable, they were bearable and sometimes, perhaps,
pleasant. During the growing season, the tramps had sources of
food other than stores, restaurants, and private homes. Farmers
and gardeners occasionally gave vegetables and eggs to hungry
wanderers. But even in such good seasons, eating was irregular and
scrounging a meal took a lot of time; and shelter and good sleeping
were chancy.
In colder weather, especially in winter, conditions were much

harsher and food and shelter a real problem. Along with all the others on the road, Loren Eiseley suffered from hunger and cold. He remembers how he felt in one town where the police had laid a trap. "I was huddled against an adobe wall in some nameless little desert town at nightfall. My teeth chattered in the cold of the high desert. I had no blanket and again no money. Sleep was impossible. In the morning I would have to search for food."[42] In that instance, the prospects were not very good. No panhandling. No stealing. And almost no escape from that particular town.

The worst of the hardships—similar to living through the pioneer winters on the prairie—were the feelings of loneliness and futility. Tom Kromer says it simply:

> I lie here and try to think back. I try to think back over the years that I have lived. But I cannot think of years any more. I can think only of the drags I have rode, of the bulls that have sapped up on me, and the mission slop I have swilled. People I have known, I remember no more. They are gone. They are out of my life. I cannot remember them at all. Even my family, my mother, is dimmed by the strings of drags with their strings of cars that are always with me in my mind through the long, cold nights. Whatever is gone before is gone. I lie here and I think, and I know that whatever is before is the same as that which is gone. My life is spent before it is started. I peer into the blackness of the ceiling, and in its blackness I try to find the riddle of why I lie here on top of this three-decker bunk with the snores of a thousand men around me.[43]

Alone, suspended in time, cut off from family and place, hopelessly estranged from everything that gives life meaning, this stiff is indeed waiting for nothing.

These were years of widespread displacement and crisis. While in 1929 there were only about 14,000 so-called transients "noticed" by the officials of the Missouri Pacific Railroad, by 1931, in just two years, that number leaped—thirteen-fold—to 186,000.[44] Even if officials observed more carefully as the number of transients grew, that increase is astounding. With the crash of 1929, thousands and thousands of men and women, and boys and girls, became drifters. They left home because of "'hard times . . . hard times'—plus the difficulties and desires of adolescence and the lure of the open road."[45] In either case, loss of a job meant not only economic dislocation and deprivation; many suffered psychic and physical collapses from which they never recovered. In some basic way, most of them were lost.

When Eiseley risked his life crossing Kansas on a passenger in almost one run, he was following an urge to return to Lincoln and get back to school. It was an impulsive and dangerous act, and he must have been almost desperate from loneliness and anxiety to do it. By taking that chance, he seemed determined to overcome his aimlessness. It is as if he had to hurry before the urge disappeared. But as he neared Lincoln, he hesitated and began once more to drift away. "I was wandering slowly westward again into the wheat. I had reversed directions."[46] He was floating—"waiting for something I didn't understand."[47] He was lost—"waiting to find a role" for himself.[48]

A freight train moving across the country with hundreds of men and women sitting in open boxcars or riding on the tops of cars became a symbol of the times. These trains also provided a perfect medium to express the "craving for locomotion"[49] that is so much a part of youth's discontented search and that reappears in older persons experiencing a crisis. With hundreds of thousands on the road, wandering became like a communal movement, and participation in it temporarily satisfied another need of young people. But this was clearly a negative participation, and as an end in itself it could contribute only to a negative sense of identity. Unless one became involved in the politics of dislocation or change, this mass movement could not satisfy an adolescent's need for an ideology or a coherent vision of experience that would overcome his sense of being displaced and help him into the world.

The late twenties and early thirties were years of personal dislocation and depression in Eiseley's life, just as they were obviously years of economic dislocation and depression in his region and the whole nation. As Eiseley grew older and his experiences of place widened to include much of the American West, as well as the plains, the correlation persisted between his inner and personal life and the historical and social environments he lived in. His personal dislocation became most severe when the economic dislocation in Nebraska and the country became extreme. By young adulthood, Eiseley's sense of place and sense of himself had become very complex. The challenge remains of explaining these relationships in any detail or with much of their real complexity, because even for Eiseley, in the 1930s *and* the 1970s, they existed on several levels. But it is clear that his senses of place and self were profoundly interwoven.

In "The Most Perfect Day in the World," a chapter from his autobiography, Loren Eiseley marks the end of his days as a drifter. On that day, he experienced a complete suspension, for he felt free of confusion, anxiety, and depression—and free from time and responsibility. It happened in Phillipsburg, Kansas, but Eiseley appropriately does not remember the exact day, the month, or the year. He and three other drifters met by accident near a water tower and a loading platform. They shared bottles of grape pop, the sun, and conversation: "We laughed and took our ease and the world could wait for us."[50] They were in no hurry because they were going nowhere.

> We slept without concern, with no ostensible future there in the late summer sun. We had no destination. It was the perfect day, the centuries had finished their work, while we dreamed there in the shade of the water tower. There was this utter pause. No trains ran, no officials passed. Even the dogs slept in the village street. I turned over, I was the only one who did. It was the most perfect day in the world, the day time stopped.[51]

This is what the running had been about—an escape from past, present, and future, and from serious psychological conflicts. On the perfect day, everything came together and stopped; for the moment, Eiseley was no longer running and not quite drifting, either. He was utterly free and ready at last to re-enter the world.

For all their shiftless, aimless, delinquent, and even self-destructive character, these eight years were necessary to Loren Eiseley's survival. They gave him the space he needed; they helped produce the poet and then the scientist. As the period became more and more prolonged, it threatened his survival. When that happened, he managed to find himself and return to school and his future. Had he instead drifted out into the world of violence forever—as he almost did—then the years would have been wholly destructive for him as they were for so many others. His crisis was that problematic. When he returned, he was no longer drifting, but he was still running—now, however, with some direction. He returned to school, finished his degree, and then in the following autumn, 1933, he went east to graduate school at the University of Pennsylvania. His association with the *Prairie Schooner*, his life as a young poet, and his participation in several archaeological expeditions for the Nebraska State museum were all critical parts of this long moratorium.

NOTES

1. *All the Strange Hours*, p. 77.
2. Ibid., p. 17.
3. *Night Country*, p. 170.
4. *All the Strange Hours*, p. 17.
5. See also *The Unexpected Universe*, p. 206, for another account of Clyde Eiseley's death.
6. Standard Certificate of Death, Bureau of Vital Statistics, Lincoln, Nebr.
7. *Night Country*, p. 170.
8. Ibid.
9. Ibid., p. 171.
10. *All the Strange Hours*, p. 83.
11. Ibid., p. 16.
12. Ibid.
13. Official Transcript of the Record of Loren C. Eiseley, The University of Nebraska, Lincoln, Feb. 6, 1936, in Penn Archives. This document helps date Eiseley's activities, but it is hardly definitive.
14. *All the Strange Hours*, p. 20.
15. Ibid., p. 22.
16. Ibid., p. 35.
17. Ibid., p. 47.
18. Ibid., p. 60.
19. Ibid., p. 55.
20. Loren Eiseley, "Riding the Peddlers," *Prairie Schooner*, 7, no. 1 (Winter, 1933), 45-50.
21. Loren Eiseley, "The Mop to K. C.," *Prairie Schooner*, 9, no. 1 (Winter, 1935), 33-39.
22. Ibid., p. 37.
23. Ibid., p. 38.
24. Ibid.
25. Ibid., p. 34.
26. Ibid., p. 37.
27. Ibid., p. 38.
28. *All the Strange Hours*, pp. 51-52.
29. Ibid., p. 9.
30. Ibid., pp. 9-10.

31. Ibid., pp. 9, 10.
32. Ibid., p. 12.
33. Ibid., p. 50.
34. Ibid., p. 47.
35. Thomas Minehan, *Boy and Girl Tramps of America* (New York: Farrar and Rinehart, 1934), p. 4.
36. Ibid., pp. 4-13.
37. *All the Strange Hours*, pp. 48-49.
38. Tom Kromer, *Waiting for Nothing* (New York: Hill and Wang, 1968), pp. 28-29.
39. *All the Strange Hours*, p. 52.
40. Ibid., p. 53.
41. U.S., Congress, Senate, Subcommittee of the Committee on Manufacturers, *Relief for Unemployed Transients*, Hearing, 72nd Cong., 2nd Sess., in David A. Shannon, ed., *The Great Depression* (Englewood Cliffs, N.J.: Prentice-Hall, 1960), p. 59.
42. *All the Strange Hours*, p. 48.
43. Kromer, *Waiting for Nothing*, pp. 186-87.
44. Shannon, *Great Depression*, p. 59.
45. Minehan, *Boy and Girl Tramps*, p. 53.
46. *All the Strange Hours*, p. 61.
47. Ibid., p. 62.
48. Ibid., p. 67.
49. Erik H. Erikson, *Identity: Youth and Crisis* (New York: W. W. Norton, 1968), p. 243.
50. *All the Strange Hours*, p. 65.
51. Ibid., p. 69.

4

The *Prairie Schooner*

A veritable stronghold of gloom.

When Loren Eiseley graduated from college in 1933, he was emerging from the longest and most difficult crisis of his life. For eight years, he had felt like a prisoner. He "could not," as he says, "get outside the ring, the ring of poverty."[1] And it is true; he was trapped by the continuing economic poverty of his family and his region. But the rings were many, and the spareness was not just economic. Eiseley was also still imprisoned by the emotional and intellectual poverty of his childhood and youth. Eventually, he broke some of those rings and managed to overcome the deprivation of his early years and to survive, as well, his identity crisis.

Insofar as one can determine phases or identify turning points in a life, Eiseley's graduation seems to be as critical as his father's death. Even though Eiseley had been writing, reading, and working, especially during the last several of those eight years, his graduation focused his efforts, initiating the reversal that carried him into the next phase of his life. It did not suddenly and radically transform him; but it did begin an almost imperceptible modulation from one phase to another. Once more, Eiseley had survived a difficult situation and turned his life toward further growth.

Years later, he published a poem called "Timberline"[2] that symbolically dramatizes the underlying character of his youth and early adulthood as well as his later life and achievement. The poem is about survival, and it describes a barren landscape where life must struggle to grow. Even though the existence is marginal and the struggle solitary, each "stunted body," wingless insect, mountain weasel, and, finally, lonely man does not retreat but crawls onward to survive and succeed. The timberline, "where elfin timber grows above tree limits and the world is dwarfed," is the place one goes to see the naked drama of life:

> This is where one comes
> to be alone; not just alone, to feel
> what life is like when one must cringe to live.

It is a marginal place where the effort to live sharply alters forms and makes struggle the rule:

> Here trees crawl forward on their knees, stretching cold roots
> upward, drag leaves after them
> upon a stunted body, but this effort
> is not to creep away, but gain a summit.

The poem offers no explanation; struggle and survival are simply facts.

> On this tremendous height there is no answer
> save the locked struggle.

Although conditions are extreme there, the timberline nevertheless represents for Eiseley what life is like—at least what his own life has been like. In the final lines he makes the connection explicit:

> Where is it the wind howls? Here. Where is it life speaks? Here.
> This is the final fell field. Who flinches here but crawls?
> I, I, against the stars.

In the simplest sense, the poem describes a terrain Eiseley knew as a youth and explored later on various archaeological expeditions. It also expresses Eiseley's sense of his own personal history. In its wider dimensions, the poem reflects his later scientific knowledge. In marginal environments, as Eiseley explained in *The Immense Journey*, one sees most clearly the impulse to live and grow, the necessity and strategies for adaptation and survival, and the mechanisms and possibilities for evolution. The struggle of life along the timberline suggests the "locked struggle" for biological adaptation and survival at the heart of all life.

The poem also has psychological overtones, for the uplands suggest all of the tight places and difficult situations where one must fight for life, or identity. In this sense, "Timberline" effectively dramatizes the fundamental conflict in each phase of Eiseley's childhood, youth, and young adulthood. As such, it represents

Eiseley's way of dealing with past and present crisis—mainly through words and form. The eight years now in question constituted for him an unusually extended but otherwise normal moratorium or identity crisis.

It is important to think of an identity crisis not simply as a period of conflict or potential breakdown, but as a necessary turning point. In this sense, a crisis involves a crucial moment—which may extend over several years—when development must move one way or another. During such a crisis, an individual marshals his resources for growth and further differentiation. Of course, he may also fail and subsequently suffer loss or breakdown of identity. Although the crisis of adolescence is often acute, and during it one's "final" identity is more or less set, the possibility of further significant turning points hardly ends with this transition.

In proposing his notion of identity theme, Heinz Lichtenstein points out that man has evolved beyond the so-called lower animals and no longer possesses a fixed, instinctual, or behavioral identity. His survival depends now on the evolution of consciousness. He has become more flexible and adaptable than other animals, and therefore he can change and grow. Man thus creates his identity; it is a peculiarly human achievement. And loss of it has become a specifically human danger.

Lichtenstein assumes that each person absorbs an underlying identity theme from its mother: "Out of the infinite potentialities within the human infant, the specific stimulus combination emanating from the individual mother 'releases' one, and only one, concrete way of being this organ, this instrument."[3] This theme is irreversible, though it is capable of virtually endless variations. It can reach great complexity and then suddenly return, as in music, to the simple basic theme. Loren Eiseley, for example, could achieve great public success, develop into a gifted, knowledgeable, and creative man, and write extraordinary books, and in the midst of it all feel desperate urges to run away and hide. In this sense of variation and complexity, identity is indeterminate, open ended, tentative, exploratory. No individual is entirely free, of course; no one can become anything he wants. Nevertheless, man has become, in Lichtenstein's terms, nearly protean in character. In Eiseley's, he is a shape-shifter.

While there may be repeated opportunities for change or variation, there are also repeated dangers of loss or breakdown and even temptations to give up our human identity. As Lichtenstein expresses it, "We . . . exist in constant tension between identity maintenance and the temptation to abandon our identity as humans altogether."[4] In this sense, identity is not only open ended; it is problematic as well.

The order I am developing for Loren Eiseley's life identifies a number of crises or turning points, some probably more critical and stressful than others. It seems helpful to speak of moments or phases in this way; it is also vital to recognize that these turning points do not break Eiseley's personal history into discrete segments. They are simply, but significantly, the most visible, dramatic, and memorable events in an unbroken life process that never is complete, until death. Although he survived and flourished in remarkable ways, to the end Eiseley was still fighting old battles and seeking new variations and achievements. He was doing so even more dramatically in 1933.

The first issue of the *Prairie Schooner* appeared on January 12, 1927. The idea for the magazine originated early in 1926 among the members of an honorary literary fraternity at the University of Nebraska and Dr. Lowry C. Wimberly, who subsequently became editor. *Prairie Schooner* began as a regional magazine with the intention of publishing regional authors and defining a body of common feelings and traditions for midwesterners. It announced its first appearance with this inscription: "The *Prairie Schooner* is an outlet for literary work in the University of Nebraska and a medium for the publication of the finest writing of the prairie country. . . ."[5] When Loren Eiseley entered the university in 1925, he already had expressed his desire to be a writer. Although he was not one of the founding group, he became an associate editor by the fourth issue, dated October, 1927, and he remained an associate through the winter issue of 1929. For the next ten years, he held the title of contributing editor, and in addition to poems and narratives, he contributed reviews and prepared a regular feature of the magazine called "Crossroads," a short section that reprinted poems from other little magazines.

Besides joining the staff for the October issue, Eiseley published his first piece ever in it, the prose sketch "Autumn—A Memory."[6] Actually, he published his first three pieces in that issue. Two of his poems were included under pseudonyms, apparently a staff practice necessary in the early years to fill out the magazine. Eiseley did his part as Eronel Croye with "Death in Autumn" and as Silas Amon with "Graveyard Studies."

Although he was barely twenty when it appeared, "Autumn—A Memory" already expressed some of the major concerns and attitudes that informed his work throughout his life. In effect, "Autumn" asks a primary question that literature, science, and fifty more years did not enable Eiseley to answer with any certainty. This prose meditation—virtually a free-verse poem—begins with a beautifully cadenced first sentence that carried the writer and his reader back into the past and to a remote place: "I remember stillness and the faint flutter of red and golden leaves down long dim shafts of sunlight through the trees." The sketch goes on to describe young Eiseley's visit to some "Aztec" ruins. With night falling, he finds himself in the silence and solitude of the ruins, "straining to catch the undernote of long dead activity, of something that lingered, that would linger till the last stone had fallen, something that would not go away." He cannot hear the voices, of course, because they cannot penetrate the void of time and death, but he senses the presence of the people in the physical remnants of their life. The people themselves are gone, and their history has disappeared with them. But he wonders, "From where did they come—and why—and what fate overtook them?" He imagines their life and their death. He envisions "the laboring copper bodies that built this place," and he thinks of their friendship and love. He speculates that "there may have come a time when the offended god turned his face away . . . or maybe the harvests burned," and he wonders if any lived to go elsewhere. Meditating on time and distance, Eiseley then sees himself and the vanished people in the perspective of vast time:

> A star burned with a steady silver flame. I was a shadow among shadows brooding over the fate of other shadows that I alone strove to summon up out of the all-pervading dusk.
>
> They had built, stone upon heavy stone. Women and men and children—children and women and men . . . To the great watching

god men's faces pass as a blur . . .
   Starlight and dust in starlight . . . Does it matter now at all?

Their lives and his turn to dust, and only the starlight remains.

   There may be a strain of youthful sentimentality and melancholy
in this "memory," but age does not banish the feelings or necessarily answer the questions with any certainty. As he meditates on
the human condition, Eiseley expresses wonder and sadness and
describes a sense of lonely futility. Underneath these feelings, we
can almost hear the anthropologist asking his questions about the
ruins—where did they come from? why did they go?—the paleon-
tologist asking his about vanished species—how did they arise?
why did they disappear?—the biologist asking his about life—how
does it originate? and what happens when it breaks down?—and
the poet or philosopher wondering if, in fact, the answers make any
difference in "starlight and dust in starlight." Later on, Eiseley had
these and other intellectual tools for asking and answering questions. The specific questions and answers may have changed, but in
a sense they also remained unchanged, as the mature man found
himself time and again facing a mystery that neither knowledge nor
time would expose. In "Autumn," his first work, Eiseley symbolically asked the first and last question and answered it with
another question. This is almost vintage Eiseley.

   "Crossroads" appeared first in the winter of 1929 and ran as
an intermittent feature through the spring, 1938, issue, with this
express purpose: "This page is the *Prairie Schooner*'s challenge to
those who think that the small magazine which does not pay for
verse never publishes material which is worthwhile. Its selections
are made only from those smaller literary magazines which are
unable to pay for contributions."[7] Eiseley chose from such magazines as *Voices*, the *Midland*, the *Frontier*, *Bozart*, and *Parnassus*,
and he normally prefaced the poems with brief remarks about the
source and the reasons for his choice. For a few years, Eiseley
edited a "Crossroads" for almost every issue, but after 1932 it was
only an occasional feature. There were no "Crossroads" in 1933 at
all, and only one in 1934. The feature returned regularly in 1935,
but then appeared only once in 1936.

   Until the break in 1933, Eiseley selected the poems and commented on them each time, except once, when Mabel Langdon
(later Eiseley) prepared the summer, 1930, section. Eiseley's illness

and extended recuperation in 1929 and 1930 may have prevented him from working on that issue. In 1933, the *Prairie Schooner* was in serious financial difficulty, and since Wimberly had to reduce considerably the number of pages in each issue, that may have temporarily eliminated the section. A few months after Eiseley graduated in 1933, he left Lincoln for Philadelphia, where he became progressively more involved with science and had less and less time for the *Schooner*, which probably explains the later irregularity and subsequent discontinuation of "Crossroads."

Although Eiseley selected a variety of poems and appended only brief comments, both his choices and remarks provide insight into his feelings and concerns during the early thirties. With some self-irony, but with seriousness as well, Eiseley described himself in the fall of 1929 as a fortress of gloom. Explaining his choice of two poems and the fascination "autumn possesses . . . for mournful men," he adds, "The editor of this column, having been assured that he is a veritable stronghold of gloom, begs to be allowed to celebrate the dark days after his own fashion."[8] He does so with "Rain Piece," a sonnet by Ted Olsen, and "Fog" by Bennet Weaver.[9] The first seems particularly mournful—"And I do not wonder that men go mad to feel / These busy needles of cruelly fluid steel"—and describes the rain as "ruthless," "malignant," and slimy. The second poem, "Fog," is indeed gloomy, dwelling on the withering and dying of life. It ends with these undistinguished, but ominous, lines:

> Silent the gathered robins crowd the South
> To their death of sunshine silently they fly.
> And I shall go down to my place with a closed mouth
> With that last silence which could not be a cry.

Autumn was always Eiseley's season, and the images in these poems fit well with his lifelong sense of melancholy and mortality.

For the preceding issue, Eiseley chose one poem about the death of love and beauty—"There Was a Girl"—that near the end says, "Love must die as youth shall cease," and he selected another about night and loneliness that ends with these lines: "We wander, dream-like, on the moonless earth. / The wind wails in the fields; / We are alone. . . ." The first strikes a "simple, human note," according to Eiseley, and even though the theme is old, "those of us not afraid of sentiment" will know the loss.[10]

The poems for the spring, 1929, number of the *Prairie Schooner* are consistent with the others Eiseley selected during the year. Instead of something optimistic, he chose another rain poem that speaks, in Eiseley's terms, of "the starkness of unturned acres under a March rain," and ends, almost predictably, "But we will not know / And we will not care / When the raindrops slow— / We will not be there." He included, as well, a poem about death and one about the futility of following a star. These are old themes, too, and melancholy youth is especially susceptible to them and sometimes acts as if no one else has ever experienced similar feelings. In a moment of such youthful pride, Eiseley points out that the poems' advice is sound, "but it will be read and never followed by the lost and the proud."[11]

It is clear that young Eiseley thought of himself as a tough-minded critic and poet who sought out sincere, powerful poems that dealt with the realities of life. He looked for poems that fit his own sense of reality, and he also chose those that broke away from thematic conventions. He not only looked for the human (read: grim) touch, but he wanted as well to avoid the sentimentality of so many popular publications. In the spring, 1930, "Crossroads," for example, he included a "powerful" poem by a "modern" woman poet. "The sugared singing of the petticoat period," he explained, "has become a thing of the past."[12]

Besides these poems, Eiseley chose verse with other subjects and styles. In the winter of 1931, the section consisted of a single piece, a long, very bitter monologue about war and its impact on one particular young man. Noting the "definite power" of the poem, Eiseley praises the small literary magazines for trying "to express the real America that the literary sophisticates too often ignore."[13] To suggest the potential quality of regional literature, Eiseley chose one poem about the frontier past and another titled "Song in Favor of the Soil" for the spring, 1931, *Schooner*.[14] But the range of his choices is, in fact, rather narrow. For three years, his selections seem almost single-minded in their severity. Time and again, in one way or another, the poems express hopelessness and grief; they speak of loneliness, misery, and death; and they resign men to the erosion of time and the permanence of earth and stars. Yet at the same time, many portray an individual's capacity to struggle and survive, for a time at least, in spite of powerful, conflicting forces.

The poetry reprinted in "Crossroads" is usually readable, and a few poems are quite good; but on the whole, Eiseley's poetry was superior. That is not surprising, because "Crossroads" drew only from publications that did not pay contributors, and except for *Voices*, Eiseley made his selections generally from less well-known magazines. He was probably the best poet publishing in most of them.

During the 1930s, Loren Eiseley contributed several poetry reviews to the *Prairie Schooner*, and he reviewed poetry for Harold Vinal's *Voices* as well. The feelings and attitudes reflected in these commentaries seem quite consistent with those expressed through "Crossroads." In the spring of 1932 he reviewed a book for the *Prairie Schooner* by a mediocre poet named Grace Stone Coates. Although he recognized the flawed character of the lyrics, he admired the woman's tough-minded restraint and her sensitivity to the "end of love" and the "end of flesh." Her work was "passionately obdurate"—a quaint phrase that describes Eiseley himself rather well.[15] In the *Schooner*, he also reviewed two books by Harold Vinal, one in 1932, the other in 1936.[16] In the first, the internal hell Vinal speaks of appealed especially to Eiseley. In the second, a narrative about people living on an island off Maine, Vinal's sketches of frustrated and trapped individuals and his descriptions of the natural realities surrounding them captured Eiseley's imagination. In the reviews, he also made a case for Vinal's accomplished use of the sonnet, for some a presumably outmoded form, but one in which Eiseley himself worked. In 1937 he raved about the natural, intimate, and hard-edged earthiness of a book by Edward Weismiller published in the Yale Series of Younger Poets. In relatively conventional and closed forms, Weismiller's poems portray a world far from the cities, and that, too, appealed to Eiseley. Although he believed that Weismiller's book might last a century, he did not fall into the trap that another reviewer in the same issue did, claiming that Weismiller promised to be an improvement over Robert Frost.[17]

Eiseley's reviews and his remarks in "Crossroads" reveal a bias against "modernists," "literary sophisticates," "literati," "Ph.D.'s," "fat complacency," and the "self satisfied and pompous." He rejects, it seems, just about everybody except those who speak for the Middle West and for the harsh realities of life outside the cities. He also implicitly rejects experiments in form and style, both in the books he reviewed and in his own early poetry. These attitudes, as we shall see, fit very well with his past and with the intent and achievement of the early volumes of the *Prairie Schooner*.

The reviews Eiseley wrote for *Voices* do not differ significantly in their expressed preferences from others he was writing, but several do reveal more about his personal life and literary interests than do the *Schooner* reviews. In the winter of 1932-33, Eiseley contributed an excellent short essay about Robinson Jeffers, expressing great admiration and commenting on features of Jeffers's poetry that Eiseley's own poetry and later prose share. At the beginning of the review he quotes Jeffers: "In literature it is only the wild that attracts us. . . . A truly good book is something as wildly natural and primitive, mysterious and marvelous, ambrosial and fertile as a fungus or lichen." In that attitude Eiseley sees Jeffers's great strength. What Eiseley most values about Jeffers "is that very rare phenomenon which happened once at Walden and a few other places, namely, the complete identification of the individual with his environment, or, rather, the extension of the environment into the individual to such a degree that the latter seems almost a lens, a gathering point through which, in some psychic and unexplainable manner, is projected a portion of the diversified and terrific forces of nature that otherwise stream helplessly away without significance to humanity."[18]

In Robinson Jeffers, Eiseley recognizes the same correlation, or identification, between an individual and a place that I have been exploring in Eiseley himself. Throughout Eiseley's childhood, youth, and young adulthood, the Nebraska prairies and high ground to the west embedded themselves permanently in his very soul. When he found that connection effectively expressed by another, he celebrated the discovery.

Because of that identification—the way the poet roots his feet to the earth—Jeffers's poetry is not nature writing in the usual sense. Eiseley remarks on the cruelty and mystery, as well as goodness, that Jeffers sees in nature; he speaks about the grim austerity of the poetry; he points out Jeffers's sense of men's great weakness; and he acknowledges the solitude and bitterness behind it. Jeffers's pain and loneliness, in Eiseley's opinion, ran far deeper than the superficial cynicism and futility of so much contemporary literature.

Eiseley probably hoped that his own voice, at least occasionally, reached those same depths. We will come back to Eiseley and Robinson Jeffers; but for now, let it stand that in 1932, in the midst of his own unhappiness, Eiseley found in Robinson Jeffers a strong voice that spoke for and to him. One lonely mind found another.

Less than a year before, also in *Voices*, Eiseley made as direct a public statement about his own personal distress as he did at any time. His autobiography (1975) and other later writings make the character of these crisis years quite clear. The review reveals his feelings at the time (1931): "As I write this review the first flakes of winter are falling past the window into the streets of my little midwestern town. I am tired; I am gnawed at by futility; I am heartsick for the things that I have lost—for the dim trails in the sage, for the green loneliness of the high Rockies. . . ."[19] Eiseley gives these confessions a literary turn, certainly, and somewhat sentimentalizes his feelings; but his distress is real. It is even possible to argue that Eiseley sentimentalizes Jeffers and through him indulges his own loneliness and pain in youthful excess. Perhaps. Sometimes the voice does sound youthfully indulgent. But given Eiseley's past, the maturity and intelligence of the Jeffers essay, and the emotional and thematic qualities of Eiseley's later, major books, we are hearing in the reviews and articles—and shortly in the poetry—the maturing of feelings and attitudes, not merely youthful effusions of fashionable cynicism or young adult morbidity that will soon pass. It was all perfectly consistent with his experiences and temperament.

Loren Eiseley's personal history and his feelings and attitudes were quite compatible with the intentions and contents of the early *Prairie Schooner*. The magazine may have been inclined more to morbidity and gloom than some liked, but that emphasis expressed the vision of its contributors and the realistic and regional intentions of its editors. In the office and pages of the *Prairie Schooner*, Eiseley found, for the time being, an intellectual and emotional home. He was beginning to build a life and an identity with language—with conventional literary expression, initially, but later with a new idiom that would be his alone.

In the first issue, the *Schooner* identified itself as a regional magazine and invited contributions both from the university and from midwestern and prairie authors. Several times during the early years, it published statements of purpose and vision. To the first *Prairie Schooner*, Bess Streeter Aldrich contributed a short essay about her own writing in which she expressed the regionalist's devotion to a place and desire to preserve something of its spirit in fiction. She also argued "that a story rings most true when it is drawn from material within the limitations of our geographical, mental, or emotional boundaries." Near the end of the magazine's second year, Lowry Wimberly, the editor, described the *Schooner* as "firmly planted on the soil of the Midwest." During the third year, he and Martin Peterson elaborated on the *Schooner*'s character, urging a realistic study of the Midwest free of pessimism or optimism and of "attitudes . . . and beatitudes": "Let us now study the Midwest more closely and more dispassionately and allow the winters to be no colder than [they are] . . . , the sandstorms no denser, the skies no brighter, and the men and women no more tolerant, no more intolerant than they are." Whatever the cause of their remarks, the regional role of the *Schooner* is very clear, as is the writer's obligation to portray a place accurately.[20]

Later in the spring, Wimberly and Russell T. Prescott spoke of a more general role for the *Prairie Schooner*. Regional verisimilitude doubtless continued as an important function, but the editors now talked about the *Schooner*'s interest "in finding a body of common feelings and traditions for midwesterners."[21] The editors hoped that the *Schooner* might define the character of the region and in some sense unite its people, as well as display the details of the prairie's past and present. The magazine wanted no sentimentality or unnecessary grimness or excess melancholy. It wanted, instead, honest, tough-minded, accurate portraits. These might be grim or even tragic, but they had to be true. Just a few years later, in 1932, Mari Sandoz spoke out, especially against sentimentality—the "saccharization of our literature." She was making a case for literature rooted in the folk and place and expressing concern over the gradual dissolution and disappearance of regional culture. America needs, she argued, "the blood and vigor of those close to the soil."[22]

When the *Prairie Schooner* began publication, the last Nebraska frontier had barely closed. The influx of homesteaders, the Kinkaiders, into northwest Nebraska continued at least until 1920. So the pioneer history of the state was really not very far away. It is easy to understand why one of the *Schooner* authors would say, in 1928, "To Nebraska students the frontier is a vital force still."[23] In writing about it, he described particular historical conditions that had become the themes of *Schooner* stories and essays—the defeat of farmers, economic tragedy, and emotional desolation. The *Schooner*'s regionalism included both a strong sense of history and realism of place.

The first issue opened, for example, with a short story by Marie Macumber, or Mari Sandoz, who later published both fiction and history about the Middle West. "The Vine" tells of a couple living on the prairie frontier, portraying the loneliness and isolation of their life and the serious conflicts between them. In the end the prairie hardships drive the wife mad. The fourth issue printed a story, "Dust," about the Sandhills region of Nebraska, and it, too, dramatized the fate of a bored, lonely, disillusioned wife. Frontier life imposed special hardships and extreme loneliness on the women, and the *Schooner* authors seemed particularly sensitive to that, for another story about a pioneer wife appeared in the second year. "The Last Move" portrays a woman who has been forced time and again to go with her wandering husband whenever he decides to move to a new place. Each time they move, their lot becomes worse, her life more desolate.[24]

In its first year, the *Prairie Schooner* also initiated a regular feature about midwestern authors. Although Bess Streeter Aldrich wrote about herself for the first issue, normally a staff member or contributor wrote the feature. By the end of its second year, the *Schooner* had printed essays about Willa Cather, Carl Sandburg, Hamlin Garland, Ruth Suckow, and others less well known. Each essay tried to describe the character and achievement of the author in question; it also provided another way for the magazine to fulfill its mission, to define midwestern regional writing. In these essays, there was more talk about the drudgery and privations of the Midlands and the bleakness of the prairies. But a feature about Willa Cather (winter, 1929) described her sense of the beauty of the prairies. The land was both stark and beautiful, a point important to understanding its appeal for Eiseley. His own experiences and the history of his family and the region taught him how harsh and bleak it could be, but nature also seduced him with the beauty and mystery of its wildness.

In 1929, the *Schooner* accepted another story, "Sadie," about a distraught wife and a cruel husband. It also printed a story called "Plans" that narrated the frustration of a young man's ambition to leave the farm and go to the university. Because of his father's illness and the youth's position as the eldest, he must stay and assume his father's role. He is trapped on the farm. One of the stories in the winter, 1930, number, "Along a Sandy Road," dramatizes the extreme emotions that could erupt under the stresses of prairie life. A mother savagely beats her daughter and drives the child to sudden suicide. Another, appearing the summer before, explores the bitter existence of a very poor family and tries to find out what makes life endurable for them.[25]

These illustrations suggest what may have prompted Lowry Wimberly's warning in 1929 about realism. The *Schooner* was not uniformly gloomy or tragic, but those readers who complained about the funereal atmosphere of the magazine had some grounds, even if their complaints were fundamentally imperceptive. The literature in the *Schooner* dealt with experiences that serious literature has always portrayed, and it did so pretty well and for the most part realistically. At one point, however, Wimberly became so sensitive to the complaints that he deliberately tried to make the winter, 1931, issue "happy." Besides responding to readers, he wanted "to relieve the gloom of economic depression."[26] Given the *Schooner*'s intent and vision, the recent and past history of the region, the severe economic depression, and the sensitivities and perceptions of writers in America during the 1920s and 1930s, the *Prairie Schooner* became exactly what one might expect.

The magazine has now been publishing for over fifty continuous years—in itself remarkable—and it has a strong reputation. But even in its early and now somewhat obscure years, the *Schooner* had a national reputation, in particular for publishing outstanding fiction. In 1929, Edward J. O'Brien, an eminent critic and editor of the annual *Best Short Stories*, gave the magazine high praise: "The quality of its stories, articles, and poems is such that the *Prairie Schooner* ranks with the *Midland*, the *Frontier*, and not more than one or two other American periodicals, as the most significant

expression of American life which we possess. As such, it focuses
the whole cultural life of a section of America. As an experienced
reader of American short stories, I find it more vital as an interpretation of American life than the *Atlantic Monthly*, the *Forum* or
Harper's Magazine."[27]

Before very long, however, the editors began to recognize the
limits of regionalism. By the early 1930s, they were publishing
work by authors from the East and West coasts as well as from
elsewhere outside the Midlands. Their strong desire to publish only
high quality writing and the great number of submissions from
other places forced them to change. In practice, they modified their
announced intention before they ever acknowledged it in print. But
that came, too. One of the first indications of uneasiness with
midwestern regional writing appeared in the summer of 1930. In
"The Midlandish Mind," Eugene Konecky argued that the prairies
were not adequate to serve as a milieu for a new American literature. The small town midlandish mind could not support an
intelligent literary culture, nor could the place itself or regional
attitudes provide a sufficiently broad subject matter for the new
literature. The essay urges the literary movement to become more
national, to synthesize regional attitudes, so that a truer picture of
midwestern life, or human life, might emerge. Konecky is warning
his audience about ignorance and provincialism; at the same time
he is justifying the *Schooner*'s realism.[28]

Two years later, Lowry Wimberly took on "the new regionalism"
himself. He is surprisingly critical of the movement, reducing its
motives mainly to a revolt by the West against the East and to a
desire to portray some presumed "distinctive quality or flavor" of
local life. Both charges are fairly trivial. In his opinion, regional
literature has no future in a country increasingly dominated by a
standard culture. For all his misunderstanding of the psychic and
biological impacts of environment and the curious way he ignores
the *Prairie Schooner* in this essay, Wimberly nevertheless perceives
a real problem. Regional literature *can* be very provincial, and for
authors and magazines with ambition to quality as well as wide
reputation, there is no future in that.[29]

In a sense Wimberly's warnings were perceptive and wise. He
was also using the essay to acknowledge and announce not so
much a new direction for the *Schooner* (and certainly not a break

with its origins) as a modification of its original intent. Authors and magazines must grow, both emotionally and intellectually. While it remained, in fact, rooted in the life of a particular place, the *Prairie Schooner* was becoming, even in the early 1930s, a more national magazine.

Like the *Schooner*, Loren Eiseley grew up firmly rooted in the Nebraska soil, but he, too, had to grow beyond that. Although the changes in his life were more radical (he left the Midlands and turned to science), he never lost his identity as an American of the middle border.

NOTES

1. *All the Strange Hours*, p. 77.
2. *Innocent Assassins*, pp. 88-89.
3. Lichtenstein, *Dilemma of Human Identity*, p. 78.
4. Ibid., p. 184.
5. *Prairie Schooner*, 1, no. 1 (Jan., 1927), 6.
6. Loren Eiseley, "Autumn—A Memory," *Prairie Schooner*, 1, no. 4 (Oct., 1927), 238-39.
7. *Prairie Schooner*, 3, no. 1 (Winter, 1929), 36.
8. Ibid., 3, no. 4 (Fall, 1929), 270.
9. Ibid., pp. 270-71.
10. Albert Richard Wetjen, "There Was a Girl"; Wilbur Gaffrey, "Fantasia: Night"; and introductory note, *Prairie Schooner*, 3, no. 3 (Summer, 1929), 208-9.
11. Introductory note and H. C. Barrowes-Donald, "We Will Not Be There," *Prairie Schooner*, 3, no. 2 (Spring, 1929), 130-31.
12. Virginia Stait, "Ci Git (Here Lies)," *Prairie Schooner*, 4, no. 2 (Spring, 1930), 116.
13. Introductory note and Albert Edward Clements, "Slacker," *Prairie Schooner*, 5, no. 1 (Winter, 1931), 63-68.
14. Norman Macleod, "Song in Favor of the Soil," *Prairie Schooner*, 5, no. 2 (Spring, 1931), 167.
15. Loren Eiseley, review of *Mead & Mangel-Wurzel, Prairie Schooner*, 6, no. 2 (Spring, 1932), 175.
16. Review of *Hymn to Chaos, Prairie Schooner*, 6, no. 2 (Spring, 1932), 175-76; review of *Hurricane*, ibid., 10, no. 2 (Summer, 1936), 165.
17. Review of *The Deer Come Down, Prairie Schooner*, 11, no. 1 (Spring, 1937), 86.
18. "Music of the Mountain," *Voices*, Dec.-Jan., 1932-33, p. 42.
19. "Wings in the Wilderness," *Voices*, Feb., 1932, p. 153.
20. Aldrich, "Midwestern Writers," *Prairie Schooner*, 1, no. 1 (Jan., 1927), 80-81; Wimberly, "The Ox Cart," ibid., 2, no. 4 (Fall, 1928),

314; Wimberly and Peterson, ibid., 3, no. 1 (Winter, 1929), 78.
21. *Prairie Schooner*, 3, no. 2 (Spring, 1929), 173.
22. Ibid., 6, no. 1 (Winter, 1932), 66-67, 66.
23. Mamie Meredith, "The Challenge of the Frontier," *Prairie Schooner*, 2, no. 3 (Summer, 1928), 210.
24. Sandoz, *Prairie Schooner*, 1, no. 1 (Jan., 1927), 7-16; Ivan Hall, "Dust," ibid., 1, no. 4 (Oct., 1927), 229-37.
25. Cornelius Marian Muilenberg, "Sadie," *Prairie Schooner*, 3, no. 2 (Spring, 1929), 132-44; Lyman L. Ross, "Plans," ibid., 3, no. 3 (Summer, 1929), 215-21; Ellen Bishop, ibid., 4, no. 1 (Winter, 1930), 1-5.
26. *Prairie Schooner*, 5, no. 1 (Winter, 1931), 85.
27. Edward J. O'Brien, *Prairie Schooner*, 3, no. 3 (Summer, 1929), 235.
28. *Prairie Schooner*, 4, no. 3 (Summer, 1930), 181-85.
29. Ibid., 6, no. 3 (Summer, 1932), 214-21.

The Young Poet

> Deep in the quiet of that earthly death
> My slow heart moved.

In its spring, 1928, issue, the *Prairie Schooner* published Loren Eiseley's first acknowledged poem, "Spiders." He was just twenty when the poem appeared, yet several of his typical themes emerge. The poem meditates on the way "spiders inherit everything." "Tiles drop from the roof— / Leaves turn mouldy under the black, slanting rain," but the spiders remain. Wherever men die or their works decay, spiders crawl or feed. The poem even compares time to a spider and the world to a fly caught in its web. Hanging there, swaying and turning, the world "desiccates" and "crumbles." From the beginning, in "Autumn—A Memory," as well as in "Spiders," Eiseley was writing about time and decay. He was speaking in a familiar voice.[1]

Through the next eight years, Loren Eiseley published at least sixty-five poems in various little magazines. After that, as he became fully involved in science, he wrote and published much less. Only thirteen poems came out between 1936 and 1945, when he stopped publishing poetry altogether for almost twenty years. Besides contributing to the *Schooner*, Eiseley offered many of his poems to the *Midland* and to *Voices*.

Like the *Prairie Schooner*, the *Midland* was an important regional magazine, published mainly in Iowa by John T. Frederick from 1915 to 1933. Scholars have generally considered it the best of the well-known regional publications, others being *Frontier*, the *New Mexico Quarterly Review*, the *Southwest Review*, and the *Prairie Schooner*. Frederick J. Hoffman even suggested that "because of its contribution to the development of regionalism, *The Midland* must be ranked alongside *The Dial, The Little Review,* and *Poetry*."[2] So it was a significant place to publish, and Eiseley's ready acceptance there suggests that his talent clearly transcended local borders. In fact, in the opinion of a later historian of the *Midland*, Loren Eiseley was probably the best poet it published in its eighteen years. His work "marks a high point toward which Midland verse as a whole was slowly moving."[3]

In contrast to the *Schooner* and the *Midland*, *Voices* definitely was not a midwestern regional magazine. Published in Boston by the well-known minor poet Harold Vinal, *Voices* resembled Harriet Monroe's *Poetry*; but although opinions are mixed, it did not quite rival *Poetry*'s achievement.[4] Nevertheless, *Voices* was better than most of its contemporaries, and in its time it published, among others, Allen Tate, Mark Van Doren, Robert Penn Warren, Kenneth Fearing, Donald Davidson, Kenneth Patchen, and Genevieve Taggard. As editor, Vinal seemed opposed to modernist or objectivist poetic tendencies (he insisted, for example, on the subjective sources and quality of poetry), and he encouraged new poets by opening his magazine to them. Eiseley fit both preferences, for he was indeed a new voice, and he wrote very personal poetry. The magazine first accepted Eiseley's work in 1930, publishing a sequence of poems titled "Bleak Upland." By 1936, *Voices* had presented thirty-one of Loren Eiseley's poems to its readers. His work clearly possessed more than a regional appeal, and its frequent appearance in *Voices* from 1930 to 1936 represents a significant achievement.

Much less frequently, Eiseley's poetry appeared in the *New York Herald-Tribune Books*, the *American Poetry Journal*, the *American Mercury*, and *Poetry*. He placed his first poem with *Poetry* in 1929, "The Deserted Homestead," and ten years later *Poetry* printed two more, in an issue that also included pieces by William Carlos Williams, Glenway Wescott, Harold Vinal, and John Malcolm Brinnin. The *American Mercury*, H. L. Mencken's famous magazine, published "Leaving September" in 1936, and in the mid-1930s the *Literary Digest* reprinted three Eiseley poems. Thus, as the decade went on, Eiseley's stature and success increased—ironically just as he began turning away from poetry to his professional scientific concerns.

In 1934, along with Witter Bynner and John Gould Fletcher, Eiseley read a requiem he had written for Mary Austin (a southwestern writer of some reputation in the 1930s) at a memorial service in Santa Fe, New Mexico.[5] Some years later, as a kind of climax to his early career as a poet, Eiseley's sonnet "October Has the Heart," originally published in the *Schooner*, was selected by Thomas Moult for *Best Poems of 1942*:

> Left to his ruin with the autumn leaf
> The spider, black and yellow, treading air
> By means of gossamer, goes like a thief
> Up, up and up—till from that trembling stair
> He launches out for some far other vine
> Where pumpkins lie like moons among the corn.
> As through some old, some bitter-clear thin wine
> The world lies still—no green leaf hides the thorn.
> October has the heart—no more dark things
> Cry in the blood; the quick uncertain storms
> Are all gone past, and with them all high wings.
> Clear in this autumn quiet something forms:
> Something to last—what Keats once bent to learn
> Painted forever on a certain urn.[6]

Although that volume included many now unknown names, it also published several famous writers, among them Walter de la Mare, Stephen Spender, Geoffrey Tillotson, Conrad Aiken, and Richard Eberhart. It is useless, of course, to speculate about Loren Eiseley's career had he somehow elected poetry rather than anthropology. When we consider that science enabled him to reach his real genius as a writer, such speculation seems idle. Nevertheless, we can say that in the 1930s Eiseley wrote a great many fine poems that still give pleasure and insight and also help us understand the prose writer he later became.

Although the four poems in "Bleak Upland"[7] are not the best of Eiseley's early poems, they represent the themes and character of that poetry very well, and they also show how closely Eiseley attended to technique. The sequence describes a harsh and barren land where the wind and dust rule and only nettles and sparse weeds grow. As the first poem, "Against Lineage," says,

> These fields are outcast, having borne
>   The nettle and the weed.
> The red and sterile sands refuse
>   To propagate such seed.

All man's efforts come to nothing, for in the face of wind and dust, "they are soon undone."

The second poem, "Upland Harvest," begins, "The upland has a bitter yield," then describes the sterility and "stony emptiness" of these western lands and the futility of man's prayers "for fertile ground." Every line in the first two poems confronts a reader with the utter barrenness of the land and the hopelessness of man's efforts.

In the third poem, Eiseley continues to speak of the bleak upland, but now he begins to express his own misery and grief more directly, comparing his pain to the wounds and woes of the earth. There is a difference, though, for the earth does not hide "old pains that should be cried aloud"; unlike the poet, it does not mask its misery. When he is finally able to express his feelings, he will—he believes—be free from them; but he will also have revealed the barrenness of his life:

> When I no longer fear to break
> This stubborn silence, nor to wear
> Heart's misery in my face, or take
> Full easement on the common air.
>
> Then I from grief too long concealed
> By guile and the dissembling word
> Shall rest—as starkly as this field
> Abandoned to the crying bird.

In the last poem of the sequence, "Be Glad You Worshippers," the young man stands as a "witness to the bitter cost" the people pay who go on planting their sterile fields and praying "to their unfruitful God." They do not, however, share the loneliness and misery of the drifting poet, for somehow their prayers insulate them from the true reality of their lives:

> Late wanderer in uplands stilled by frost
> Where the year turns in sterile solitude,
> I have been witness to the bitter cost
> Of failing harvest and the meagre food;
> And, coming where a freezing crossroad lies
> By a worn church, heard, at the preacher's nod,
> The sullen voices in crescendo rise
> Laboring at prayers to their unfruitful God.

O you who kneel beneath a blackened cross,
Be glad you know no stars far overhead;
Be glad of your sleep's surety, nor toss
And cry out in the night, nor rise to tread
Alone down darkened fields where no one heeds
The hand of the Great Sower, sowing weeds!

Eiseley's portrait of the "bleak upland" has a personal, as well as a regional, significance. In one sense, the barren land projects the poet's inner space. His own life has had a "bitter yield," and so, possessed by grief and bitterness, he is crying out in pain and anger, trying somehow to rid himself of his misery.

In another sense, the poems speak of an entire region and people for whom struggle, poverty, and failure were life. In "The Deserted Homestead," published a few months earlier in *Poetry*, Eiseley narrated one of those failures:

The wind is desolate in the fields;
And round the house at night
The autumn smoulder of decay
Creeps like a blight.

His standing corn with mildew rusts
Forsaken on the hill.
The wild will cover up the road
Now his hands are still.

Only a sparrow, like a leaf,
Skips along the eaves,
Half lonely for a human voice
In the hush of leaves.

This ending that is old as earth
Sorrow cannot break.
Our doors are open to the wind,
And the wind will take.

The jeweled phrase is worthless here.
The blackbird and the crow,
Bleak criers over windswept land,
Alone may sow

Dark syllables across the wind;
Or, in the ruined field,

> Deride the hackneyed misery—
> Earth's only yield.[8]

Besides showing a likely historical event, this poem resonates with the feelings and insights of "Autumn—A Memory." Like an ancient ruin, the homestead reveals the passing and dying of people and the extinction of a way of life.

The settings of "Bleak Upland" and "The Deserted Homestead" are general enough to suggest not only historical conditions but also the pioneer struggles going on in the northwest corner of the state during Eiseley's early years and the depressed farm conditions of the 1920s. In some ways, Nebraska life did not change from the 1850s until Loren Eiseley's youth. He has incorporated those timeless features into these poems, concentrating and intensifying the picture to achieve force, to develop his metaphor, and to write in the regional manner.

In these early poems, Eiseley is beginning to work with the interplay between inner and outer space—a rhythm and metaphor basic to all of his writing. This is not an unusual literary device, but for Eiseley it functioned as far more than that. It expressed his awareness of how deeply he and the land were intertwined. Close correlations existed between Eiseley's inner space and the places he inhabited and explored from childhood onward. Later, science gave depth and dimension to his understanding of the movement between inner and outer, but Nebraska and the land beyond—seen in "Bleak Upland" through a regionalist's eyes and then later in new dimensions by the scientist—provide the major place and symbol for Eiseley's imagination. The plains, the uplands and mountains, and the Southwest—the hard, barren, rocky country that infuses so many of his poems and so much of his life—not only provide a basic imagery but fundamentally shape his mind and imagination. In his autobiography, as we noted earlier, he claims to be "a creature molded of plains' dust,"[9] and he says of himself and his family, "We were Americans of the middle border."[10] Already in "Bleak Upland" one can see the literary manifestations of this past.

The four poems develop through conventional, tightly controlled forms, but within the sequence they vary a great deal. One is a sonnet. The others follow different but consistent patterns: the rhymes are true; the lines are relatively short and end on a strong stress; only the sonnet runs to pentameter. These are obviously poems of a young poet learning his craft and working, therefore, with various lines and rhymes. Sometimes the poems are a little forced or awkward; the lines simply don't flow as they might. They are rough, like the young poet and the world he is describing. They are also poems of a young man struggling for control and survival, and so the tight forms were probably necessary to contain the feelings erupting within him. "Bleak Upland" is an important sequence because it sets the texture, terms, feelings, and attitudes that Eiseley developed throughout the decade.

In his 1931 poem "Earthward," for example, Eiseley expresses some of his feelings about the land, especially his longing to escape "the confining shell of the mind" and to "mix" with the earth:

> In the old irrigation ditch on the Terrel ranch
> Brown water still flows—watering the cactus now
> And the jewel weed. Stray feet seldom come here,
> But all afternoon the dragonfly flits through the weedy coverts
> And his larvae crawl from the water to shed
> Their tight water-shrunk skins for a crystal and gold expansion,
> The unquestioning flight
> Along the blue air.
>
> Men have said this before, but some few
> Must learn for themselves: I find it suddenly good
> Not to think anymore, but to mix with brown water and earth smells;
> To split the confining shell of the mind
> And relax on this oldest,
> Most certain breast.[11]

Not only does Eiseley find a way to escape painful memories and present distress; he discovers, as well, beauty and goodness in the irrigation ditch. Although the imagery may seem regressive, Eiseley is in fact writing about places where life sustains itself in its simplest forms. So this regression is clearly in service of the ego, and as such it perfectly dramatizes this particular period of his life, at the same time it touches on needs and desires everyone experiences. In the poem Eiseley has relaxed, appropriately, the characteristically tight lines of his other early sonnets, and he has thereby achieved fluency and vitality. In its form and focus, "Earthward" is typical of his best work, although later in the decade he was writing even better poems.

His poems about animals often reveal similar longings. In "Song for the Wolf's Coat," Eiseley contrasts the bitterness of human life and consciousness with the instinctual freedom of a wolf:

> Under the wind's cold roof what shelter have we—
> What tattered garment can the flesh put on?
> Walk in the wolf's coat, you would be more happy;
> Stare with a wolf's eyes—you would greet the sun
>
> Only as warmth from rain. In the hollow bracken
> Stretching your toes and fiercely at peace,
> The minutes would run and your wild thought be unshaken,
> By the side of death you would doze and take your ease.
>
> We, in the fury of thought, drink bitter water,
> The crystal springs of the mind are like acid pools—
> Under the wind's cold roof we are lost and homeless,
> And the flesh is flesh—we have cast that garment of fools.
>
> But better we might have run in the wolf's coat, shaggy,
> Fierce, with the yellow eyes of death in the sun,
> In the flesh of beasts, with the blood like a boiling caldron—
> In the flesh of beasts it had been better to run.[12]

This poem speaks less of the beauty and surety of nature than of its ferocious and mindless vitality. Instead of expressing relief at escaping the burdens of thought, the poem evokes the furies of thought and the poet's desperate need to get away. While the underlying impulse may resemble the desire in "Earthward"—to escape memory and thought—the quality of feeling differs very much. This one burns, while the other soothes.

Less than a year later, Eiseley published two poems about foxes. In "Fox Curse" he speaks at first for the foxes, cursing anyone who forgets them, and then he identifies with their wildness and defiance:

> This curse is for you,
> Neighbor, you so grim-
> Purposed though your hands
> Are already dim:
>
> May you never have
> Land so deep in corn
> That you will forget
> Fox fur on a thorn.

> May you never drive
> Iron in this ground,
> But a fox's bark
> Still will turn you round.
>
> Though I meekly pass
> Where you plow and fire
> Everywhere I leave
> Fox fur on the wire—
>
> And a fox's face,
> Masked in human skin,
> Something wild and sharp,
> Hold its laughter in . . . . .[13]

In "Incident in the Zoo" he stands outside a cage of "little Fennec foxes" and observes with fascination their delicacy and beauty. They do not belong there, for they shudder at "the city's iron pulse" and fear "the shaking ground."

> They move in memory among mint leaves.
> Their lives are bound
> To a lost land, all night their ears have captured
> No friendly sound.[14]

But when they hear a roar from the lion's house, their "wild hearts" are touched, and they respond.

Although the range of feeling in these animal poems is broad (Eiseley captures their ferocity, wildness, mystery, delicacy, and beauty), he is consistent in his fascination, particularly with foxes, and his longing to escape into the animal world—impulses that reached their finest expression in "The Innocent Fox," the next-to-last chapter of *The Unexpected Universe* (1969). Both "Fox Curse" and "Incident in the Zoo" were reprinted in 1934 in the *Literary Digest*.

Many of these poems clearly allude to Loren Eiseley's own life, and given his life history, one might expect that loss, loneliness, sorrow, depression, and struggle would act as underlying formative impulses and appear frequently as themes. Those experiences, in part at least, led to his feelings about the earth, the wolf's coat, and the foxes' den. In the spring of 1933, *Voices* published a second group of Eiseley's poems, "Fire in the Wind," and these, perhaps more than any others, express the deprivation, depression, and

bitterness in his life. The group consists of seven poems, four of
them in a short sonnet sequence titled "Sonnets for a Second
Death." Eiseley was now twenty-six, about to complete his undergraduate degree at the university.

Written apparently out of profound despair, "Note at Midnight,"
the second poem in the group, compresses years of grief and
confusion into two compelling and moving sonnets:

Written to you, this letter out of pain
And sick despair, and longing for a night
With no day after—I have slept again,
Once, and awakened, I have chattered light
Gossip with neighbors, I have eaten, read
A book or two—and all this I have done
Unseeing and unhearing—I am dead
Though upright with swift pulses in the sun.
To have walked cold through this still living house,
Looking on all things with malignant eyes,
Hating the light, the sun, the fool's applause,
Is to have measured how the narrow skies
Contract to dark, how easily one word
Shatters the green leaf and the singing bird.

It may be when my broken mouth shall grin
Out of parched rubble at a wintry sky
With shifted stars, I may have found within
The dark some answer. Oh, no doubt that I—
Lord of blown nothing and the king of waste,
The counsellor of leaves upon the blast—
Will have some message, have in somewise faced
The evil master of our wretched past.
But now no fist of thunder at the door
Receives reply, save echoed knocking thrown
Back from lost stairs, and on the moonlit floor
Of space, no answer, and Time's hinges groan
Inward on vacancy—wherein grows plain
The dark's puffed cheeks above the lantern brain.[15]

It is not difficult to imagine that this poem describes Eiseley's
near breakdown after his father's death. Trapped in the midst of
grief and despair, he can look only with malignant eyes on everything that lives, and he can only hope that relief will somehow

come. This troubled state of mind could well be the source of insomnia, anxiety, and sorrow sufficient to drive a young man halfway across a continent. It could be the source of his longing to escape memory and thought and, in a sense, to die without losing either the earth or animal vitality.

In "Sonnets for a Second Death," Eiseley attempts an even more ambitious poetic account of pain and despair—or living death. The four sonnets trace a journey "on the road to death" that leads, after three days, to a resurrection. Each poem portrays one day of the journey and shows the poet and his companion, another whose life has turned to ashes, passing into darkness and beside an "evil wood" as they follow the road "from Night to Nothing":

> We walked five miles, chance met, and going on
> Whatever roads the dead walk, till at last
> They lay their dead limbs down, in earnest gone
> Back to the windy dust heaps of the past.

But in the midst of his despair, the poet begins to awaken:

> Deep in the quiet of that earthly death
> My slow heart moved.

Like Lazarus, after three days in the tomb, the poet arises to "sunlight" and the "greening leaf," and once more he experiences wonder and love. His resurrection, however, does not permit him to forget, and the sequence ends in tension. Eiseley is divided between the impulse to love and enjoy and his recognition that love and life invariably end in sorrow. Nothing in these four sonnets resolves the conflict. They end with love, but also with anxiety.

The "Fire in the Wind" poems differ a great deal from poems like "Earthward," and they are more mature and skillful than "Bleak Upland." Eiseley has worked on a complex and intricate intertwining of natural, literary, and biblical imagery. He has developed greater fluency and facility with his lines, effectively sustaining a consistent style and theme through several poems. And he has written well-formed poems. "Note at Midnight," for example, moves easily from imagery of spring and light to winter and darkness; later, in the sestet of the second sonnet, it develops, interestingly, from seasonal images for describing his psychic state to imagery dramatizing an unanswered call. In "Fire in the Wind," the young poet is reaching for an intricate, tightly controlled, symbolic expression of grief and inward death; and in many ways he has succeeded.

But intriguing as they are, they are less satisfying and effective than poems like "Earthward." The "Sonnets for a Second Death" sequence, especially, seems forced and artificial and, compared to "Earthward," too literary and conventional. Although Eiseley has attempted an ambitious sequence and written well, he has not written in his most natural and gifted mode—the mode, for example, of "Coyote Country," one of the best of his very early poems:

> If you should go, soft-footed and alert,
> Down the long slope of shale
> Into a tumbled land of scarp and butte
> Beyond the pale
> Of the herding men, where water is under stone,
> You would be in coyote country. It is the place
> Where tumbleweed is blown
> Four ways at once, and your neighbors are not seen
> Except as loping shapes
> Or tangible dust.
> Once, if you're lucky, something may pause and lift
> One paw and two grey ears
> In a moment's trust
> That is gone like wind.
>
> This is the road. Go down
> Over the harsh way. If you dare, go down
> Into the waste, where lonely and apart
> The road runs north. Somewhere here is my heart
> If anywhere. I spy
> Nothing at all—and you in turn may try
> The thistle and subtle stones,
> Or you may go
> Southward tonight—be certain you will not know
> More of me than is found
> In two poised ears
> Or feet gone without sound.[16]

Besides imagining himself as one with the fox or the wolf, or absorbed into the earth, he also envisions situations where he can stop loving and no longer be subject to passion or pain. In "Word for the Frost"[17] Eiseley speaks of the relief and contentment renunciation would bring. In place of the fury and fire of love, he would have the coolness and stillness of the frost, for only in that state could he survive. But it is a strange survival, because, as before, he is imagining a kind of death in the stoniness of the earth. And so we are once more in the world of "Earthward" and "Song for the Wolf's Coat."

When he speaks of renouncing love—"I have let love go like quicksilver through a wall"—as well as escaping pain,[18] Eiseley might also be revealing one of his motives for turning to science. Not only was he able, finally, to commit himself; he may have needed, at precisely this time, what he perceived to be the coolness, impersonality, and control of science. Years later, in "The Star-thrower," he would write of his past as the "skull of emptiness" and the "endlessly revolving light without pity," the passionless eye with which "science looks upon the world."[19] By then, such a death is no longer desirable, for Eiseley is clearly committed to life and a humane science. But in the mid-1930s that pitiless eye may have been just what he wanted, as "Words for Forgetting" suggests:

> Go forward on these simple roads,
>   Do not turn back.
> The stars behind you in the wind will blow,
>   The coyote's track.
>
> Delicately replace the lifted dust
>   Of your own heel.
> Go forward and the dark will close
>   About you. You will feel
>
> The fragrant emptiness of prairie miles.
>   Now you will own
> Nothing that is not yours, yourself
>   Down to the naked bone.[20]

As one might expect, he could not dissociate himself completely. His agony might diminish and eventually disappear, but the memory stayed. This he recognizes in "Leaving September":

> If I have once forgotten on this field
> The long light of the dusk, or far away
> The sheep on tawny grass, how stones will yield
> Small bitter puffballs, or a cricket stay

To wring wry tunes from emptiness and dearth,
Let me remember; let me hold them now
Close to the heart—while I upon the earth
Am the stone field and pain the heavy plow.
Not in wide measures is the harvest culled,
Not by disaster, nor by cutting hail
Is the loss seen, the grief in somewise dulled—
Being done at last. Ours is a different scale—
Leaving September stars and a little smoke
And memory tight as a lichen to an oak.[21]

From the mid-1930s onward, Eiseley began to write about love
and life in a different way. In the midst of desolation, he discovered
that somehow love, "this undying madness," persists and that one
need not renounce it or give up consciousness in order to survive.
He expressed this as early as 1933 in the first poem of "Fire in the
Wind," "If He Hears No Sound."[22] His vision is still harsh, for the
love and life he writes about are minimal: it is love like a burr, not a
flower, and life, cringing and struggling on the edge of existence.
The last two quatrains of the poem express this simply and elo-
quently:

In the slant of the rain by the house unshuttered
And left to men's stare,
Let me remember love harsh as a bowlder,
Unchanging and bare.

Not to flower—with the gesture of springtime,
Harvest nor fruit—
Beautiful I find it—this undying madness
Where nothing has root.

In the spring of 1935, Eiseley published six poems in *Voices*[23]
that explore several aspects of this emerging belief. Although he
still speaks of "the homeless, the embittered, the lost one" and
continues to recognize that nothing lasts, he nevertheless thinks
now of the beauty and value of love, rather than of the need to
renounce or escape it. It *is* better to have loved.

"Now the Singing Is Done," the finest poem in this group,
describes, once again, love's torment and life's harshness, but in it
Eiseley gives thanks, nonetheless, for the love he has had:

They are burning the cornfields now. In the mellow dusk,
In the leaf-mold moon when the pumpkins go to town
They are burning the cornfields up, and wind-warped smoke
Trails mountain-blue in the fields and the stubborn brown

Hills go quietly dark. Now the singing is done
In the harvesters' throats. As the dense grass catches fire
I think of the fuel I have been to a fiercer flame—
In the darkness I shrink, and yet with the old desire

Tormented I stand, but know in my veins no more
The rush of the blood. On that mad invisible tide
I have leaned the last time. The iron and flint at the core
Strike darkness at last. I am glad that the night is wide.

I am glad that over my shoulder no greater shadow than this
Leans. . . . . You are gone. The world is as still as death.
I have had it all—the bitter loving by stealth
And the open love. For the harsh and the tortured breath

I give my thanks—for the bodies I could not hold,
For the mouths abandoned and lost. Far better be sieve to the deep
Waters that always move than to dry to an acrid pool,
Be a mocker at love. . . . . *I shall sleep with fire when I sleep.*

Apparently Eiseley has moved beyond love in this poem, and his most acute suffering has passed. He has partly achieved his desire, but he is no longer trying to forget. Indeed, he wants to "sleep with" the *memory* of love's fire—the passion *and* pain, the satisfaction *and* sorrow. Resigned to loss and believing that desire has ended, he writes as if a major part of his life were over—and he is just twenty-eight. Within the poem, Eiseley achieves stability and some peace, but clearly at a cost. He may be free of some burdens ("no greater shadow than this") and even relatively content with remembrances, but he has virtually given up life. The Eiseley of this poem still strives for an ambivalent—if not impossible—state: to retain life without participating in it. He is a long way from the end of his psychic journey.

"Now the Singing Is Done" shows a noticeable growth in Eiseley's skill as a poet. The lines are no longer tight and forced, and Eiseley is able to work with variations in meter and stress. As a result, the poem flows across end lines and over stanza breaks. He has achieved the fluency of his open forms; yet at the same time he has imposed the control and beauty of rhyme and fairly regular stresses. His lines hover between free verse and the regularity of meter and rhyme—a delicate and effective balance.

The thematic structure of the poem also illustrates his skill. Through the complex and interesting meanings he develops for fire, Eiseley effectively correlates outer and inner space—the burning in the cornfields and the burning within himself. In fact, the significance of fire includes not only these two possibilities. It comprehends, as well, the fire of nature's dying, the end of a season when all life burns and dries up; the fire of life's energy that eventually burns up and out in each of us; and the burning fire of love's passion, along with the protective fire of love's warmth. Eiseley has also given the poem richness and interest by expressing its movement through several related images: from light or dusk to dark, from action or burning to stillness, from the sound of singing to silence ("the world is as still as death"), from wakefulness to sleep, and finally, from life to death.

"Now the Singing Is Done" represents a considerable achievement in control, subtlety, and complexity, although it reflects no new idiom, no new perspective; the images, themes, and forms of the poem are all conventional, as well as personal. Still, in this Eiseley was perfecting a significant poetic voice that assuredly transcends its regional origin. Only later would he develop a truly new idiom, when he fused science with literature in a series of excellent books of prose and several outstanding late poems.

The other poems in that 1935 group develop similar themes and suggest that Eiseley was emerging from the most critical years of his identity crisis. "On the Pecos Dunes," for example, is one of the first poems that Eiseley based on his anthropological fieldwork. In it he speaks of the continuing presence of the people and culture in "a long dead town" that scientists have evidently been excavating. The poem explores Eiseley's interest in time and his sense that life and the earth endure even though all things pass. "The love they spoke to the winds has gone," but even so, "the root stays / And the root seeds"—as if the sources of love and life remain to somehow grow again. There is no logic in this; Eiseley's mind keeps telling him that everything eventually disappears and dies. The last poem of the six speaks once more of this "undying madness"—the illogical permanence of love. In this poem, "Song without Logic," he feels so strongly that he can even throw love in the blind teeth of death:

> When worms upon the damp wall of the brain
> Inscribe their passage and the feeding root
> Goes footless over what will not again
> Stir with blind life—then, from this devious, mute
> Organ of sentience subtract the sum,
> Subtract the sunlight and subtract the dew.
> What you will have will be the open, dumb
> Stare of the bone and minus every clew—
> Minus the chart, minus the silver nerve,
> The singing wires on which the flesh was hung—
> What will you say, what savagery will swerve
> Space from its arc, rearm the emptied tongue?
>
> But this to death—in the blind teeth thereof:
> *The honey of chaos is the honey of love.*

There is nothing soft and sentimental about this love; it is, as Eiseley said, "harsh as a bowlder, unchanging and bare."

These poems were published when Eiseley was twenty-seven years old. By this time, he was settling into a relatively stable personal life. The acute emotional crisis that had lasted for eight years had passed. His grief over his father's death had diminished. His years of riding trains and of irregular study at the University of Nebraska were over. In the fall of 1933, he had gone on to the University of Pennsylvania to study anthropology. For two years, he spent the academic year in school and his summers as a fieldworker on expeditions sponsored by the university and the Smithsonian. In 1935, he completed his M.A., then returned to Lincoln for a year to work as an assistant sociologist[24] and write for the Nebraska Federal Writers' Project.[25] After that, he went back to Philadelphia to study for his Ph.D. Besides emerging from a personal crisis, Eiseley was also settling into a profession that would focus and organize his intellectual and emotional life and in a few years force a suspension of poetry.

In no sense, however, did Eiseley free himself from loneliness, fear, or pain. His poems from 1936 to 1937 show that. Nevertheless, his poetry and his life did in fact change—if only a little—and that slight change led to a significant and, over time, a dramatic new phase.

In the early 1940s he published two poems that in a sense complete the development I have been describing. "Say It Is Thus with the Heart"[26] urges acceptance of the fact that nothing "but a leaf from a long ago wind" will last:

> The rain has been drunk from these bald and sun-beaten ridges;
> Only the bowlders have kept
> Through the weathers of time the marks where the feet of a lizard
> Scurried and crept,
>
> Or a strange leaf out of a strange autumn
> Far off and long past,
> Or a small blue shell that was one of thousands
> Whose shape did not last.
>
> These are the things that the past and the future cherish—
> Not wisdom, not grace
> But a small blue shell or the mud where a scaled beast stumbled
> May last for a space.
>
> Say it is thus with the heart, say that only
> Tricks of season and snow
> Are victors at last. Without anger
> Say that no one could know
>
> Your face that a hundred had sworn to remember forever
> Comes as well to this end—
> Replaced by a voice, by a fancy, by nothing
> But a leaf from a long ago wind.

Although there is a strong sense of resignation here (some readers might find the poem even bleak), Eiseley no longer seems tormented or confused, and that is the point. For the moment, he has reached an accommodation with death, although he would never fully resolve his feelings about it. But he now can say it with his heart, and so he is no longer divided. His intellect and emotions are one, and he seems to be relatively content. When this poem appeared, Eiseley had been teaching at the University of Kansas for almost five years, and he had been married for almost three.

The second poem, "Winter Sign," seems to describe the poet's recovered capacity to love.[27] "Having stumbled into this season of grief," he intends for now to "reflect on the life that is here and about" and to express the hard core of love within him:

A spider web pulled tight between two stones
With nothing left but autumn leaves to catch
Is maybe a winter sign or the thin blue bones
Of a hare picked clean by ants. A man can attach

Meanings enough to the wind when his luck is out,
But, having stumbled into this season of grief
I mean to reflect on the life that is here and about
In the fall of the leaves—not on the dying leaf.

Something more tough, reliable, and stark
Carries the blood of life toward a farther spring—
Something that lies concealed in the soundless dark
Of burr and pod—in the seeds that hook and sting.

I have learned from these that love which endures the night
May smoulder in outward death while the colors blaze,
But trust my love—it is small burr-coated and tight.
It will stick to the bone. It will last through the autumn days.

Once again, Eiseley uses the natural image of seeds to suggest the resilience and persistence of love and life. Here the seeds have evolved critical survival mechanisms that enable the plant to multiply and radiate. Like these burr-coated seeds, Eiseley's love was tough, persistent, and reliable. Although it sometimes may have seemed minimal or even invisible, it could be trusted, and it would last.

After the mid-1930s Eiseley developed critical psychological and verbal capacities that enabled him to survive. Gradually, he became resigned to sorrow and loss; more than that, he discovered a renewed willingness and desire to love. Even though it speaks of the persistence and reliability of his love, "Winter Sign" is in no sense sentimental or melodramatic. In it his own life, as well as life generally, remains unchanged: it *is* a season of grief, a marginal struggle for survival. But now Eiseley could accept that and live actively and with some satisfaction. Able to control and direct his life to some extent, he was learning to love the world without either trusting it or being wholly absorbed by it.

Besides dramatizing Eiseley's struggle and his emergence from a critical part of his life into a successful personal and professional life, his poetry developed an increasing sensitivity, variety, and complexity that extends its significance and interest beyond the experience of a particular young man or a particular regional literature. The poetry also displays a progressive strengthening of the poet's language and form. Eiseley began writing in conventional, regular, closed forms, and he achieved considerable skill with those. As he became more confident and probably more secure personally, the poems became more fluid, and he began experimenting with variations on conventional meter and with somewhat looser and more open forms. "Say It Is Thus with the Heart" and "Winter Sign" illustrate his best achievements in both. And Eiseley's language developed, as well. Tough enough from the beginning, it grew in passion, strength, and firmness as he himself did.

The parallel is obvious: the poetry traces Eiseley's personal growth, and it illustrates his poetic development. These achievements are also reciprocal. On the one hand, the poems played an essential role in strengthening Eiseley psychically; they helped him endure, understand, and probably control his feelings. On the other, his increasing psychic strength contributed to the development of his technique. For the first time, we can see clearly how identity and language were emerging together in Loren Eiseley's life.

NOTES

1. Loren Eiseley, "Spiders," *Prairie Schooner*, 2, no. 2 (Spring, 1928), 92. Most of Eiseley's early poems have been reprinted in *All the Night Wings* (New York: Times Books, 1979); see the Checklist for additional detail.
2. Frederick J. Hoffman, Charles Allen, and Carolyn F. Ulrich, *The Little Magazine: A History and a Bibliography* (Princeton, N.J.: Princeton University Press, 1946), p. 147.
3. Milton M. Reigelman, *The Midland: A Venture in Literary Regionalism* (Iowa City: University of Iowa Press, 1976), p. 99.
4. Hoffman et al., *Little Magazine*, p. 264.
5. "Ox Cart," *Prairie Schooner*, 8, no. 3 (Spring, 1934), 161.
6. Loren Eiseley, "October Has the Heart," in *The Best Poems of 1942*, comp. Thomas Moult (New York: Harcourt, Brace, 1943), p. 55; originally published in *Prairie Schooner*, 15, no. 3 (Fall, 1941), 151.
7. Loren Eiseley, "Bleak Upland," *Voices*, No. 55 (1930), pp. 158-60.

8. Loren Eiseley, "The Deserted Homestead," *Poetry*, 35, no. 3 (Dec., 1929), 142-43.
9. *All the Strange Hours*, p. 25.
10. Ibid., p. 27.
11. Loren Eiseley, "Earthward," *Midland*, 18, no. 2 (June, 1931), 54.
12. Loren Eiseley, "Song for the Wolf's Coat," *Voices*, No. 71 (Aug.-Sept., 1933), p. 26.
13. Loren Eiseley, "Fox Curse," *Voices*, No. 74 (Feb.-Mar., 1934), p. 13; reprinted in the *Literary Digest*, May 19, 1934.
14. Loren Eiseley, "Incident in the Zoo," *Prairie Schooner*, 8, no. 3 (Summer, 1934), 120; reprinted in the *Literary Digest*, Nov. 10, 1934, p. 32.
15. Loren Eiseley, "Note at Midnight," *Voices*, No. 69 (Apr.-May, 1933), p. 17.
16. Loren Eiseley, "Coyote Country," *Midland*, 19, no. 2 (Mar.-Apr., 1932), 49.
17. Loren Eiseley, "Word for the Frost," *Voices*, No. 74 (Feb.-Mar., 1934), p. 13.
18. Loren Eiseley, "Letter of Parting," *Voices*, No. 74 (Feb.-Mar., 1934), p. 14.
19. *Unexpected Universe*, p. 68.
20. Loren Eiseley, "Words for Forgetting," *Prairie Schooner*, 8, no. 3 (Summer, 1934), 118.
21. Loren Eiseley, "Leaving September," *American Mercury*, 39, no. 153 (Sept., 1936), 90.
22. Loren Eiseley, "If He Hears No Sound," *Voices*, No. 69 (Apr.-May, 1933), p. 16.
23. Loren Eiseley, "Six Poems," *Voices*, No. 81 (Apr.-May, 1935), pp. 16-19.
24. "Loren Eiseley," in *Current Biography Yearbook, 1960*, ed. Charles Moritz (New York: H. W. Wilson, 1960), pp. 125-27.
25. Jerre Mangione, *The Dream and the Deal: The Federal Writers' Project, 1935-1943* (Boston: Little, Brown, 1972), p. 109.
26. Loren Eiseley, "Say It Is Thus with the Heart," *Prairie Schooner*, 16, no. 1 (Spring, 1942), 23.
27. Loren Eiseley, "Winter Sign," *Prairie Schooner*, 17, no. 3 (Fall, 1943), 163.

6

Excavations in a Timeless Land

Somewhere here is my heart.

Near the end of his autobiography, Loren Eiseley confesses that he cannot account for himself. After almost seventy years of living and after several recent years of systematic excavation into his own life, he cannot explain who he truly is or by what series of events he has become this man—this writer, scholar, and scientist. In his mind, he holds the "splintered glass of a mirror dropped and broken long ago"—fragments of memory, pieces of his life—and he has written these into his book. He possesses a sense of the onward impulse of his life, but he has no sense that he has directed it, and surely he does not believe that he has measured or successfully explained it. So one of his primary questions—How does one choose one's life?—remains unanswered, even in its past tense: How *did* I choose? *How* did I live? In fact, he came to believe that he did not *choose* at all.

In two of his later poems, "Other Dimensions"[1] and "The Double,"[2] Eiseley speaks about the accidental quality of his life and the other lives he might easily have led had events or chance broken in another way. He recollects some of the alternatives he experienced briefly, and he imagines his fate had he not escaped them.

"Other Dimensions" names specific jobs—night watchman, hatchery worker, truck driver, seaman—but these are less important than the poem's focus on the inexplicable, random quality of the young man's life. Thinking about the years before he finished his degree, Eiseley imagines that he might have drifted into "any eddy" and "remained there," either arrested in his development or prematurely extinguished. Although he can trace his personal evolution, much as paleontologists can trace the development of a species, he cannot explain the mechanism of "why one path *was chosen* [emphasis added] and not the other."

"The Double" concentrates on the man he might have become had he continued to drift and hide. Through the image of a dream, Eiseley projects the "conclusive ending" to his "youthful years":

the brutal, battered face, relentless, wild, the fugitive
grown old, nothing left now but a fierce cunning, and illiterate hate.

Although in one sense this man is lost in the past, he is nevertheless the "double" because something of that battered savage fugitive still lives within the scholarly man and lurks somewhere in his book-lined study. For a moment, Eiseley holds the two identities in tension ("I . . . knew two lives at once"), but in the end he yields to the grizzled "alternate" of his dream and takes "the road / into [his] final and most desperate day." He yields less to that life than to its desperate ending in death.

The impulse to escape, or die, is even more explicit in "Other Dimensions," where he thinks of the silence and peace that would follow a sudden death under the wheels of a speeding train. Once again, in his sixties when he wrote the poem, Eiseley gave in to this impulse, imaginatively at least: "The life that almost ended / draws me with a strange attraction."

Even at the end of his life, the tensions of his youth and the psychic patterns he had developed were still with him. He had to struggle to maintain a balance between impulses to escape, hide, or die and those to continue surviving and growing in a social world. By then he could at least look back on a remarkable life, accidental and inexplicable as it may have seemed. During his youth, however, he had no such achievements, and he was dangerously close to the bleak, savage future of his double. But he was neither defeated nor paralyzed. In 1931 he took a first major step toward science, thereby initiating a future that would focus his intellectual and emotional energies in new ways and begin to provide new kinds of answers to questions he had been asking for years. Those symbolic first questions in "Autumn—A Memory" were about to become professional matters for Loren Eiseley.

Eiseley joined his first scientific field expedition in the summer of 1931. Through the influence of his friend Bertrand Schultz, Eiseley was hired by the Nebraska State Museum to work with the South

Party of the Morrill Paleontological Expedition for that summer. He joined the South Party again during the summers of 1932 and 1933.[3] Schultz had been leading field parties for the museum since the late 1920s,[4] and so he was a regular. He was also "one of those fortunate people who knew his course and did not wander."[5] The two had met in anthropology classes at the university, where Eiseley majored in both anthropology and sociology.[6] As their interests developed, Schultz continued in vertebrate paleontology, while Eiseley went on in anthropology. At one point, they planned to do a book together— *The Hunt of the Mammoth*—each writing his own complementary part. But the war interfered; their prospective publisher became uneasy; and then, in 1944, Eiseley moved to Oberlin College, in Ohio, and later even further east. At the end of the war, the manuscript was out of date and their professional lives were separating, so no book ever came about. Their friendship continued, however, and to the end of his life Eiseley remembered the important influence Bert Schultz had had on his future.

The Nebraska State Museum has been in existence since 1871,[7] and it has been sending out field parties almost since that time. The museum's serious fieldwork began with the opening of the Agate Springs fossil quarries, perhaps the most famous of the beds in Nebraska. Discovered in the late 1870s, they remained undeveloped until the summer of 1904 when the Carnegie Museum of Pittsburgh began excavating. A year later the Nebraska State Museum opened a quarry at an adjacent site, and with that the museum initiated its long history of exploration and excavation.[8]

Until around 1930, field activities were modest and not very systematic. Even though the state had been a center for the collection of mammal fossils since the 1850s, significant quarrying had barely begun. The parties that Eiseley joined were some of the first large ones dispatched, and they virtually opened the phase of fossil hunting that Schultz calls "the systematic stratigraphic collecting period." Before that, paleontologists collected somewhat randomly and did not, as a rule, compare specimens or interpret phylogenetic trends within a stratigraphic frame. In fact, they often disregarded geologic evidence altogether. But paleontology was changing, and the South Party played an important role in that. In 1931, the museum sent out ten workers, six of them in the South Party; later in the thirties, after Eiseley had gone east to graduate school, there were as many as ninety people either collecting in the field or preparing fossils in the museum's laboratory. During this strati-graphic phase, the museum collected more than 80 percent of its vertebrate fossils.[9]

Ironically, a period of drought and depression in Nebraska and the nation turned into a boom time for fossil hunting. During the extended drought in the early 1930s, many deposits were exposed that would not otherwise have been visible. (Now grass or vegeta-tion covers perhaps 60 percent of those exposures.) Besides this "advantage," the expeditions had generous financial support, in spite of widespread hard times, from private donors. Over a long period, for example, Charles H. Morrill donated more than $100,000 to the museum, most of which supported museum field-work.[10] Near the end of the decade, WPA, CCC, and NYA money helped support and enlarge the museum's collection activity.[11] In these early years, a young man like Loren Eiseley could make more money in the field than he could by staying in Lincoln, or by drifting across the country; moreover, he could begin learning about a science during one of its most productive periods.

Eiseley surely needed the money; the job also gave him a chance to keep running. The field parties worked mostly in western Ne-braska in high plains or rugged badland country, far from cities and, at best, near only very small towns. Scottsbluff was the largest; in the early thirties only about eight thousand people lived there. The parties usually camped out in the field, and so their main contacts were with one another. Working six days a week, they rarely went to town except for supplies or on a Sunday holiday. Much of their activity isolated the crew members even from each other. If they did not work alone, they frequently worked in twos. Out there, a young man could spend many long, silent, solitary hours searching for fossils, digging through strata, uncovering bones, sifting soil—and thinking. "In [that] timeless land," Eiseley says, "I could remain hidden."[12]

Before the main collecting season began in 1931, Eiseley accom-panied Bertrand Schultz to a site southwest of Milford, Nebraska, twenty-five to thirty miles west of Lincoln, where a well-preserved mastodon skull had been unearthed.[13] They worked there in late March and returned briefly in April. They were able to secure some skeletal parts, skull chunks, and a tusk, but flood conditions prevented any further excavation until June, when the South Party—six members, including Loren Eiseley and Bertrand Schultz, and also Schultz's wife, Marian—left Lincoln for a summer in the field. After returning briefly to the mastodon quarry on the West Fork, Big Blue River, near Milford, they started working their way west in Nebraska, ending their summer collecting season with sustained exploration and excavation in three western Nebraska counties, Scottsbluff, Banner, and Morrill.

Throughout the summer, they worked almost daily in the bone quarries. Leaving the Milford site, they moved to a quarry southwest of Long Island, Kansas. In July, the party was excavating along the Platte River, near Grand Island, Nebraska, where they found some human artifacts in association with extinct bison bones. In early August they moved their camp to a farm north of Cambridge, and then two weeks later the crew went further west to Max, Nebraska. They were working their way through south-central Nebraska and northern Kansas, digging fossils and looking for new sites. From the Max campsite, for example, three of the party explored west into northeast Colorado, while Eiseley and Schultz ventured north and east to Enderson, Nebraska, where they found good exposures but no bones. The South Party was obviously covering a lot of territory—looking for quarries, listening to the local people for hints of bone finds, and asking questions.

By late August, they were in the far western part of Nebraska, mostly along the Wildcat Range and Pumpkin Creek. Oddly enough, other major museums had looked at the area and declared it barren of fossils; but within days after they arrived, the party discovered the fossil remains of a Miocene dog, and early in September, Eiseley and Emery Blue located a quarry east of Harrisburg, also in the Pumpkin Creek area. Besides these finds, the party unearthed of group of young and adult oreodonts near Birdcage Gap in Morrill County. That summer they opened up a whole new fossil field, forty miles long, that ran from Morrill County west into Wyoming.

By late spring of 1932, Eiseley was eager to get out into the field again. He saw money to make and, perhaps, commitments to avoid. He evidently talked the Schultzes into opening the season early, and the three of them—Loren Eiseley and Bertrand and Marian Schultz—left Lincoln on May 3. Although they worked at several sites between Lincoln and the west, they returned almost directly to Wildcat Ridge in the western uplands to continue exploring the field they had discovered the previous summer. Before the month was out, on May 30, 1932, they discovered a remarkable new quarry[14]—perhaps the "five million years of the planet's history" that Eiseley has written about so effectively in "The Relic Men."

According to his narrative, he and the others learned that a member of a local religious sect had found a huge fossil bone. They decided to investigate. Since they were geologists and paleontologists and the man was a fundamentalist, they were uneasy about how they might be received. But as soon as Eiseley saw the man he felt relieved: "He had the merry, wondering, wandering eye of the born naturalist. Poor, uneducated, reared in a sect which frowns upon natural science, some wind out of the Pliocene had touched him. He threw wide the door and made a great, sweeping gesture that propelled us almost bodily into the room."[15]

As it turned out, the bone was an authentic "elephant" femur that the old man, "Mr. Mullens," as Eiseley calls him, had found twenty years before out in the hills. That one bone was exciting enough, although the time lapse worried them, but when Mullens told them that the site was covered with bones, they could barely contain themselves. The man seemed certain that he could find the place again, and he agreed to lead them. The experience of that trek—driving over sand banks and prairies and walking up and down seemingly endless hills, with the old man wheezing and choking from heart trouble—is a story in itself. But when they found it, the fatigue and anxiety of that journey—as well as all the discomfort, boredom, and monotony of fieldwork—disappeared in the thrill of discovery.

> There was a late afternoon sun playing on that hillside, and I can remember still the way my eyes traveled down it from boulder to gray boulder between the spines of Spanish bayonet. And then I saw it. Maybe this won't mean anything to you. Maybe you don't understand this game, or why men follow it. But I saw it. I tell you I saw five million years of the planet's history lying there on that hillside with the yucca growing over it and the roots working through it, just the way the old man had remembered it from a day long ago in the sun.

I saw the ivory from the tusks of elephants scattered like broken china that the rain has washed. I saw the splintered, mineralized enamel of huge unknown teeth. I paused over the bones of ferocious bear-dog carnivores. I saw, protruding from an eroding gully, the jaw of a shovel-tusked amebelodont that has been gone twice a million years into the night of geologic time. I tell you I saw it with my own eyes and I knew, even as I looked at it, that I would never see anything like it again.[16]

According to museum records, in late May, Schultz and Eiseley were exploring sites as far west as Scottsbluff. On May 30, 1932, Roy Swanson led them to a large bison fossil deposit near Signal Butte, sixteen miles west and three miles south of Scottsbluff. Several hundred yards from the base of the butte, Spring Creek had exposed part of an old river channel; the bison bones were embedded in the gravel of the old stream.[17] The quarry was opened shortly afterward, and in August, the party discovered eight pre-Folsom artifacts among the bison bones.

In "The Relic Men," Eiseley speaks of the "tusks of elephants," the bones of bear-dog carnivores, and long-extinct amebelodonts. They did not find these fossils at Scottsbluff, for that was mainly a bison quarry. And the location does not match Eiseley's topography. But these variances do not lessen the thrill Eiseley felt or the excitement he evokes when he describes that moment. In fact, Eiseley seems to have fused several different discoveries into one. While Signal Butte may be the main one, Eiseley could also have had in mind a bison quarry near Crawford, Nebraska, that a Mr. Everson helped them find in 1933, the Bridgeport rhino quarry some of the party worked in 1933, the quarry Eiseley located in 1931, as well as many others they discovered and opened. There were, after all, *many* new quarries in those days. By concentrating several experiences into one (if that is what he has done), Eiseley has given us an epiphany of discovery and simultaneously a realistic moment in his life as a bone hunter.

With the South Party, camp life was fairly primitive and the work was demanding. The crew lived in tents near the quarries, although one summer Marian and Bert Schultz moved into an abandoned cabin while the others slept in tents. (Eiseley wrote about that cabin in "The Bird and the Machine.") Marian Schultz had joined the South Party in 1931, soon after she and Bertrand were married. She cooked for the men (they cleaned up), and she also helped dig. Camping and working in the field, they were subject to the heat and sun of dry prairie summers. Hardened as they might become, the sun still burned, and the dust coated and sometimes choked them. If they were lucky, they could cool themselves after work in a nearby river or pond. On the rare occasion when heavy rains came and flooded an area where they were working (as happened, for example, on July 24, 1932), the party had to spend most of the next day trying to dry out. Once in a while a flood down a canyon forced them to move to higher ground. And once, several summers before, a tornado had destroyed the camp of a field party led by Schultz. If the parties stayed out too late in the fall, then they had snow and cold to face, as they did in 1932, when some of the crew worked well into October. But in drought-stricken Nebraska in the summer, they suffered mainly from dust, wind, and heat.

Weather and territorial conditions made already difficult work even harder. If they weren't walking in the heat mile after mile over mostly barren ground, they were digging for bones in it, and that was never easy. Their work required everything from removing several feet of overburden to subtle sifting and brushing, and in those days there were no dozers or other modern advantages. The South Party worked with horses, ploughs, scrapers, and shovels. Their techniques were not primitive, but the work demanded a lot of physical energy and stamina, and it required patience. They weren't always uncovering mastodons or finding new, spectacular digs; in fact, much of the work was quite tedious. Eiseley recalled the season when he seemed to do nothing but dig up interminable rhino footbones:

> In this case, we did not go on. There was an eroding hill in the vicinity, and on top of that hill, just below sod cover, were the foot bones, hundreds of them, of some lost Tertiary species of American rhinoceros. It is useless to ask why we found only foot bones or why we gathered the mineralized things in such fantastic quantities that they must still lie stacked in some museum storeroom. Maybe the creatures had been immured standing up in a waterhole and in the millions of succeeding years the rest of the carcasses had eroded away from the hilltop stratum. But there were the foot bones, and the orders had come down, so we dug carpals and metacarpals till we cursed like an army platoon that headquarters has forgotten.[18]

Travel for the party was slow and uncomfortable. Few roads in western Nebraska were paved. Most of the state highways were surfaced only with gravel; and the upland roads, when there were any, were rutted and passable only with difficulty. They drove Model T's and sometimes old Plymouth and Chevy trucks—hardly Land Rovers in durability, reliability, or comfort. Once a member of the party had to fix three flat tires just going from camp to Bridgeport for groceries.

The South Party normally worked six days a week, sometimes seven. If anyone did work on Sunday, he went to a different site or worked at an altogether different job. Breaking the tedium of the week's work was important. They never worked on holidays, and so on the Fourth of July, in 1932, the crew went to a local rodeo. Once in a long while, they took an extended break. In the summer of 1933, for example, a number of the party made a week-long trip from Scottsbluff into Colorado and New Mexico, going as far as Santa Fe; and then for an August weekend several of them drove north through the Black Hills as far as Rapid City, South Dakota. That month they had been working the badlands area of northwestern Nebraska, near Harrison, Crawford, and Chadron. Occasionally there were breaks and distractions, but for the most part the South Party had little leisure and virtually no entertainment.

Nor was the work itself particularly glamorous:

> Bone hunting is not really a very romantic occupation. One walks day after day along miles of frequently unrewarding outcrop. One grows browner, leaner, and tougher, it is true, but one is far from the bright lights, and the prospect, barring a big strike, like a mammoth, is always to abandon camp and go on. It was really a gypsy profession, then, for those who did the field collecting.[19]

It was also a very solitary, lonely occupation, as Eiseley expressed in a letter to Lowry Wimberly, his friend and the *Schooner* editor: "The work progresses here but all in all it is lonely here and the days pass slowly. An occasional coyote met in the hills, the heat and the quiet and the bones of dead beasts make up our day. . . . There is a whole heaven full of stars and I can only repeat again inarticulately that it is lonely . . . lonely. You can't believe civilization exists here."[20] There was obviously time—especially during long evenings—for an unsettled young man to think and write. Sometimes in the evening Eiseley recited his own poems for the group while they sat on a hillside under a tree.[21] Whether he actually wrote very much isn't clear. But he did keep notebooks, and between his first and second summers in the field he published two poems, "Spring in This Town" and "Coyote Country," which seem to reflect his state of mind.

"Coyote Country" (see chap. 5) describes a dry, stony upland, beyond the grazing country, where tumbleweeds and dust blow. That is coyote country, and the only neighbors are the loping shapes of the animals and the "tangible dust." It is Loren Eiseley's country, too—"Somewhere here is my heart." He feels at home there, where he imagines he can escape pain and confusion and become one with the coyote:

> . . . be certain you will not know
> More of me than is found
> In two poised ears
> Or feet gone without sound.

The poem and Eiseley's actual experience correlate very closely, for coyote country is obviously fossil country, and the scarps and buttes, rough roads and dust of the poem are the same places Eiseley roamed through the heat of three summers searching for bones. He absorbed that country as completely as he had the open spaces around Lincoln when he was a boy, and out there he tried to find both a retreat and a home. But he could not really hide, any more than he could get away from trouble on the trains, for he carried his burdens into the quarries and camps of the South Party.

"Coyote Country" does not express Eiseley's emotions so directly as "Note at Midnight," which begins:

> Written to you, this letter out of pain
> And sick despair, and longing for a night
> With no day after . . .

But "Coyote Country" does suggest how unsettled Eiseley still was in 1932, and it reveals, as well, how carefully he observed the country and continued to internalize it.

Exactly when fieldwork turned from escape into vocation is not clear. There was obviously no single moment of recognition or transformation. During these years, one set of impulses and motives slowly came to dominate another, but neither completely disappeared at any time. Even as Eiseley became a successful academic anthropologist and a public figure, anthropology continued to provide him with opportunities for escape or evasion, and it let him stay close to the earth, the prehistoric past, and the animal world. As much as it permitted the public man to emerge, anthropology sustained the private man—the outcast and fugitive. As he aged, Eiseley's impulse to withdraw seemed to grow stronger, even while the tension between that and his public persona continued to be very great.

It took Eiseley eight years to complete college. Even at the end, as Eiseley reports it—on the final day of his last examinations—he came dangerously close to giving up again:

> I knew I was ill with influenza from the moment I awoke in the rooming house where I was quartered, some blocks from the university. It was the final day of examinations—and this one examination in particular, if passed successfully, would complete the requirements for my undergraduate degree. Nominally then I would be labeled as of the class of '33, though the people I had started college with in 1925 were all vanished into the outer world, people with children, jobs, careers—doctors, lawyers, teachers.
>
> I had flunked courses before in my interminable and intermittent despair. I sat on my bed amidst a growing feeling of sickness. What I thought was not pleasant. The head of that particular department in which my ordeal was to take place was a harridan who would have been creditable only as a guard at Buchenwald. If I appeared later I would have been sure to get the kind of examination she reserved especially for people like me.
>
> I had acquired in those years some small fragments of worldly wisdom. The time was now. One more impediment and I knew what would happen. I would drift out into the world of violence forever. There was a letter lying on my desk from an old companion suggesting a prospecting trip in the Canadian Rockies. I dressed slowly, walked to school, and took the examination. My immediate instructor, a very lovely and understanding woman, was killed shortly thereafter in an auto accident. I had passed, however, and my record was never again to trouble the files of my university.[22]

The balance had shifted just enough that he could finish.

The relatively good salary paid by the Morrill Expedition enabled Eiseley to save a small amount of money. With that, some assistance from his uncle, and later a small scholarship, Eiseley put together enough to go to Penn. His uncle, William Buchanan

Price, was an attorney who had been moderately successful financially all along, even into the depression. In 1932 he had been elected state auditor, swept in by the Roosevelt landslide.[23] Eiseley's mother had been living with the Prices—her sister Grace—in Lincoln, and Loren had lived there for several years himself. William Price could evidently afford the assistance. He also seemed to believe in young Eiseley, which further persuaded him to help make the young man's future possible.

By the summer of 1933, then, Loren Eiseley was emerging from the worst part of his crisis. Flight was changing into quest. Fieldwork was turning into vocation. And so, when Eiseley returned to western Nebraska with the South Party in 1933, this final summer in Nebraska must have been more directed than the others. He still went simply as a field man, not as a leader or even an official recorder; but now it was becoming clear that he would be a professional.

By early July, Eiseley was back in the field exploring the Ogallala formations (Pliocene exposures) near Lewellen and Belmer. Then he spent a week with Emery Blue and several other South Party members driving through Colorado and New Mexico. He did not actually join the main group for work until late July. They were digging north of Harrison in the Nebraska badlands in the extreme northwest corner of the state. After arriving there, Eiseley spent the rest of the summer excavating further into the past than he had gone before. Throughout August he worked the Oligocene beds northwest of Crawford, as far as Toadstool Park. In that area he was uncovering the remains of life over 20 million years old. He was digging up titanotheres, chadron turtles, and no doubt more oreodonts. Outwardly, the summer of 1933 differed very little from the others. The crew worked long days in the heat and dust; they camped out at night; they made their way from place to place over rough, unpaved roads. Although Schultz and several others stayed out until late October, Eiseley returned to Lincoln on September 4, then left for Philadelphia.

In his autobiography, he condenses virtually all of his field experience into a few paragraphs:

> Save for occasional visits to far-off towns, no news penetrated to us. We lived in a timeless solitude that had already existed when Egypt was first rising from the mudflats of the Nile. We wandered

among gullies and pinnacles cut by wind and rare desert rains. Vegetation stopped at the edge of those declivities; there were canyons, volcanic clays over which toppled sandstones, tilted like the giant menhirs and dolmens of megalithic Europe.

Few people outside of the realm of paleontology realize that these runneled, sun-baked ridges which extend far into South Dakota are one of the great fossil beds of the North American Age of Mammals. Bones lay in the washes or projected from cliffs. Titanotheres, dirk-tooth cats, oreodonts, to mention but a few, had left their bones in these sterile clays. The place was as haunted as the Valley of the Kings, but by great beasts who had ruled the planet when man was only a wispy experiment in the highlands of Kenya. These creatures had never had the misfortune to look upon a human face. Most of what we knew of mammalian evolution in North America had come from this region. All the great paleontologists had worked here. New species of animals still occasionally turned up.[24]

During these summers in the field, Loren Eiseley was exploring his "territory" as he never had before. Throughout his childhood and youth, he had progressively expanded his sense of place—from home, to the spaces near Lincoln, outward to the prairies, and to the West beyond; now, in his middle twenties, he had started excavating, rather than simply enlarging his territory. Literally digging beneath the surface, he was psychically breaking through time and space barriers into the distant past and ultimately into his own future. He was exploring his land and himself as well, and in doing so, he had begun to move backward and forward in almost unimaginable time dimensions.

Each time he had moved outward before, he discovered a new place and experienced something new; each occasion had also involved a repetition or an extension of places and experiences he had absorbed from history or known as a child. Over and over, he had sought—or even fled to—the same kinds of places for the same unchanging reasons. The fossil fields of western Nebraska were no exception. Like the snowstorms, the solitary fields, and the caves of his childhood, the remote uplands could hide and protect him and help avoid confrontation and choice.

The fossil fields and western badlands were perfectly compatible with Eiseley's inner landscape and the territories he had known before. But they differed in two respects. They were even more distant, barren, and solitary than the places of his youth, and they eventually gave him a home and a future. In those bone quarries, Eiseley ventured beyond the nearby fields and prairies, beyond the distant places reached by trains, into the remote uplands of western Nebraska and back millions of years into prehistoric time and space. There he could imaginatively escape human life almost completely and become, for a time, one with animals that "never had the misfortune to look upon a human face." He could run in the wolf's coat and hide like a fox. In those remote ages, he could simply lose himself. But he could also feel lonely and foreign—even there the pattern repeated itself. The country that most possessed his imagination neither yielded peace nor provided a perfect home. He still felt homeless, dispossessed.

This time, however, Eiseley went for more than flight or survival. Through his work with the South Party, Eiseley found knowledge, discipline, and a profession. At least he discovered their beginnings, and he brought conflicting impulses into balance. This profession formally addressed questions Eiseley had been asking for many years. Instead of losing himself in the distant past or in remote areas of the present, or even in his own psychic turmoil, he in fact discovered himself and his future there. What had been conflicting and divisive impulses now became complementary. They were by no means resolved or harmonized, but they were in sufficient balance for Eiseley to move, with his psychic geography fundamentally unchanged, beyond the most critical years of his life.

That country impressed itself into Eiseley's mind in still other ways. By digging millions of years into the past of his own territory, Eiseley extended his knowledge of place about as far as he could, in the most concrete, intimate, and specific ways. The fossil beds also extended his knowledge of life's history and confirmed everything he had learned so far. The desolation of the past—all that death— corresponded closely to the inner wasteland he had experienced for years. Extinction, he realized once again—not survival—is the rule. Many species had gone under. Some survived, but not without a struggle—and then only in significantly altered forms. They "cringe to live" and "crawl forward on their knees," like life at the timber-line or like the Snout that Eiseley writes about in *The Immense Journey.*

Six months before his last summer in Nebraska, in the December-January, 1932-33, issue of *Voices*, Eiseley wrote about Robinson

Jeffers and his complete identification with his environment. Besides describing a kindred sensibility, Eiseley could very well have been describing himself, for at this point in his life he and his environment—the places and worlds he had explored and excavated—were thoroughly intertwined. This kind of identification did not lead to "mere 'nature writing' in the ordinary sense"; rather, Jeffers's "thoughts [grew] as naturally as the pines at Point Lobos out of the same rock." And so with Eiseley: his own feelings and thoughts grew naturally from the territories he discovered, internalized, and wrote about from childhood to adulthood.

The prairies and uplands in the West had become like a second body for him. In some obvious yet inexplicable way, we reside within our bodies; we can hide there behind a demeanor or a gesture—behind our physical presence. Our corporeality protects and insulates us. So, too, the solitary places Eiseley sought became extensions of his own body that hid and protected him.

Our bodies also insert us into space and establish continuity between our inner selves and the external world. In this sense, place as second body physically extended Eiseley further into space and time. He perceived the world not only with his own bodily senses but also through his extended body, acting as the edge of his corporeal or sensuous presence in the world. There is nothing mystical about this. The notion of second body simply emphasizes the physical, as well as psychic, wholeness of Loren Eiseley's life: body, place, and mind are intricately intertwined in a complex, unanalyzable whole.

NOTES

1. *Notes of an Alchemist*, pp. 110-14.
2. *Innocent Assassins*, pp. 27-28.
3. *All the Strange Hours*, p. 87; *Current Biography, 1960*, p. 126. Much of the information in this chapter about the Morrill expeditions comes from several volumes of field notes taken by its members— C. B. Schultz, Frank Denton, E. L. Blue, and Eugene Vanderpool. The field notes are in the Nebraska State Museum.
4. *University of Nebraska News*, "Museum Notes," No. 22 (Oct., 1963), p. 4. Throughout this chapter, I am indebted to Professor C. Bertrand Schultz for information conveyed in our conversations in Lincoln, in November, 1976.
5. *All the Strange Hours*, p. 87.

6. Mabel A. Elliott, assistant professor of sociology, University of Kansas, to L. Guy Brown, Oberlin College, June 16, 1944, in Penn Archives; Loren Eiseley transcript, University of Nebraska, in Penn Archives.
7. "Museum Notes," No. 45 (Mar., 1971).
8. Ibid., No. 30 (Mar., 1966).
9. Ibid., No. 22 (Oct., 1963).
10. Ibid., No. 45 (Mar., 1971).
11. Ibid.
12. *All the Strange Hours*, p. 87.
13. Erwin H. Barbour, "The Milford Mastodon," *Bulletin of the University of Nebraska State Museum*, 1, no. 24 (1931).
14. Identified in the field notes but also cited in Bertrand Schultz and Loren Eiseley, "Paleontological Evidence for the Antiquity of the Scottsbluff Bison Quarry and Its Associated Artifacts," *American Anthropologist*, 37 (Apr., 1935), 307.
15. *Night Country*, p. 119.
16. Ibid., pp. 121-22.
17. In addition to the field notes and Schultz and Eiseley, "Paleontological Evidence," the find is discussed by Erwin Barbour and Bertrand Schultz in "The Scottsbluff Bison Quarry and Its Artifacts," *Bulletin of the University of Nebraska State Museum*, 34 (1932).
18. *Unexpected Universe*, pp. 220-21.
19. Ibid., p. 220.
20. Eiseley to Wimberly, June 22, 1933, in University Archives, Love Memorial Library, University of Nebraska, Lincoln.
21. Frank Crabill to Mabel Eiseley, Jan. 13, 1978, in Penn Archives.
22. *All the Strange Hours*, pp. 77-78.
23. Ibid., p. 87.
24. Ibid., pp. 86-87.

7

The Turn toward Science

> Get knowledge, but get it with
> understanding.

The first day of registration at Penn almost drove Eiseley to distraction.[1] He had come directly from the silence and solitude of western Nebraska to the noises and crowds of a major city. He had spent little time in large cities, and he had never gone far from Nebraska with the intention of staying for an extended period. Now he had left friends behind to go to a place where he knew no one. And he went from a university he knew well to a school where he had never been before. This was no casual move from one place to another; Eiseley had, in fact, altered the basic balance of his life. Before the first day ended, the noise became nerve shattering. It exacerbated his sense of displacement and increased his anxiety, and so he fled to a deserted cemetery where he could regain his composure and, for the moment, restore the silence and solitude of the fossil graveyards from which he had just come.

Within a few days, Eiseley explains, his "tolerance of noise levels increased,"[2] and he began to adjust to the ways of the city. But he did not adjust very quickly. He had taken a major step in his life, one that would cause anyone considerable stress. For a young man of Eiseley's temperament and history, the stress was even greater. He experienced a long autumn and a miserable winter during which he felt neither very happy nor very secure.

Because he had little money, he could not afford a dormitory room and had to live alone off campus, which limited his personal contacts. His budget provided very little money for entertainment or diversion. The wretched autumn and winter weather that year ("the rain seemed never to cease") depressed him more. As if that weren't enough, he suffered frequently from colds.

Besides these difficulties, he soon discovered that he was in a very demanding graduate school, harried by the work load and anxious about finishing his degree in the time he had hoped. In November he wrote to his old mentor, Lowry Wimberly, "I despair of being able to get my degree in the one school year." He explained that he was carrying a full schedule, "and it's well nigh running me to death."[3] He also felt uneasy about his initial meetings with Frank Speck, the chairman of the department and, later, Eiseley's graduate mentor and friend. In those days the anthropology department was very small. It consisted of Speck and one other person, later two others. A student's relationship with the chairman was critical, since he was virtually the department. Eiseley and his friend Ricky Faust understandably worried a lot about their "inability to make much human contact" with Frank Speck.[4]

In class one day early in the semester, Eiseley seemed to make matters worse by failing to play one of Speck's characteristic games. The chairman had poured out "a little heap of square-cut flints" on the seminar table and then initiated the game.

> "What are these?" he barked. "Any of you know?" He looked at me. I was supposed to be the archaeologist in the group.
>
> I examined them, and a western memory with an absolute surety came back. "They are not Indian at all. They are eighteenth-century guns flints for flintlock rifles."
>
> A titter ran about among the students at the table. They were sure the old man had tripped me.
>
> "What makes you so sure?" he said menacingly, trying to make me back down. "Sir," I said, "I just know. They're square-cut European flint. I've seen them on the guns themselves. I am sure I'm not mistaken."
>
> "You are right," he growled reluctantly. The tittering ceased. "Class is dismissed."
>
> "Jeez," whispered my companion. "The old man will make you pay for that. He likes to win those games. Why didn't you shut up?"
>
> "I couldn't," I said logically. "He asked me directly. I had to answer." Ricky shook his head.[5]

The consequences were not very serious after all, for soon after the incident Lou Korn, one of the advanced graduate students in the department, explained the rules for getting along with Frank Speck. Apparently Speck had been both impressed and put off by losing the game, but once Loren learned how Speck wanted his students to behave, he had no more difficulty, and soon he and Speck became very close.

Before that, however, Eiseley had further reason for uneasiness and distress over his relations with Speck. One of his most troubling experiences that winter occurred during a brief episode of partial deafness. Eiseley's right ear became inflamed from a severe cold, but having no money and no "sense for city survival," he failed to seek medical aid until after his eardrum broke. As it happened, he was scheduled for a seminar report during this period, and his apparent deafness seemed to give Speck yet another reason to be put off. "I gave my lecture, but to my horror I was failing to hear some questions directed at me from the back of the room. I was not heartened to hear later that Speck had remarked in his gruffest manner, 'He's deaf as a post.' Coming from him this could only mean impending doom."[6]

Besides the embarrassment and humiliation, one can imagine the unexpressed fears Eiseley may have felt. Uneasy about seeking medical aid, even after his friends told him about the first-rate care at the university hospital, Eiseley obviously had not forgotten his mistreatment and the mistaken diagnosis he received at the dispensary in Lincoln. His fears may have run even deeper. By his late twenties, he had already known enough illness to be wary, frightened, and depressed by any sickness. Illness had become—and would remain—a troubling and threatening experience.

Although he does not mention his mother's deafness in association with this episode, he must have experienced some of the apprehensions in 1934 that possessed him later, during another loss of hearing, longer and more serious, in 1948. Eiseley never really separated his mother's deafness from her madness; throughout his life he feared that he might have inherited a strain of family instability. "Out of deepest childhood," he wrote, "I remember the mad Shepards as I heard the name whispered among my mother's people."[7] They were somewhere in his line of descent, and when he was difficult as a child, his mother's people would link those mad Shepards with his name. That might not have made such a devastating impression had his own mother not been seriously psychotic. But the combination made the fear acute. It is difficult to know exactly how troubling or significant this experience was; at the least, the episode evoked distressing experiences from the past and underscored his difficult adjustment to Penn and Philadelphia.

Although the year was difficult, it was obviously not intolerable, because Eiseley in fact stayed. A year or two earlier, he might not have. He stayed because he was more settled within himself and also because he had reason to. During the year, he made several good friends, two of whom became particularly close, Duke (Francis Tachibana) and Ricky (Richard A. Faust). In October and November of 1933, Duke was living in an old building on Locust Street, and every day after lunch Loren and Ricky stopped in to pass time until class, talking and sometimes playing their game of very low budget blackjack.[8] Relations with Speck seemed to improve as the year passed, and for all of Eiseley's anxiety, he was succeeding in a difficult graduate program. Occasionally he got up to New York, where at least once he met Harold Vinal and spent an evening at the theater with him. Eiseley was also still active with the *Schooner*, and he was publishing many poems. When he wrote Lowry Wimberly about his meeting with Vinal, Eiseley mentioned that he had obtained "a really good" poem from him for the *Schooner* and was trying to get more from Vinal and his friends.[9] In the summer of 1934, he was invited to read a poem at the Mary Austin memorial in Santa Fe, and that same summer he worked with a University of Pennsylvania expedition to the Southwest. These satisfying features of his life provided the basis for a fruitful and successful second year at Penn.

When school resumed in the fall of 1934, Eiseley and his two friends took a room together in the International House, an old mansion near campus.[10] Duke, an American-born Japanese, obtained a job there,[11] and evidently because the foreign student population had been severely reduced by the depression, all three were able to move in. Ricky would have felt comfortable because he'd been born in Japan and spoke Japanese.[12] Not only were the three close among themselves; they were also, as Eiseley explains, "amicably interracial in [their] friends and connections."[13] It seemed perfectly appropriate for them to be there.

The three men acquired the former master bedroom of the house, which gave them ample space for books, personal belongings, and living. (They were delighted to find that their wardrobes had tripled.)[14] They got on well and became close friends—Eiseley and Duke, or Tachi, especially. Duke even typed some of Eiseley's poems for him.[15] Other residents of the house and friends often dropped in, and they developed quite a warm circle there at the International House.

That second year turned out to be one of the happiest in Eiseley's life. After a troublesome transition year, he found friends to over-come his loneliness and a place he felt attached to, and through them he was also beginning to feel part of the university and his profession.

In no sense, however, did Eiseley forget or give up his friends in Nebraska. He continued to correspond with Lowry Wimberly, expressing in one letter his yearning "for the old armchair in the office."[16] During his years at Penn, he returned several times to Nebraska, where his mother still lived. He kept in touch with Bert Schultz, and according to him, Loren rode back and forth from the East once or twice with the Schultzes. And of course Mabel Lang-don was still living and working in Lincoln. She and Eiseley were close throughout his college years, and they became engaged before he left for Penn,[17] though they were not married until 1938. After he finished his master's degree and before going on for his Ph.D., he returned to Lincoln to live and work briefly as an assistant sociologist at the university.[18] While he was there (first semester, 1935-36), he took several sociology courses and German for grad-uates.[19] He also joined the Nebraska Federal Writers' Project and wrote parts of the Nebraska guidebook in the American Guide Series.[20]

In very basic ways, Lincoln remained his home. He had obviously not left his original territory altogether, and psychically, part of him would never leave, even though his years there had been very painful and Philadelphia had clearly made him happier.

The warm relationships, the peace, and the innocence of that second year did not last, however. The depression continued to exact its toll; some graduate students had to leave the profession because there were so few jobs. But the eruption of war in the Far East and the threat of war elsewhere caused the most profound change in their lives. It affected Eiseley's Oriental friends first. The families of his Chinese friends, for example, were threatened by the Japanese invasion. When Duke returned to Japan in 1936 to visit his family and arrange for a transfer of his inheritance, he was not permitted to exchange money and became the subject of police surveillance. Subsequently, even though he was an American citizen, he was not allowed to leave Japan.[21] At some point in the mid-thirties, Ricky became discouraged with the job market and left the university for high school teaching. The friends were scattering, the mood disintegrating. Never again would Eiseley "encounter the genuine peace" he had experienced with them.[22]

Even though these relationships were very important, the most profound influence during those years seems to have been Frank Speck. Eiseley wrote first about his mentor in *The Unexpected Universe*. There he relates an incident from Speck's student days when he astonished a linguistics professor at Columbia with his knowledge of Mohegan (or Mohican)—a presumably extinct northeastern Indian language.[23] Speck had learned Mohegan from an Indian widow in Connecticut who had raised him from childhood to age fourteen. Her knowledge of the language, her Indian heritage, and her love of natural history affected Speck very deeply. In fact, he became so identified with his Indian friends and their culture that he felt more at home in their world than in his. In a real sense, Speck's whole career extended and fulfilled the attachments and interests he developed while he lived with Mrs. Fielding. When he entered Columbia, he had enrolled in a theology program, but that surprised linguistics professor and Franz Boas persuaded him to become an anthropologist. Under Boas's guidance, Speck's knowledge of the Indians became greatly enriched and focused by systematic scholarship. Speck went on to become one of the foremost ethnohistorians of the first half of the twentieth century.[24]

When Eiseley encountered him at Penn, Frank Speck had been teaching there for over twenty years and had been chairman or acting chairman for most of that time. Before he joined the faculty, there were only a few anthropology courses; he virtually originated the department and then presided over its development for many years—until, interestingly enough, Loren Eiseley returned to Penn in 1947 as chairman. When he first met Speck, however, Eiseley was new and unknown, while Speck was an important man and a formidable presence. The young man from Nebraska was entering Speck's territory—his creation—and until Loren learned the rules

and proved himself, he would feel uneasy and confused. He began
by properly identifying the flints, and soon after he learned Frank's
style.

After Lou Korn had advised Eiseley and Ricky about getting
along with the chairman, Eiseley began to realize how lonely Frank
Speck was:

> I learned a lot about Lou Korn in those few moments. Secure,
> himself a favorite, he had gone out of his way to inform two
> helplessly floundering newcomers who had not grown up as under-
> graduates under the old man's tutelage. Frank, in a strange way
> which I was never totally to understand, was lonely. His initial
> growl, which I had not anticipated from my correspondence before
> coming to Penn, was an assertion of his own independence. He
> expected perception. If you saw through the gruffness, if you liked
> books, snakes, the life of the hunting peoples, if you were a good
> companion, he would do anything to help you.[25]

Like a few other favored students, Eiseley could fulfill a need in
Speck's life; and as it turned out, Speck could satisfy a desperate
need in Eiseley's.

In *All the Strange Hours*, Eiseley narrates only a few episodes
involving Speck and himself, but typically, these serve as representative moments that express a great deal about their relationship.
One is the flint game. Another reveals their common attitude
toward science and the modern world. One day, while they were
walking at the zoo (Speck often had to get away), he surprised
Eiseley by asking, "quite softly and uncertainly," about the ducks
they were watching: "Loren . . . tell me honestly. Do you believe
unaided natural selection produced that pattern? Do you believe
that it has that much significance to the bird's survival?" Eiseley
responded with his now well known doubts about scientific explanation:

> I feel right now, as though the universe were too frighteningly queer
> to be understood by minds like ours. It's not a popular view. One is
> supposed to flourish Occam's razor and reduce hypotheses about a
> complex world to human proportions. Certainly I try. Mostly I
> come out feeling that whatever else the universe may be, its so-called
> simplicity is a trick, perhaps like that bird out there. I know we have

learned a lot, but the scope is too vast for us. Every now and then if we look behind us, everything has changed. It isn't precisely that nature tricks us. We trick ourselves with our own ingenuity. I don't believe in simplicity.[26]

The words are those of a mature man, but they nevertheless express the quality of his doubts as a young man. In that kind of exchange, Eiseley and Speck found one another. On this particular occasion, Speck presumably replied, "Loren . . . I feel as you do, maybe even more, because I really live far back with the simpler peoples."[27] Eiseley shared that sense. Although he would discover over the years that *his* true home lay "back on the *altiplano* with the great grey beasts of the crossing," rather than with "primitive" Indian tribes, he knew even then that he, too, did not quite belong in the modern world. Like Frank Speck, "a true changeling," Eiseley often felt like a substitute child, and late in his life he literally described himself in just such terms:

So is it now. The fox, the wolf, the coyote,
                    the last
              contenders against traps and poison
                    hold with grim teeth
                          slowly retreating
              into waste lands where only coyotes run.
I am born of these,
                    their changeling.
              Who first rocked
              my cradle
              or what wild thing left me
              upon my parents' doorstep
              is a mystery
                    although
through this means I can see
              faces where faces are not
                    and I know
              a nature still
                    as time is still
                    beyond the reach of man.[28]

Both men were lonely and fundamentally displaced, and that bond established a deep kinship between them. They shared mutual doubts about the validity of scientific explanation, even though they were scientists; each had been captured in some way by the past; and each felt strong impulses—even as adults—to flee the modern world. They shared a lot; but most importantly, Frank Speck became Eiseley's teacher and guide—his second father.

When Eiseley described "the day time stopped" for him—that perfect day when he lay in the sun of a Kansas City railroad yard—he explained how he had felt without a father to guide him: "I was merely lost, waiting to find a role for myself. Other youths, in the world I had left, had fathers who pointed the way. I had none. All I had was knowledge that the world was complex and dangerous. I was young. Someday something would happen to decide my course."[29]

In the mid-1930s he had friends, work, and poetry, and over time he was slowly finding a vocation. But not until he discovered a person and a set of beliefs that pointed the way could Eiseley fully emerge from his crisis. Frank Speck was the man; and science, as he practiced it, was the guiding ideology. "I have always regarded this man as an extraordinary individual," Eiseley writes of him. "To this day, fragments of his unused wisdom remain stuffed in some back attic of my mind. Much of it I have never found the opportunity to employ, yet it has somehow colored my whole adult existence. I belong to that elderly professor in somewhat the same way that he, in turn, had become the wood child of a hidden forest mother."[30] Eiseley had found not only an intellectual father, but an emotional one as well.

There were other friends or relatives in Eiseley's life before he met Speck who might have fulfilled that role, but they were either wrong for it, or the time simply wasn't right. Eiseley owed a great deal to Lowry C. Wimberly, for example. But Wimberly remained only a good friend and associate; their tastes and temperaments were quite different.[31] Eiseley's uncle by marriage, William Buchanan "Buck" Price, had helped him at a critical point in his youth, and Eiseley felt great affection for him. In 1923, when Eiseley was sixteen, his uncle Buck gave him a copy of Henry F. Osborn's *The Origin and Evolution of Life: On the Theory of Actions, Reactions, and Interaction of Energy*. It was inscribed "Get knowledge, but with it get understanding. From your 'buck.'"[32] Price invited Loren and his mother to live with them after Clyde Eiseley died, and then in 1933, his faith and financial assistance helped Eiseley get to Penn. Price died in 1936. Years later Eiseley dedicated *All the Strange Hours* to him. Although Eiseley remembered him warmly throughout his life, he valued him as his uncle. With Frank Speck it was different.

Although Eiseley enrolled in Speck's courses and wrote his dissertation under him, he learned more, he says, during after-class conversations in Speck's office and "over cups of coffee in a dingy campus restaurant" when they talked about things centuries older than either of them—about "snakes, scapulimancy, and other forgotten rites of benighted forest hunters." Eiseley also learned about science and about one particular man of science during afternoons at the zoo, or on walks in the "pine barrens," or on hair-raising canoe trips. "He was an excellent canoeman," Eiseley reports, "but he took me to places where I fully expected to drown before securing my degree."[33]

Speck and Eiseley formally identified their intellectual relationship by publishing an article together in the *American Anthropologist*. Titled "Significance of Hunting Territory Systems of the Algonkian in Social Theory," it discusses eastern Canadian Indians, the fur trade, the Indians' nomadic movements, and the organization of their property in the seventeenth and eighteenth centuries. These were Frank Speck's main concerns and rather different from Eiseley's own field experience and primary interest in the Quaternary period. In fact, Eiseley published very little about Indians in the eastern United States and Canada. But as Speck's student, he would have known his mentor's work and so could have easily been an informed author. More than anything, the article gave Speck's public sanction to Loren Eiseley and helped initiate the young anthropologist's scientific career. Important as that announcement is, it reveals nothing of the deeper kinship between them.

At the University of Pennsylvania, Eiseley met new friends, and for a brief interlude, he experienced a peace and tranquility unlike anything he had known before. In Frank Speck, he found not only a man he could admire and learn from, but one he could trust and love as well. The University gave him knowledge and confirmed him in a vocation. These were years of restoration, stability, and growth.

In June of 1937, Loren Eiseley received his doctorate, certifying his knowledge of anthropology and the fulfillment of a series of requirements. "I knew a good deal of ethnological lore from the Jesuit Relations of the seventeenth century, about divination through the use of oracle bones. I knew also about the distribution of rabbit-skin blankets in pre-Columbian America and the four-day fire rites for the departing dead. And mammoths gone ten thousand years, I knew them, too."[34] And he had written a dissertation, "Three Indices of Quaternary Time: A Critique." His knowledge, however, was not so miscellaneous or "happily irrelevant"[35] as his brief account might suggest. His master's thesis and his dissertation—as well as his earlier work in Nebraska—provide the best access to that.

During the summers Eiseley worked for the Nebraska State Museum, he learned a great deal of paleontology and anthropology. That work led Bertrand Schultz and Eiseley to collaborate on a detailed analysis of the age of the Scottsbluff bison quarry. In 1935, they published their account, "Paleontological Evidence for the Antiquity of the Scottsbluff Bison Quarry and Its Associated Artifacts."[36] Although the article focuses on a single quarry and tries to date the fossils and artifacts found in association there, it was in fact part of a larger effort by scientists to determine the arrival date of early man in North America. Scholars could not agree whether man migrated to this continent in the Pleistocene—during either pre- or late Wisconsin periods—or within the last ten thousand years, the Recent period.

In the article Schultz and Eiseley carefully review the relevant scholarship and examine the evidence from the quarry. Using the record of invertebrate life there to supplement the fragmentary character of the geological knowledge about western Nebraska and the confused state of bison taxonomy, they cautiously propose a somewhat earlier date for that site, and thus for Folsom culture, than others had indicated. "In fact," they assert, "the appearance of these forms [fossil invertebrates] taken in conjunction with the evidence derived from faunal change and the occurrence of fossil bison seems, if one cannot put it in stronger terms, at least suggestive of considerable antiquity."[37] They are arguing in effect for a dating of 12,000 to 15,000 years ago—"at least late Wisconsin"[38] and significantly earlier than Recent. Although Schultz and Eiseley say that many puzzles remain, they seem confident of their findings. A year later, in "An Added Note," they speak more forcefully, and even a little testily, in support of their argument.[39]

These issues bear directly on Eiseley's master's thesis, completed in the spring of 1935.[40] As its title indicates—"Review of the Paleontological Evidence Bearing upon the Age of the Scottsbluff Bison Quarry"—the thesis relies heavily on the Nebraska work but develops those findings in more detail than the slightly earlier article permitted. By writing his paper, Eiseley hoped to throw light on "a little known people"—the Folsom culture, whose artifacts had been discovered near Folsom, New Mexico, and at the Scotts-bluff site. Eiseley is arguing against the notion that Solutrean man could not possibly have penetrated North America until after the withdrawal of the Wisconsin ice sheet; he proposes instead that early man could have migrated to this continent after the onset of the glacier and before its withdrawal. By examining the existing knowledge about North American and European ice sheets and using a recently published argument that the Mackenzie River valley had been open for 25,000 to 30,000 years, Eiseley decides—cautiously, once again—that America was indeed open to Aurignacian and Solutrean invasion. At that time, scientists dated these cultures at 15,000 to 20,000 years into the past. Eiseley's detailed account of the fossil and artifact evidence found at Scottsbluff helps support the more general argument about early man's appearance in America.

The longest part of the thirty-six-page thesis describes the evidence from Scottsbluff and develops Eiseley's argument about its date. There seems to be nothing new from Nebraska, but in his conclusion Eiseley does add evidence from another High Plains site near Yuma, Colorado. In the summer of 1934, on an expedition for Penn, he saw an extensive collection of invertebrates from sand blowouts that had also yielded "the largest number and most beautiful examples of the ungrooved Folsom or 'Yuma' point." This analogous evidence, along with the primary material from Scottsbluff, enables Eiseley to extend the Nebraska site into the tundra period of the late Wisconsin or even into a slightly earlier and milder period between the Iowan advance and the early Wisconsin. As far as he can guess (the difficulties and the need for caution have not changed), the quarry dates "in the neighborhood of 15,000 years ago." The thesis ends by identifying this quarry as simply one discovery in what he believes will be a series that will reveal more and more about one of the earliest peoples in North America.

Since the article and the thesis are almost contemporaneous, they obviously do not differ very much. They rely almost entirely on the same evidence and conclusions. They display Eiseley's critical and analytical ability, as well as his interest in field research. They also reveal his way of seeing particular events or phenomena in larger contexts—a single quarry in the framework of early man's migration to America. If anything, Eiseley had thought about the thesis a little longer and written it all himself, so that it reflects his personal way of seeing the material. More coherent and fluent than the article, it is a well-written, mature piece of scientific investigation and reasoning.

Two years later, Eiseley finished his dissertation. Although it is also closely related to the work he had done before, it is almost entirely analytical and critical. Rather than report and analyze the results of fieldwork or research, Eiseley examines the use of invertebrate (mollusca) and vertebrate faunal successions and pollen analytical methods as measurements of glacial and postglacial (Quaternary) time. According to the abstract in the University of Pennsylvania Archives, Eiseley's conclusions were essentially negative. Pollen analysis and mollusca were apparently not very reliable indices for dating archaeological horizons in America. Vertebrate faunal successions, however, were more reliable and had, in fact, helped Eiseley and Schultz date the Scottsbluff quarry.

Listed in the card catalog of the library at Penn, described in an abstract, and indexed in volume 34 of the Xerox University Microfilms *Comprehensive Dissertation Index*, a single document as such does not exist. One cannot, in other words, go to Penn and read Loren Eiseley's dissertation. Evidently Eiseley, his director, Frank Speck, and the dean of the Graduate School agreed that the separate publication of the three parts of the dissertation, with copies furnished to the Graduate School, would satisfy the degree requirement. Speck had read the entire thesis in draft and approved it. According to a May 6, 1937, letter from D. S. Davidson, president of the Philadelphia Anthropological Society and the third and newest member of the anthropology department, one part of the dissertation ("Index Mollusca and Their Bearing on Certain Problems of Prehistory: A Critique") would be published in the twenty-fifth anniversary studies of the Philadelphia Anthropological Society.[41] That collection, with Eiseley's paper, did appear in May or June of 1937. The remainder of the dissertation had been accepted for publication in the Daniel Garrison Brinton centenary volume, edited by Speck. That volume never appeared, but another part of Eiseley's dissertation did. In 1939, *American Antiquity* printed "Pollen Analysis and Its Bearing upon American Prehistory: A Critique."[42] Eiseley's critique of the third index, vertebrate faunal successions, was apparently not published in its dissertation form, although this method figured significantly in his own work.

The pollen analytical method attempted to establish a postglacial chronology that was based upon climatic fluctuation. Through analysis of pollens—preserved mainly in peat bogs—scientists hoped to identify characteristic vegetation and from this determine climate. According to Eiseley, the techniques had been more fully and reliably developed in Europe, where scientists had available several cross-checks—faunal sequences, land movement, and archaeological remains—that were not applicable in America. Although Paul B. Sears had made "an enviable start" with the method in the East, his findings had not been verified, and moreover, they were inapplicable to the High Plains region.

"If we now survey," Eiseley writes, "that area in which our oldest culture seems definitively recognizable, we come to the added realization that the pollen analytical method seems altogether inapplicable—not so much because it is in an embryological state of development as because of the lack of necessary successions of preserved pollen." Up to that time, each attempt to establish chronologies for the High Plains through pollen analysis "ended in total failure."

At the time Eiseley wrote, scientists had experienced no better success establishing invertebrate successions—the index mollusca. They had started using mollusks to determine age because of the obvious limitations of pollen analysis. But serious disagreement existed about fundamental approaches, and very little data was available. Promising as the technique may have been, it was not well enough developed, according to Eiseley, to be very useful.

"The safest attitude," he concludes, "would seem to be to await more comprehensive collections and more intensive general faunal surveys of the area of the High Plains."

"Three Indices of Quaternary Time" is more abstract than Eiseley's earlier writing. It is based primarily on his analysis and critique of published work, rather than on his own or his colleagues' field study. In it, he is examining and evaluating the methods of his science, and not simply learning or applying it. This work shows considerable competence. In June, 1937, when he received his Ph.D., Eiseley was already an informed and mature anthropologist with a systematic and comprehensive grasp of his field. He knew far more than the irrelevant odds and ends of information he mentions in *All the Strange Hours.*

During these years of preparation, he was not only learning anthropology and archaeology; he was experiencing and learning time as well. For Eiseley, "time was never a textbook abstraction." Throughout his youth and young adulthood, its "remnants" had lain openly about him "in arroyos, in the teetering, eroded pinnacles of Toadstool Park, or farther north in the dinosaur beds of Wyoming."[43] He had physically excavated centuries, millenia, and ages, and he had pursued time through libraries and studied it analytically and critically. As a scientist, he came to know it experientially and intellectually—its rocks, bones, and artifacts, its life—so that, as he says, "through some strange mental osmosis these extinct, fragmented creatures merged with and became part of my own identity."[44]

This process did not begin with science, however, for Eiseley's awareness of time—his fascination with it—go much farther back. Like his sense of place, his sense of the past originated during his childhood. He tried to explain this once to W. H. Auden when the two were dining together not long before Auden's death. Auden had asked Eiseley what public event he remembered first from childhood. In struggling to answer, Eiseley talked about the prison break, and then about the stones and fossils he collected as a child. He spoke also of the gold crosses he once made for dead animals or for a dead hero he had read about. Auden interpreted his answer as the "child's effort against time" and then proposed that the archae-

ologist "is just that child grown up."[45] As a young boy collecting
fossils, perhaps he *was*, as Eiseley himself suggests, "groping . . .
childishly into time, into the universe,"[46] and in that way struggling
against it. For isn't his impulse to understand and thereby control
it an "effort against time"? Although many layers of experience and
knowledge lay between the child and the archaeologist, time is the
common element running through them all.

Eiseley's sense of time is layered much like his sense of place, and
in fact, they are not really distinct. As he pushed the spatial
dimensions of his life farther and farther outward and deeper and
deeper into the land, he pushed the time dimensions of his life back
even beyond history, gradually developing a greater understanding
of each layer.

Starting with childhood games and ending with his dissertation,
Eiseley had been exploring time for at least twenty-five years. The
layers are identifiable: family, regional, archaeological, paleontological; the time frames are recognizable: decades, centuries, mil-
lennia, epochs, geological periods. But the layers are not really
distinguishable from one another, for even though Eiseley's mind
generally moved deeper and deeper into the past, the strata were
not laid down separately or in a systematic order as geological
strata might be. Several of these psychological and intellectual
strata were in effect being laid down simultaneously, so that they
interleaved one another in the complex wholeness of Eiseley's
mind.

With the completion of his doctoral work, Loren Eiseley added
still more layers: detailed knowledge about the arrival of early man
on the prairies, extensive knowledge of High Plains vertebrate
paleontology, and a thorough understanding of the techniques for
dating this prehistory. As he learned and discovered more, the
distant past became increasingly present to him, and he began
thinking of the ways that he and it were intertwined, so that
eventually these epochs and their "extinct, fragmented creatures
merged with and became part of [his] identity." In 1937 the fusion
was not quite complete, but even then Eiseley was beginning to
reflect on time, as science defined it for him, and he was also
writing about the personal and imaginative significance of his
knowledge.

"On the Pecos Dunes" (1935) draws directly on Eiseley's anthropological fieldwork. In it, he meditates on some red pottery shards shifted from the sand by fieldworkers, and he imagines the song "the far-away people" might have sung to express their sense of the way all things pass and only the earth endures:

> They made red bowls and these were not lasting,
> The love they spoke to the winds has gone
> But they cry this word from the rabbit's burrow,
> When the wind shifts north you can hear it strong:
>
> > That the root stays
> > And the root seeds
>
> They have left this word like a fighting song.[47]

Several years later in "Say It Is Thus with the Heart" (see chap. 5), Eiseley seems to be working out his personal response to the facts of paleontology and archaeology. He has learned that over long periods of time nothing remains but a few fossils and some shells, and he is trying to accept that without anger and perhaps even with love. The last four lines give the poem great personal force, and in a compressed image, typical of his later manner, Eiseley places *his* present moment in the context of epochs.

The young scientist was not yet using time and evolution as fact and metaphor, as he would some twenty years later in *The Immense Journey*, nor was he yet writing about time as historic and unreturning, as he would also in *The Immense Journey* and later in *The Firmament of Time* and *The Unexpected Universe*. Eiseley was, however, beginning to explore the mythic dimensions of time and the magical presence of the past; those "far-away people" do mysteriously have a voice. This is not too surprising, given the odd and irrelevant pieces of knowledge he says he had accumulated by the time he received his degree. His graduate work had involved his mind and imagination in magic as well as hard facts.

The young man was also beginning to sense that his true home lay not only on the High Plains but far back in the past as well, on "the cold bleak uplands of the ice-age world." Later, Eiseley's mind and imagination would enable him to transcend time, as most of us experience it. The prehistoric past would become a more and more powerful psychological reality and imaginative presence. In some ways, Eiseley would come to live in another dimension, intersecting ours, but with a trajectory reaching far behind and far beyond our conventional time-bound dimension.

Science gave a formal definition and a firm base to Loren Eiseley's fascination and experience with time and to his imaginative explorations of its significance. The explicit and intuitive senses of the past Eiseley had developed by 1937 underlie his major scientific and literary work. But science, in fact, functioned much more complexly in his development.

In the early 1930s, when Nebraska was suffering with the rest of America in the depths of the Great Depression, prospects were not very promising for a young man trying to finish college. Eiseley saw no professional, no paying future in poetry or, as he once said, in philosophy. Science seemed at least possible, and Eiseley believed he could make a living at it. After all, he had been paid pretty well in the field when there were no jobs to speak of in Lincoln, and he had not been paid anything for his poetry or prose. Moreover, he felt concern for his mother's welfare, in spite of her irresponsibility toward him, and in 1936, when his uncle Buck died, Eiseley assumed actual responsibility for both his mother and his aunt. To become a scientist, therefore, made economic sense. It was the practical thing to do.

Besides that, it was a psychologically necessary choice. Eiseley had been poor for so long that he feared poverty perhaps as much as anything. To be poor would bring back all of his troubling past and in a sense return him helplessly to it, thus denying everything he had gained. It was a question of status and identity, as well as a matter of making a living and supporting relatives. At some point, Eiseley seems to have vowed deep within—so that it became almost compulsive—never to be poor again. Even in the last year of his life, with an apparently assured financial future and no one to support but himself and his wife, he still worried almost obsessively about money. Having once been poor, he could not forget.

Science may also have appealed to Eiseley because of its apparent systematic, rational, and impersonal character. It may have seemed like the one profession where love and kindness did not matter, where he could safely defend himself from personal crisis. Although Eiseley said very little about such motives, his poetry and "The Star Thrower" indirectly suggest this.

   The turmoil of Eiseley's early adult years had fragmented completely whatever sense of wholeness remained after his youth, but after a period of confusion, he began to realign his life. Fieldwork and scientific education were his first major steps toward organization and engagement. By giving himself totally to science, by assuming a mask of orderly and objective knowledge, he could neutralize his more intense and painful feelings, and he could go about the world in a publicly accepted disguise. Science protected him, at the same time it became his entrance into a community and the world.

   Science filled out and ordered the fragmented image of life that Eiseley had been able to express but not altogether deal with. It confirmed, for example, his sense that life is dominated by conflict and crisis, that all organisms live constantly under the threat of death or extinction. The record of the past, revealed and explained by science, showed him this vision. It linked Eiseley's own history with the prehistory of mankind and nature. These coherent explanations restored some continuity to his broken life, for they were tied to the town and the territory that were his home. This constitutes the most important personal function that Eiseley's sciences—anthropology, archaeology, paleontology—performed.

   "Men should discover their past," Eiseley says in his autobiography, and in 1937 that was becoming his profession. Whether Eiseley was excavating in the field or digging through libraries, he was simultaneously acting out his own psychic life as a wanderer, a creature of impulse, and a fugitive—but now in an orderly, acceptable way. He was also acting out the life of his ancestors, of early man, and of extinct animals—all those wandering, unsettled species that preceded him. In a real sense, Eiseley was beginning to discover that biologically, psychologically, and imaginatively he bore all of his historical predecessors with him.

   These generalizations appear true enough, though they make a very gradual and problematic transition seem like a total and permanent conversion. In fact, Eiseley's turn to science was neither complete nor final; throughout his life, he felt ambivalent toward the field. These same explanations could also suggest that his conflicts had been resolved by science, rather than simply brought into tension and problematic balance. By the time he graduated in June, 1937, his intellectual and emotional energies were organized and directed toward a future in science, and thus he passed successfully through another critical phase of development and moved with some confidence into his profession. But in no sense was Eiseley free from his past. The interplay between forces contributing to high expectations, emotional security, and basic confidence and forces making for disappointment, insecurity, and distrust continued for the rest of his life.

At the beginning of his last year in graduate school, in the fall of 1936, Eiseley once again felt a strong impulse to leave—this time to go to sea with Tim Riley. Eiseley had met him early one morning on the New York-to-Philadelphia express and learned that Riley, now a sea captain, had left home at age fifteen and had been a sailor ever since. He had broken off all contact and did not even know if his father was dead or alive. Although Eiseley had more or less settled down, he recognized in Tim Riley the homeless wanderer that in some ways he still was.[48]

In the course of their conversation, Riley mentioned a woman he had recently met—"a real girl" with whom he'd made plans—but now he had to ship out again. Although Eiseley urged him to come back to her at the end of the voyage, it seemed as if Tim could not break the pattern; he would go on wandering, a homeless stranger, for the rest of his life. Instead of acknowledging Eiseley's plea, Riley urged him to come along. "'Look do you like what you're doing? . . . 'Cause if you don't, you can come with me. I'll get you signed on.'"[49]

Just then, things were difficult for Eiseley. Besides the residue of instability from his recent past, Eiseley felt tired and the future looked grim. He saw no job prospects. Several of his friends had already given up and turned to something else, "to anything but this meaningless treadmill of the depression." So when Riley said, "Come with me," Eiseley felt an enormous desire to go, leaving fatigue, hard work, and depression behind. At virtually the same moment, however, he thought of Frank Speck, a man as alone as himself, "who had guided and chided [his] graduate career," and of his uncle, William Buchanan Price. If he left, he would probably betray himself; more importantly, he would betray his uncle, and Frank Speck, especially.[50]

After his father died, Eiseley had no one to be loyal to, and before that, his home life had been almost unbearable. Now it was

different. He had a "father," a way of life, and a possible future. So
he stayed. The delicate balance was inclined toward science. "In the
end," he tells us, "I stood up alone without friends or relatives and
received my doctorate."

NOTES

1. If not otherwise indicated, the details about the University of Pennsylvania in the first part of this chapter are based on Eiseley's *All
   the Strange Hours.*
2. Ibid., p. 88.
3. Eiseley to Wimberly, Nov. 14, 1933, in University Archives, Love
   Memorial Library, University of Nebraska, Lincoln.
4. *All the Strange Hours*, p. 89.
5. Ibid., pp. 89-90.
6. Ibid., p. 112.
7. Ibid., p. 26.
8. Francis Tachibana to Mabel Eiseley, July 22, 1977, in Penn Archives.
9. Ibid. The Penn Archives contain a personal letter from Vinal to
   Eiseley, dated August 11, 1935, indicating that the two were fairly
   good friends and that Vinal knew both Eiseley and (then) Mabel
   Langdon (later Mrs. Eiseley).
10. *All the Strange Hours*, pp. 113-14.
11. Tachibana to Mabel Eiseley, July 22, 1977.
12. *All the Strange Hours*, p. 113.
13. Ibid., p. 114.
14. Tachibana to Mabel Eiseley, July 22, 1977.
15. Ibid.
16. Eiseley to Wimberly, Nov. 14, 1933.
17. Loren Eiseley, "Lengthier Biography," 6-page typescript in Penn
    Archives, evidently written in connection with the publication of
    The Immense Journey.
18. *Current Biography, 1960*, p. 105.
19. Transcript, University of Nebraska, in Penn Archives.
20. Mangione, *Dream and the Deal*, p. 109: "Eiseley wrote parts of the
    essays on paleontology and archaeology."
21. *All the Strange Hours*, p. 118; Duke [Tachibana] to Eiseley, Oct.
    9, 1939, in Penn Archives.
22. *All the Strange Hours*, p. 115. See also Richard A. Faust to Eiseley,
    Dec. 9, 1975, in Penn Archives.
23. *Unexpected Universe*, p. 86.
24. Beside Eiseley's own accounts in *The Unexpected Universe, All the
    Strange Hours*, and *The Invisible Pyramid*, see Irving Hallowell's
    obituary for Speck in *American Anthropologist*, 53 (Jan.-Mar., 1951),

67-87, and John Witthoft's brief sketch in *Dictionary of American Biography, Supplement 4, 1946-1950* (New York: Charles Scribner's Sons, 1974), pp. 761-63.

25. *All the Strange Hours*, p. 91.
26. Ibid., pp. 94-95.
27. Ibid., p. 95.
28. *Notes of an Alchemist*, pp. 21-22.
29. *All the Strange Hours*, p. 67.
30. *Unexpected Universe*, p. 63.
31. This is suggested in Eiseley to Rudolph Umland, Jan. 26, 1967, in Penn Archives.
32. Caroline E. Werkeley, Report of the Loren Eiseley Collection, type-script, July, 1978, in Penn Archives.
33. *Unexpected Universe*, p. 63.
34. *All the Strange Hours*, p. 130.
35. Ibid., p. 130.
36. *American Anthropologist*, 37 (Apr., 1935), 306-19.
37. Ibid., p. 317.
38. Ibid.
39. "An Added Note on the Scottsbluff Quarry," *American Anthro-pologist*, 38 (July-Sept., 1936) 521-24.
40. Available at the University of Pennsylvania Library.
41. The abstract and relevant letters are in the Penn Archives. "Index Mollusca" appeared in *Twenty-fifth Anniversary Studies of the Phila-delphia Anthropological Society*, ed. D. S. Davidson (Philadelphia: University of Pennsylvania Press, 1937), pp. 77-93.
42. *American Antiquity*, 5, no. 2 (Oct., 1939), 115-40.
43. *Innocent Assassins*, p. 11.
44. Ibid., pp. 11-12.
45. *All the Strange Hours*, p. 29.
46. Ibid., p. 28.
47. Loren Eiseley, "On the Pecos Dunes," *Voices*, No. 81 (Apr.-May, 1935), pp. 16-19.
48. *All the Strange Hours*, pp. 122-32.
49. Ibid., pp. 128-29.
50. Ibid., p. 129.

8

The Writer as Scientist

Words can sometimes be more penetrating
probes into the nature of the universe than
any instrument wielded in a laboratory.

Because of the depression, when Eiseley completed his degree, he
believed that he had "no real hope"[1] of finding a university job, and
he began looking for newspaper work. But that summer he did, in
fact, get a job at the University of Kansas teaching in the Department of Sociology and Anthropology. There he began a distin-
guished forty-year career as a university teacher and administrator.

Within another year, Eiseley and Mabel Langdon were married.
They had known one another since Eiseley's undergraduate days at
the University of Nebraska. She had graduated from there in
1925—the year he enrolled—and after that she worked as an assistant curator at the art gallery on campus and also enrolled as a
graduate student. She, too, worked for the *Prairie Schooner* and
occasionally wrote poems, prose sketches, and reviews for it. The
wedding ceremony took place on August 29, 1938, in Albuquerque,
New Mexico.

It is difficult to say anything more about their marriage because
it has been so tightly closed to any but the most disrespectful kind
of outside scrutiny. Neither would write or talk about their life
together (she still declines to do so), and their friends have been
rightly reluctant to intrude on that privacy. But at the least, the
marriage and the job identify critical symbolic moments in Eiseley's
life. At this point both his professional and personal lives were
moving into new phases of growth and development.

If he had ever succeeded in suspending love and passion, he
evidently no longer needed to withhold either so completely. He
published very little that helps here. The few poems that did appear
in the early 1940s suggest some resolution of the tensions that he

experienced and expressed in poems like "Fabric for the Moth." "Winter Sign," a poem from 1943, expresses the love and commitment implicit in Eiseley's decision to marry. He speaks about a love that is tough, persistent, and reliable: "It will stick to the bone. It will last through the autumn days."[2] And it did.

Concealed as the record is, it nevertheless seems reasonable to say that "love"—Eiseley's capacity to feel, share, and give, as well as his *belief* in love—defines one of the major dimensions of this new phase. Science, obviously, identifies the other. Although one seems private and the other professional, the two are not separate. They were aspects of one whole or unified space—his life—and they were also mutually sustaining. The changes Eiseley experienced during the mid-1930s, for example, helped generate the psychic and emotional energy necessary to sustain both of his major commitments. Each required passion, devotion, and a sense of responsibility. At first, this kind of commitment expressed itself mainly in science as intellectual passion and intensity; but later the true sources of Eiseley's own scientific commitment became clearer to him, and he recognized the function of love in his professional life. Likewise, for several years, science had helped Eiseley explain, endure, maintain, and then develop his private life. It supported, in a sense, the renewal of passion, devotion, and commitment there.

The beginning of his career and his marriage clearly marked a new phase in Eiseley's life. They did not define a radical break, however, any more than earlier crises or turning points had, so much as identify significant points in an unbroken life process and thereby help explain the flow of the writer's life. From one phase to another, many things remained unchanged.

Eiseley indicates as much when he describes the lifelong uneasiness he felt as a teacher and administrator. It began with his first year of teaching at Kansas. The experience was traumatic, and he did everything he could to keep ahead of the class and gain the approval of at least a few students:

> At the close of the first year I had acquired . . . some followers. I had learned figuratively to bow and I was destined to keep right on bowing through the next thirty years. There was no escape. . . . An actor, and this means no reflection upon teaching, has to have at least a few adoring followers. Otherwise he will begin to doubt himself and shrink inward, or take to muttering over outworn notes. . . . I had emerged as a rather shy, introverted lad, to exhort others

from a platform. . . . It has been a lifelong battle with anxiety.[3]

His needs and his profession required him to face large groups of people and eventually become a public figure; at the same time other needs required solitude and protection.

Years later, in 1965, Eiseley wrote another essay about Robinson Jeffers. He identified, in Jeffers, a conflict that he himself suffered, that extended deep into his past and penetrated every part of his personal and professional life. Near the end of the essay, Eiseley refers to a Jeffers character "whose great compassion for life was so intense that she became life's victim." She was in some way Jeffers's alter ego. "Thus," Eiseley concludes, "[he] confronts the paradox of his daemon: to escape and not to love; to love and not escape. . . . [He] projected through another mask than his own the agony of that love which encompasses both man and creatures . . . the infinite capacity for love which makes man so pitiably vulnerable."[4] This was Eiseley's demon, too—"to escape and not to love; to love and not escape." It is a major theme in his writing and his life, and it makes a difference in his science.

The job at Kansas was not quite the piece of luck Eiseley suggests. He had had other offers. He was apparently a desirable candidate, and the administration there took "heroic measures" to come up with a competitive salary that would persuade Eiseley to go to Kansas and not to Detroit or Penn State.[5] He stayed at the University of Kansas for seven years, where he was an assistant professor of anthropology and sociology until 1942, when the university promoted him to associate professor. While he was there, Eiseley worked hard at his courses. Perhaps each year was a little like the first:

> Each night I studied beyond midnight and wrote outlines that I rarely followed. I paced restlessly before the class, in which even the campus dogs were welcome so long as they nodded their heads sagely in approval. In a few weeks I began to feel like the proverbial Russian fleeing in a sleigh across the steppes before a wolf pack. I am sure that Carroll Clark, my good-natured chairman, realized that a highly unorthodox brand of sociology was being dispensed in his domain, but he held his peace. By then everything from anecdotes of fossil hunting to observations upon Victorian Darwinism were being hurled headlong from the rear of the sleigh. The last object to

go would be myself. Fortunately for me, the end of the semester came just in time.[6]

He also continued active fieldwork. During the school year and the summer of 1938, for example, he began excavating an ancient campsite in Smith County, Kansas. An important archaeological discovery, this site helped fill the time gap between Folsom culture and more recent pottery-making and agricultural Indians (as recent as 1,000 years). The Kansas people were evidently nomadic hunters who inhabited the region some 5,000 to 7,000 years before. In January, 1939, Eiseley and a colleague, geologist H. T. U. Smith, whose assistance Eiseley requested, reported their findings to the American Anthropological Association.[7]

During this period, Eiseley also co-authored two articles about eastern Indians with Frank Speck; two parts of his dissertation appeared in print; and he began writing articles about the extinction of a particular species of bison. In 1940 he was awarded a Social Science Research Council grant that enabled him to spend fifteen months studying in New York City at the American Museum of Natural History. There Eiseley specialized in physical anthropology, learning essential techniques of skeletal measurement, studying human osteology and dentition, and acquainting himself with the kinds of pathological and anomolous variations found in any large series of remains. The months at the museum gave Eiseley laboratory opportunities he had never had before. He had hundreds of specimens to work with, and he could thereby perfect his technique and the accuracy of his observations. The grant paid him $2,500 and provided generous travel expenses. He was the only postdoctoral fellow selected from Kansas by the council.[8] His career was clearly on the rise.

At Kansas, Eiseley and his wife became part of a small group of junior faculty who were drawn together by their common situation (they were young and new) and their opposition to a relatively hostile upper administration. Everyone in the group was trying to establish and maintain a sense of professional identity and integrity, but Eiseley stood out, strong, independent, determined; he seemed to have a sense of destiny beyond all the rest.[9] That inner strength that had helped him survive was now focused on growth and success. The Eiseleys also became close friends with his chairman, Carroll D. Clark, and his wife. Years later, Clark recalled those

times, "before the war disrupted the Department," as providing
some of the happiest associations of his life. And Eiseley remembered their relationship well: "My memories come flooding back as
though they were but yesterday, and I feel that in some invisible
reality we have just put on our coats and started down the hill
together for an evening of good music, with Mabel at the keys of
the piano and you playing on the saxophone."[10]

In those years (and for the rest of his life, really), Loren Eiseley
and his wife depended profoundly on one another. Their mutually
supportive relationship sustained him; he now had a home, some
security, and love. In turn, his professional success gave him a way
of making a life for Mabel and sustaining their relationship. Although there was nothing idyllic about the Kansas years, they were
apparently good.

As before, however, things changed. "The change was mixed
with many things in my life," Eiseley reflected, "a growing dis-
illusionment with some aspects of scientific values, personal problems, abrasive administrators, humanity itself. In short, the war
had finally come to Kansas and transformed the pleasant, sleepy
little town of Lawrence overnight."[11] The war and these other
concerns were surely important. But they may have released distress already in Eiseley rather than create wholly new problems. In
an unpublished account of these experiences, for example, he
alludes to his haunted past: "There came also a comprehension of
the stubborn power of the mad Shepards who slumbered in my
own ancestry."[12] It had happened before in Philadelphia when the
effects of depression and war in the Far East disrupted the peace
and tranquility of Eiseley's second year at Penn. Earlier still, before
he left Nebraska, public events and conditions had had a profound
psychic effect on him. But more than *cause* his depression or
dissatisfaction, these factors primarily reinforced characteristic
feelings and responses. For Eiseley, external events were so intertwined with his inner experience that it seems impossible to identify
clear causal relationships.

In Kansas, there happened to be those "abrasive administrators"
whom Eiseley still resented when he wrote his autobiography
almost thirty years later. The unpublished version treats them
much more harshly and in more detail than does his published

narrative.[13] He also continued to undergo serious personal and financial pressures; his mother and his aunt were "totally dependent" on his support, and his wife had developed a malignancy that required surgery.[14] Besides that he felt a strong obligation to join the war effort, but to his disappointment he was rejected, either because of physical defects (a bad ear and eyes) or because of his mother's and aunt's dependence on him.

With the onset of war, Eiseley began teaching enlisted reservists in the premedical program. His training in physical anthropology and his background in anatomy and biology made his services essential. While he was with the medical program, he experienced a very distressing incident—the "small death" he describes in *All the Strange Hours*—that reinforced his growing doubts about scientific values.

As it chanced, I was assisting one of my medical superiors in a cadaver dissection. He was a kind and able teacher, but a researcher hardened to the bitter necessities of his profession. He took the notion that a living demonstration of the venous flow through certain of the abdominal veins would be desirable. "Come with me to the animal house," he said. "We'll get a dog for the purpose." I followed him reluctantly.

We entered. My colleague was humane. He carried a hypodermic, but whatever dog he selected would be dead in an hour. Now dogs kept penned together, I rapidly began to see, were like men in a concentration camp, who one after the other see that something unspeakable is going to happen to them. As we entered this place of doleful barks and howlings, a brisk-footed, intelligent-looking mongrel of big terrier affinities began to trot rapidly about. I stood white-gowned in the background trying to be professional, while my stomach twisted.

My medical friend (and he was and is my friend and is infinitely kind to patients) cornered the dog. The dog, judging from his restless reactions, had seen all this happen before. Perhaps because I stood in the background, perhaps because in some intuitive way he read my eyes, perhaps—oh, who knows what goes on among the miserable of the world?—he started to approach me. At that instant my associate seized him. The hypodermic shot home. A few more paces and it was over. The dog staggered, dropped, and was asleep. The dose was kindly intended to be a lethal one. He would be totally unconscious throughout the demonstration. He would never wake again. We carried him away to the dissecting room. My professional friend performed his task. A few, a very few, out of that large class, crowded around closely enough to see.

The light was pushing toward evening. The dog was going; this had been his last day. He was gone. The medical students attended to their cadavers and filed out. I still stood by the window trying to see the last sun for him. I had been commanded. I knew that, even if I had not been in the animal house, the same thing would have happened that day or another. But he had looked at me with that unutterable expression. "I do not know why I am here. Save me. I have seen other dogs fall and be carried away. Why do you do this? Why?"[15]

In contrast to this distressing incident, Eiseley's work in the medical program also led to one of his most satisfying experiences in Lawrence. Shortly before he accepted the headship of the sociology and anthropology department at Oberlin College in 1944, he was offered an opportunity to attend medical school by the chairman of anatomy at Kansas, Henry Tracy. Eiseley felt moved and complimented, although he could not accept. His age (he was almost thirty-seven), the good opportunity in Ohio, his dependent mother and aunt, his wife's continuing need for care, his need for money, and surely some resistance to starting over in another profession all made it impossible. It was simply too late. Besides, there was no real need. When he left Kansas, he was definitely moving up. Just three years later, he would be on his way back to the University of Pennsylvania to assume the chair of the department his mentor, Frank Speck, had headed for years.

By the time Eiseley had been at Kansas for two years, he had written or co-authored five publications for important professional journals. As his scientific output increased, his publications as a poet understandably began to decrease. In 1936, for example, his last really productive year as a poet, he published a total of seven poems in the *Prairie Schooner*, *Voices*, and the *American Mercury*. But over the next three years, there were only four. This small number contrasts sharply with Eiseley's productivity from 1928 through 1936—a period during which he published at least sixty-five poems, wrote literary articles and reviews, and edited "Cross-roads." His interests and needs as a writer were obviously changing as his emotional and intellectual commitments turned almost exclusively to science.

For several years, Eiseley had not been able to give much time to his work as a contributing editor for the *Schooner*, either. And so in 1938 "Crossroads" was discontinued, and sometime during the next year he gave up his editorship. With that, he cut his last formal, and perhaps symbolic, tie with the literary world that had sustained him emotionally for almost a decade. Although nine poems did appear in the *Schooner* between 1940 and 1945, he was nevertheless directing his time, energy, and attention elsewhere. For the next twenty years he published no poetry whatsoever. By the late 1940s, however, he was beginning to develop the new prose idiom that eventually fused his poetic and scientific worlds into an undivided whole.

After publishing no professional articles for two years (1940-41), Eiseley's output increased markedly. Suddenly he was writing about science for almost everybody. He was writing for specialist professional journals, like the *American Anthropologist*, as well as for *Science, Scientific American, Scientific Monthly*, and even for *Prairie Schooner*. From 1942 through 1946, he published over twenty articles—eight in 1943 alone. Although the character of his published work had changed dramatically, he was still a writer, and he still needed to write. For a few years, the new form of his work satisfied the demands of his profession, and it thereby satisfied his personal needs for stability and success. But more than that, through this scientific idiom, he was developing a new sense of himself. The idiom helped define and express the man he was becoming. In immediate practical terms, he was publishing his way out of Kansas, through Oberlin, and back to Penn. But this professional type of writing would not satisfy him emotionally and intellectually for very long.

While he was at Kansas, Eiseley wrote three scientific papers for the *Transactions of the Kansas Academy of Science*. In these, he is writing and thinking strictly as a physical anthropologist. The first, published in 1943,[16] reports the results of a close study of one of the "anthropological 'bric-a-brac' from the earlier years," the Foxhall mandible from Suffolk, England. Although the actual specimen had been lost, Eiseley read all of the available literature and carefully examined a detailed line engraving of the jawbone. Based on his observation of a rare feature shown in the drawing, he argues not for a place or a date, but for the need to pay more attention "to the mental foramen in reports on modern and ancient physical remains." The paper develops in a straightforward scientific manner; it is relatively impersonal; and the style, although more fluent than some scientific writing, sounds appropriately professional:

> The find, in 1937, of a human occipital and parietal bone in a stratum at Swanscombe, England, assignable to the Mindel-Riss interglacial, has aroused debate once more as to the antiquity of men of the *sapiens* type. Similarly the Mount Carmel finds regarded by McCown and Keith as transitional to *sapiens* have been just as reasonably interpreted by others as indicative merely of cross-breeding between *neanderthalensis* and *sapiens*, thus suggesting again, a greater antiquity for the latter.[17]

This is a scholarly, a library or research article, and not a report of fieldwork. Eiseley probably worked on it during his year in New York. Besides its odd scientific interest, the subject may have intrigued him because of its mysteriousness: the point could be neither falsified nor verified.

The second of these articles is much more statistical than the first.[18] In it Eiseley reports the results of extensive research at the American Museum of Natural History in New York. After examining a wide range of racial stocks, he has developed, he argues, a more thorough statistical analysis of the intertemporal-interangular index than any previous researcher. This index is (and the definition speaks for the style and technical character of the paper)

> actually made up of the minimum frontal width (i.e. intertemporal width) and the maximum width of the supra-orbital torus (interangular width). In the majority of cases the greatest interangular width of modern man lies at the fronto-malar suture. In the more primitive species of men, and occasionally among rugged modern males, the outer ends of the supraorbital process tend to bulge outward, and hence the measurement at this point is sometimes

slightly in excess of the distance measured between the outer borders of the two fronto-malar sutures.[19]

The paper develops around five statistical tables that present data for fossil man and several extant racial groups. According to Eiseley, the data "augment" current knowledge in a relatively neglected field.

Eiseley collaborated with C. Willet Alsing in a 1944 report entitled "An Extreme Case of Scaphocephaly from a Mound Burial near Troy, Kansas."[20] The skull in question had been found many years before and given to the museum at the University of Kansas, where the authors noticed it in an exhibit case. Since few descriptions of such skulls existed and it was rare for "both physician and anthropologist" to obtain such a complete specimen, they decided to "place on record a thorough description of [this] scaphocephalic cranium." The account itself is relatively long and detailed. It includes measurements, photographs, and a narrative description of the skull, and it also explains the possible etiology of the skull's deformity. The conclusion simply emphasizes their purpose—to record—and briefly summarizes their observations. Like the other two *Transactions* papers, this one is a classic scientific report. Eiseley had learned the style well. The article also illustrates the kind of work that prompted Henry Tracy to recommend medical school to him.

Beginning with the articles he wrote with Bertrand Schultz, Eiseley had worked steadily on a number of papers, including his thesis and dissertation, that explored the association of bison fossils and Folsom artifacts—what one might call "the bison group." Two of these, published in the forties, represent another dimension of Eiseley's scientific writing. More speculative and written for a wider audience, they are less technical and conventional. They are interesting to compare because they cover virtually the same material.

In the first, "The Folsom Mystery," printed in *Scientific American* in 1942,[21] Eiseley presents a carefully reasoned case based on evidence he had been developing for years about the relationships among certain living and extinct bison species. His argument bears directly on the problem of "dating those mysterious forerunners of the American Indian in the Great Plains"—Folsom man. The evidence is specific and the case is systematic, but the article contains no measurement data or descriptions of specimens. It is not technical or scientific in that sense. And its style is more informal and interesting than that in *Transactions*, as the first paragraph illustrates:

> No mystery in American archeology has been more fascinating than that of the Folsom culture. In the 15 years that have elapsed since the original site was excavated at Folsom, New Mexico, archeologists have diligently pursued every clue that might shed a ray of light on the shadowy "first" Americans. Their subsequently discovered sites, scattered over a wide area in the High Plains region of the United States, reveal little about them except that they were hunters of animals long since vanished: extinct American camels, bison larger than the historic variety, strange South American sloths, and even the huge American elephants, the mammoths. Their characteristic hunting tool, a grooved, exquisitely fashioned "point," superior in workmanship to any other variety of point known from the New World, speaks eloquently of their artistry and skill. But, so far, there is little else except these peculiarly shaped, beautifully made "Folsom" points to speak for the intrepid hunters who made them. Tantalizingly, his unmistakable weapon, but not Folsom Man himself, appears in site after site associated with the now extinct animals which he hunted.[22]

Eiseley's expressed fascination with the culture, his description of the beauty of the artifacts, and the fluency of his writing make the difference. He reveals his interest in mysteries, in old books, and in the adventure of pursuing difficult trails into the past: "Hidden away in old books, . . . discussed by naturalists interested only in existing animals, a curious broken thread of clues winds backward into the days of the first voyagers who explored the Great Northwest. If these clues are comprehended in relation to the archeological picture which we have just discussed, they take on a strange and almost startling significance."[23]

This article is more personal than *Scientific American* articles (not to speak of technical papers) usually are. Moreover, it suggests something of Eiseley's own sense of paleontology and anthropology. With only "broken threads" and fragmentary records, these sciences try to recover the human and faunal past of our continent. It is a fascinating and difficult quest, one that he described over a decade later as an "immense journey." Nevertheless, even with these other dimensions, the article is solidly scientific. It offers only foreshadowings of his later prose style.

The second of the two articles appeared in *Scientific Monthly*, a journal directed more to a lay audience. Although the organization is virtually the same as the first, and paragraphs in fact correspond from one to the other, the article, "Did the Folsom Bison Survive in Canada?,"[24] is more dramatic. Eiseley is trying to interest an even wider readership. This one begins:

> In 1927 a wave of incredulous surprise swept the archeological world. The discovery, at Folsom, New Mexico, of the bones of a supposedly extinct Ice Age bison in association with implements of human manufacture, shook to its foundations the theory of conservative archeologists that man had been a late arrival in America. Instead, a series of discoveries scattered over the High Plains region of the United States has revealed that man reached the American continent in time to see the last of the giant mammals of the Ice Age—the mammoth, the huge and lumbering sloths and the now extinct American horses and camels. All this is now archeological history. The specialist no longer scoffs as the earth continues to yield up evidence of these thinly scattered mammoth hunters remotely ancestral to the American Indians of to-day. The sole question not entirely answered to the archeologist's satisfaction, as yet, is the exact date at which the last of these extinct animals disappeared. And since these early people hunted the huge buffalo of the time with marked success, particular interest has lingered about these longhorned relatives of our family American bison of to-day.[25]

It ends with his characteristic caution: "Only more extended exploration of the Canadian wilderness and the intensive comparison of its fossil bisons will illuminate the whole problem. Until that time, however, a question must exist as to whether the 'extinct' Folsom bison lingered on into historic time, at least as an attenuated and mixed remnant on the northern fringe of that great continental bison range which the early travelers described as 'making the earth one robe.'"[26] Together the two articles reveal Eiseley's early interest in writing about science for a nonspecialist audience.

In the 1940s Eiseley published a number of articles about the extinction of the terminal Pleistocene (postglacial) fauna, continuing and extending his earlier studies. In some way, each publication in this group offers careful criticism of certain then-current

explanations for these massive extinctions. Scientists were proposing many related and even overlapping possibilities—the effect
of early man's presence, hunters using fire drives, dramatic reduc-
tions in populations that forced species into evolutionary traps,
radical climate changes—and Eiseley had examined these carefully.
In the two long articles, one published in 1943 and the other in
1946,[27] he analyzes a recently proposed theory in detail and finds
serious fault with it. He argues pointedly and vigorously, as he does
also in short notes or brief communications about other mistaken
notions.[28] He sets high expectations for himself as well as others.
And in each case, he urges care and caution.

Sometimes he simply identifies all that a given theory has failed
to consider, then lets its inadequacy speak for itself. He tempers
comments about other scientists: "This survey of Dr. [Carl] Sauer's
main contentions reveals, I believe, the impossibility of using any
one specific explanation to dispose of so complicated an array of
events."[29] At other times, he seems impatient (or slightly incredu-
lous) with obvious weak (or foolish) explanations: "The researcher
who uses facts is helpless before the individual who conveniently
explains every case of extinction as the result of the mysterious
failure of some life instinct in that particular form. . . . If we are to
explain extinction in this manner, we might just as well retire to the
armchair and the study and emerge for field work no more."[30]
Occasionally, he is crisp, even sardonic, especially in response to
those who disagree with his own work. In refuting one such theory,
Eiseley expresses wonder over the enormity of early man's role in
exterminating hosts of species:

> *Bison taylori*, the extinct species, so far as paleontology can tell
> us, was an animal whose habits were essentially the same. Yet
> according to this view, small hunting groups in the early days of an
> enormous empty continent exterminated their own game more suc-
> cessfully than any of the succeeding higher cultures. Not alone did
> they exterminate *taylori*, but in some mysterious way they permitted
> *Bison bison* at the same time to go unhunted and expand in numbers.
> Nor were they content to confine their exterminating activities to the
> bison. They destroyed mastodon, mammoth, horse, camel and a
> variety of other forms as well.[31]

He ends this particular critique with a series of strongly worded
sentences: "I must confess that I cannot. . . . I fail . . . to see. . . . I

further assert. . . ." All this falls, of course, within the range of respectable academic prose and may even seem bland. But the slight differences within the academic mode do reveal strong feelings. Taken as a group, these articles help define the changes in Eiseley's scientific writing, and they also help identify his style of doing science.

It would be easy enough to overread the articles and attribute a particular scientific style to Loren Eiseley rather than identify one. But his repeated admonitions about care and caution and the dominance in his work of the critique suggest an individual style, one consistent with his personality, as well as with his earlier work and with general scientific principles of evidence and theory formation. In these articles, and elsewhere, Eiseley is watchful, critical, suspicious, and somewhat contentious. He is very careful, and he exposes himself very little. He does not, for example, develop counterproposals that, like the theories he refutes, would be subject to attack or exposure. Nor does he advance his own independent theories that would really expose him to attack. He remains protected—and scientifically authoritative as well.

Even though this "extinction group" of articles is seriously scientific, they are more fluent and personal than, say, his earlier pieces in the *American Anthropologist* or the three *Transactions* publications. Sometimes they are even narrative and anecdotal, and they do reveal certain feelings about his profession. He seems to be pressing against the conventional limitations of scientific style, searching for a more comprehensive and human style, as well as a more complete and comprehensive self.

In "Myth and Mammoth in Archaeology," an article dating from about the same time,[32] Eiseley writes with a narrative and personal style that gives his exposition of archaeological history a strong storylike quality. He is still addressing a professional audience and urging "continued archaeological pursuit of the time of extinction." But he has broadened his concern to include the cultural milieu within which myths were read as evidence. Rather than simply discredit the "evidence," he tries to explain its historical origins and thus make a human or cultural point as well as a scientific one. At this time, in the mid-1940s, Eiseley seems to be thinking and sensing on two levels—the professional and the personal, the scientific and, in a sense, the poetic.

When "Myth and Mammoth" appeared, Eiseley had already moved to Oberlin College, with the rank of professor and head of the Department of Sociology and Anthropology. He continued to study and write with great energy and productivity. Three of the "extinction" articles were written and published while he taught there, from 1945 through 1947. In all, ten of his articles and essays appeared during that period.

In *All the Strange Hours*, Eiseley refers only once to his three years at Oberlin, and then he does not name the school, although he did in an early draft: "The beachheads were finally established. The Germans' last desperate offensive toward Bastogne and the Channel ports was contained. Japan's sea empire was tottering. Men of my age and condition were freer to move again. I was proffered an administrative post and a full professorship at an Ohio college under a dean who was both a fine historian and a great man."[33] It was at that point that Henry Tracy asked Eiseley about medical school. Besides age, the problems of dependents, money, and so on, the "very good post in Ohio" made it impossible for him to change his profession.

Although there was some opposition to his appointment at Oberlin from the sociology department (something about "the anthropological tail might eventually wag the sociological dog"), Eiseley received assurance from Dean Carl Wittke that "the storm" would be over before he got there. Evidently it was, for once appointed and there, Eiseley was welcomed and much appreciated. Colleagues recognized that he was an exceptionally well trained man with an unusual range of qualifications, and they realized, as well, that few at Oberlin possessed "anything resembling [his] intellectual equipment."[34]

Since there were only three faculty members in the department, Eiseley's administrative duties were very slight. Except for an evening seminar, he scheduled his classes early in the morning, at eight and nine; during the rest of the day and some evenings he read and wrote. He taught mostly general courses—an introduction to physical anthropology and prehistoric archaeology, cultural anthropology, the Neolithic, population, introductory sociology, social problems, and an anthropology seminar. During his tenure at Oberlin, his interest in the history of science developed, and he ordered many historical books for the college library.[35] Although he was a close friend of Carl Wittke, Eiseley still seemed to be a very private person, and distant. He had social acquaintances but few close friends. While there, his sense of profession and personal vocation also continued to change.

Just after he arrived at Oberlin, his essay "Apes Almost Men" appeared in the autumn, 1944, *Prairie Schooner*. Along with a similar piece, "There *Were* Giants," published the next year,[36] it marks a noticeable transition and return. Although Eiseley was writing several kinds of articles and essays during this period, it is clear that his work was moving in a new direction. In both essays, he selects a subject, takes a point of view, and works with techniques similar to those he developed later for *The Immense Journey*.

"Apes Almost Men" deals with then-current knowledge about *Australopithecus* fossils. The essay reviews the history of the famous finds by Raymond Dart and Robert Broom and summarizes the evidence for certain conclusions about the relationship of *Australopithecus* to early man. In short, Eiseley is giving the *Schooner* readers a general account and interpretation of these early "humanoid" (hominid) fossils. He narrates and explains the science in ways quite similar to his popular articles for *Scientific American* and *Scientific Monthly*. Even though some of the "facts" have changed—the dating of *Australopithecus*, for example, and the belief that it was a cave dweller—the scientific character of the essay is clear.

This essay differs from the others in the way Eiseley dramatizes and, in effect, humanizes his subject. He begins by speaking mysteriously of a new species of human ancestor. Then he evokes the remote and largely unknown "time depths" when the transition from ape to man occurred:

> The transition point lies somewhere below the Pleistocene, or Ice Age, in remoter time depths as yet unplumbed by the archeologist. We know, as a matter of fact, only the later period of man's evolution. Something even more strange might await the man who succeeded in uncovering fossils from the time beyond the ice, from that great seven-million-year-long period which the geologists call the Pliocene. Out of that far darkness had emerged our forebears, heavy of bone and brow, but with club and hand-ax already gripped

in purposeful hands. Somewhere beyond them lay the more impenetrable mystery, the mystery shrouding the threshold between man and beast. Only the border between life and death could be more strange.[37]

The style plays on "strange," "mystery," "remote." It expresses Eiseley's fascination with that darkness and appeals to similar feelings in his readers. Although he says that *Australopithecus* "is not *human*"—and that remains the fact of the matter—he describes such creatures as our cousins (contemporaries of more direct ancestors) and speaks of them as almost human:

> Apes though they are, however, we must not underrate these obscure cave folk. Their brains, in proportion to body weight, are better developed than that of the existing gorilla, which is a much larger animal. In terms of possible upper range of cranial capacity they do not lie far below the minimum range recorded for one of the new Pithecanthropus fossils at 850 cubic centimeters. It well may be that though not, as yet, toolmakers in terms of socially transmitted cultural tradition or techniques, they were nevertheless capable of making instrumental use of chance sticks and stones. Moreover, the males, lacking as they did the great shearing canines of the existing apes, may have been less combative and more socially agreeable. These creatures probably represented a stage so close to the borderline between fossil man and a completely ape mentality that much archeological effort will have to be expended before we can safely assert that their level of attainment was completely and entirely animal. There is no existing form of life which enables us to observe in the flesh the play of mind at that dim borderline above the existing apes and below the margin which we call human. But whatever the coming years may yield us in the way of additional information, we can quote in justice to Raymond Dart's early and much debated discovery, the final words of Dr. Gregory and Dr. Hellman, two of the world's most distinguished comparative anatomists: "As a result of our studies we affirm with Broom that in South Africa there once lived apes which had almost become men."[38]

The effect and interest Eiseley achieves is partly a matter of emphasis. He dwells on connections more than differences and even describes differences as if they were connections: "In terms of possible upper range of cranial capacity they do not lie far below the minimum range recorded for one of the new Pithecanthropus [homo erectus] fossils at 850 cubic centimeters." Imagine the effect of a different emphasis: Their cranial capacity is significantly less, 450 to 650 cubic centimeters, than the smallest recorded capacity, 850 c.c., for *Pithecanthropus*. The emphasis is also a matter of purpose—to dramatize—and of temperament—to discover relationships and true ancestors.

"There *Were* Giants" is very similar in purpose, effect, and structure. It explains the history of a particular fossil jawbone, "cast on primitive but human lines," that presumably revealed an extinct species of giant, early humans. The find was dramatic enough in itself, and Eiseley's summary of the history and evidence makes its significance clear. It was indeed something new. But Eiseley's treatment of it heightens the drama virtually to cultural, mythic proportions, and this is quite different from his other "popularizations." Just after the discoverer of the fossils, G. H. R. von Koenigswald, mailed his find from Java to the United States, he disappeared, presumably in the Japanese invasion of the island. Eiseley begins with that adventure: "In 1941, one of the last boats to leave Java carried in the mail bags below deck, a small package. . . ." But then "the Japs stormed ashore in Java, and the sender of that obscure little package vanished into Oriental darkness." Such an opening creates a mysterious and ominous air, and Eiseley continues to allude to the war as if it were an attack on science by hordes of "little yellow men" (he wrote this, remember, during the hostilities). After evoking that atmosphere, Eiseley describes the fossil as "one of the darkest and strangest secrets in the whole history of man's mysterious past."[39] So not only was war involved, the scientific significance was presumably very great. Eiseley lays on further meaning by invoking Greek myths and biblical legends to suggest man's fascination with giants throughout recorded time. And as he does, he continually connects the fossil (*Goliath javanicus* it was then named) with man. At the end he is speaking of these extinct animals as our brothers:

> But of this we *can* be sure. The discovery of "Goliath" will immensely complicate the study of human evolution and introduce a myriad problems just as it seemed that a reasonable outline of our remote history was becoming possible. For now, at least, we know that somewhere in the jungles of a million years ago there roamed a

mighty brother of the men from whom we seem to be descended. And of all the wild, incredible human faces which, age by age have stared at their own reflections in the ancient drinking holes of the Solo River, none, surely, were more formidable than his.[40]

Like the other *Schooner* essay, this one is obviously trying to interest readers, to show them that science is a great adventure with sometimes high risks. Eiseley is also trying to explain science and its significance to readers for whom he had not been writing just a few years earlier. "There *Were* Giants" is another of his early attempts to bring the past alive and closer, so that he, as well as we, could understand it and ourselves better.

In "Myth and Mammoth in Archaeology," "Apes Almost Men," and "There *Were* Giants," Loren Eiseley is clearly moving toward the complex and comprehensive style of *The Immense Journey*. Each essay develops from a firm scientific base as Eiseley explores or analyzes some new find or some aspect of anthropology or paleontology. But rather than simply report findings, each essay tries to relate the past to the present: Eiseley speaks about extinct species of apes and hominids as our cousins and brothers, and in this sense, perhaps, his anthropology was becoming unconventional. Each article also experiments with a richer, more evocative prose style, as Eiseley makes his writing more personal and literary. Although he continued to publish professionally in the *American Anthropologist* in both 1947 and 1948 and did not therefore change his style all at once, the transition and new direction do seem very clear.

Doubtless, Eiseley felt more secure professionally and therefore freer to write as he chose—although he would pay a certain professional price later on. It also seems fair to say that he was changing his style to make money from writing, for it was during these years that he began publishing in *Harper's*. He was, after all, a writer (though seldom a paid one) before he was a scientist. Moreover, his genuine need for money—as well as his great anxiety about it—persisted through these years. Beyond these apparent reasons, there were probably other, deeper ones, even if we can only guess at them. Almost from the beginning, Eiseley felt some ambivalence about science. Although he seemed temporarily satisfied by his near total involvement in it, orthodox science was clearly not going to be enough; Eiseley was probably trying to recover some of the dimensions of expression, sensitivity, and insight that he had developed as a poet but felt denied as a scientist. He was also letting his impulse to explore unknown territory—and his desire to find something of himself in the past—reappear. Although he did not write about Nebraska and the Great Plains in these essays, he was beginning, once again, to excavate his own human past in what continued to be a lifelong effort to find a home.

That the *Schooner* essays were not science in the usual sense does not mean that Eiseley was becoming unscientific. Rather, he was *extending* science. He was pointing the way toward what he later called a science "for the uses of life."

When Loren Eiseley left Oberlin College in 1947 to return to the University of Pennsylvania, he experienced perhaps his ultimate success as a scientist. In 1947, he was not yet known as a writer; that career and fame lay ahead. Over the years, he would go much farther as an academic and an administrator, eventually becoming the provost of his university. He would also become a well-known public figure—author, lecturer, holder of over thirty-five honorary degrees. But when he returned to his graduate school as chairman of his department and successor to Frank Speck, he was being recognized primarily for his achievements as an anthropologist.

That return must have been a great psychological moment, too. Not only was he being recognized as a superior professional by the university he had entered just fourteen years earlier as a naive, confused, and distressed young man; he was returning, in effect, to succeed and replace his "father." The son had at last proven himself. Still "moody," he was now a "genius" for all the world to see. No longer a second son, he was now the first, the inheritor of his (second) father's estate. Clyde Eiseley had died almost twenty years before, leaving his son with a strong image of failure. Although he preserved and valued his father's great capacity for love, he could not build his life in the image of Clyde Eiseley. With this success—a triumph, really—Loren Eiseley seemed to have finally escaped the ring of poverty, failure, illness, anxiety, and confusion. At the moment of his greatest triumph, however, he was about to undergo still another major change and slip away to something else.

NOTES

1. *All the Strange Hours*, p. 136.
2. Loren Eiseley, "Winter Sign," *Prairie Schooner*, 17, no. 3 (Fall, 1943), 163.
3. *All the Strange Hours*, pp. 136-37.
4. Loren Eiseley, "Foreword," in *Not Man Apart: Lines from Robinson Jeffers: Photographs of the Big Sur Coast*, ed. David Brower (San Francisco: Sierra Club, 1965).
5. Carroll D. Clark to Eiseley, May 1, 1937; Willard Waller to Eiseley, May 12, 1937; in Penn Archives.
6. *All the Strange Hours*, p. 136.
7. See the various newspaper articles, also a typescript by Harold T. U. Smith, in the Penn Archives.
8. Newspaper articles; typescript copy, Jan. 27, 1941, of Eiseley's request to the Committee on Social Science Personnel for a three-month extension; manuscript, "The Small Death" (early version of "A Small Death," *All the Strange Hours*); in Penn Archives.
9. Suggested during my conversation with John and Max Virtue, acquaintances of Eiseley's at Kansas.
10. Eiseley to Clark, Dec. 12, 1967; Clark to Loren and Mabel Eiseley, Mar. 27, 1968; in Penn Archives.
11. *All the Strange Hours*, p. 146.
12. "The Small Death," p. 1.
13. Ibid., pp. 3-4.
14. Ibid., p. 2.
15. *All the Strange Hours*, pp. 148-49.
16. "A Neglected Anatomical Feature of the Foxhall Jaw," *Transactions of the Kansas Academy of Science*, 46 (1943), 57-59.
17. Ibid., p. 57.
18. "Racial and Phylogenetic Distinctions in the Intertemporal Interangular Index," *Transactions of the Kansas Academy of Science,* 46 (1943), 60-65.
19. Ibid., p. 61.
20. Loren Eiseley and C. Willet Alsing, "An Extreme Case of Scaphocephaly from a Mound Burial near Troy, Kansas," *Transactions of the Kansas Academy of Science*, 47, no. 2 (Dec., 1944), 241-55.
21. "The Folsom Mystery," *Scientific American*, 167, no. 6 (Dec., 1942), 260-61.
22. Ibid., p. 260.
23. Ibid., p. 260.
24. "Did the Folsom Bison Survive in Canada?," *Scientific Monthly*, 56 (1943), 468-72.
25. Ibid., p. 468.
26. Ibid., p. 472.
27. "Archaeological Observations on the Problem of Post-Glacial Extinctions," *American Antiquity*, 8, no. 3 (Jan., 1943), 209-17; "The Fire

Drive and the Extinction of the Terminal Pleistocene Fauna," *American Anthropologist*, 48, no. 1 (Jan.-Mar., 1946), 54-59.

28. "Indian Mythology and Extinct Fossil Vertebrates," *American Anthropologist*, 47, no. 2 (Apr.-June, 1945), 318-20; "The Fire and the Fauna," ibid., 49, no. 4 (Oct.-Dec., 1947), 678-80.

29. "The Fire Drive," pp. 58-59.

30. "The Fire and the Fauna," p. 679.

31. "Archaeological Observations," p. 213.

32. "Myth and Mammoth in Archaeology," *American Antiquity*, 11, no. 2 (Oct., 1945), 84-87.

33. *All the Strange Hours*, p. 150.

34. Hope Hibbard to Carlisle, Apr. 26, 1978; Wittke to Eiseley, May 19, 1944, and July 11, 1944, in Penn Archives.

35. George E. Simpson to Carlisle, July 26, 1977.

36. Loren Eiseley, "Apes Almost Men," *Prairie Schooner*, 18, no. 3 (Fall, 1944), 170-76; "There *Were* Giants," ibid., 19, no. 3 (Fall, 1945), 189-93.

37. "Apes Almost Men," pp. 170-71.

38. Ibid., pp. 175-76.

39. "There *Were* Giants," p. 189.

40. Ibid., p. 193.

9

The Obituary of a Bone Hunter

> I have crawled in many caverns, stooped
> with infinite aching patience over the
> bones of many men. I have made no
> great discoveries.

At virtually the same moment Loren Eiseley returned to Penn—
successful and chosen—*Harper's* magazine published his essay
"Obituary of a Bone Hunter." In it Eiseley relates three autobiographical incidents that define what he calls "the life of a small
bone-hunter." "I have made no great discoveries," he concludes,
after explaining his career as a relatively minor and unimportant
researcher. "There will be no further chances."[1]

These words sound very strange coming from a man who had
only turned forty a month before the essay appeared. But his
appraisal of his career evidently did not change, for twenty-four
years later he included the "Obituary," virtually unrevised, in his
autobiographical collection, *The Night Country*. While the essay
does accurately define one dimension of Eiseley's scientific life, it
says much more. It marks, in fact, another critical turning point
and the beginning of a new phase in his life and career. Eiseley
would continue to move toward greater and greater professional
and public success in his "visible profession," but now he would
simultaneously withdraw from its orthodoxies and into himself to
create a unique new vision and prose idiom. Ultimately, he would
forge a more comprehensive, more human science.

Near the beginning of his "obituary," Eiseley explains the difference between big and small bone hunters. "The little bone
hunters may hunt big bones," he writes, but "they are the consistent
losers," for they never find them; and so they are little, or minor, all
the same. Like others, Eiseley looked and hoped for a big find, and
according to his essay, he may have had three chances. But he

"muffed them all."[2] Each incident apparently happened in the
1930s.

The first occurred west of Carlsbad, New Mexico, "in the
Guadalupe country,"[3] probably on one of the Penn expeditions.
Eiseley and his colleagues were cave hunting, and up the side of a
canyon they found a cave with a blocked entrance. After several
days of digging in the area for Basket Maker artifacts, they blasted
open the cave entrance. Eiseley decided to investigate, hoping that
he might find evidence of an even older human culture. He had to
crawl on his belly a long way in the dark until he came to a small
chamber. There he set his light beside him and started to dig. But
then he became aware that something was beginning to fall from
the ceiling—soft, velvety things—and suddenly the fear got him.
There were millions of daddy longlegs on the ceiling, and when the
light touched any of them, they dropped. Eiseley could think only
of escape.

> If I could have stood up it would have been different. If they had not
> been overhead it would have been different. But they had me on my
> knees and they were above and all around. Millions upon millions.
> How they got there I don't know. All I know is that up out of the
> instinctive well of my being flowed some ancient, primal fear of the
> crawler, the walker by night. One clambered over my hand. And
> above they dangled, dangled. . . . What if they all began to drop at
> once?[4]

He succeeded in getting out, as well as in hiding his fear from his
co-workers, but he failed to find Neanderthal man, if he was even
there.

The second missed opportunity happened in another cave in
similar country. This time Eiseley was searching alone and discovered a small opening high up a canyon wall. The location and
fire-blackened cave roof suggested that "ancient men had been
there." It was a difficult climb. On the way up he lost his knapsack
and his pick, but he managed to reach the cave mouth. Just as he
started to crawl in—certain that something was there—a huge owl
burst out of the darkness, forcing Eiseley flat on his face in the dirt.
He was determined, however; "no owl was going to stop [him]."[5]

> I twitched my ripped shirt into my pants and crawled on. It wasn't
> much farther. Over the heap of debris down which the great owl had

charged at me, I found the last low chamber, the place I was seeking. And there in a pile of sticks lay an egg, an impressive egg, glimmering palely in the cavernous gloom, full of potentialities, and fraught, if I may say so, with destiny.

I affected at first to ignore it. I was after the buried treasures that lay beneath its nest in the cave floor. The egg was simply going to have to look after itself. Its parent had gone, and in a pretty rude fashion, too. I was no vandal, but I was going to be firm. If an owl's egg stood in the path of science—But suddenly the egg seemed very helpless, very much alone. I probed in the earth around the nest. The nest got in the way. This was a time for decision.[6]

Eiseley chose not to pursue the purposes of science, but to yield, instead, to the purposes of the living. And so once more he failed to find "the skull that could have made [him] famous."[7]

The third incident involved a crazy old man and a fragment of what may have been a fossil human jawbone. According to Eiseley, this happened "years later," but other evidence suggests that it was no later than 1937. One day the old man came to Eiseley's office—presumably at the University of Kansas—to challenge a statement Eiseley had made in a speech about the migration of early man to North America. Eiseley had probably talked about his and others' work on early man, and he may have mentioned that man appeared here very late, only 10,000 to 15,000 years before. The old man insisted, however, that a great civilization had existed in the Miocene (20,000,000 years ago). Then he showed Eiseley the jawbone, which from across the room looked like a valuable human fossil. He claimed that he had found it in a cave in Missouri, but he would not let Eiseley hold or examine it carefully; nor would he tell him of the cave's location, unless Eiseley made a "statement to the papers that the Golden Age is true." Eiseley protested. The man persisted, and then he started to leave: "I will not come back. You must make a choice."

For one long moment we looked at each other across the fantastic barriers of our individual minds. Then, on his heavy oakwood cane, he hobbled to the door and was gone. I watched through the window as he crossed the street in a patch of autumn sunlight as phantasmal and unreal as he. Leaves fell raggedly around him until, a tatter among tatters, he passed from sight.

I rubbed a hand over my eyes, and it seemed the secretary looked at me strangely. How was it that I had failed this time? By unbelief?

But the man was mad. I could not possibly have made such a statement as he wanted.[8]

So for a third time Eiseley missed his chance. From then on he had few, if any, other opportunities, and as he said, he made no great discoveries. "Thirty years have passed," he noted in 1971, "since the old man came to see me. I have crawled in many caverns, stooped with infinite aching patience over the bones of many men. I have made no great discoveries."[9]

In the end, Eiseley attributes his failure—his life as a small bone hunter—to "the folly of doubt" rather than to bad luck or scientific incompetence. At critical moments, especially in the cave with the egg and in his office with the old man, Eiseley had chosen the values of life over those of science. Unlike a primatologist he knew who would "lift a rifle and shoot a baby monkey out of its mother's arms for the sake of science,"[10] Eiseley could not destroy a potential life, the egg, in his search for fossils. Afterward, he was tormented more by his fear that the frightened bird may never have returned to its nest than by the loss of any skull.

He could not knowingly lie, either, in order to obtain a potentially valuable fossil. He held back in these instances—and perhaps from science generally—because of serious doubts about scientific values. The folly of doubt was really the folly of reverence or the folly of love. He hesitated, turned aside, and then failed to make the great discovery. If he did not do well by science, he had at least "done well by life."

On the face of it, "Obituary of a Bone Hunter" provides an entertaining and mildly ironic self-portrait of a successful academic scientist who happened never to make a major discovery. The essay also appeals widely to everyone's sense of failure and recollection of lost opportunities. The moral interpretation it gives to Eiseley's motives for not pursuing human fossils is reminiscent of a poem, "Credo," that Eiseley published a few years before. It urges us to "be heedful of the heart" and seems thus quite different from some of his earlier poems and not altogether consistent with his original motives for turning to science.

> Go with the feet of autumn—when a hawk
> Climbs a high spiral into whitening air—
> Go with the feet of autumn! Heed the talk
> Of the harsh crow; be insolent, be bare

Of lands you wished for, of possessions, things
Held in time's teeth. Less than the winter store
Of seeds a mouse might keep would weight your wings.
Abandon all. Be glad there is no more.

This the heart wills. Be heedful of the heart—
Conceived in ecstasy and nursed in pain.
Thirst is its excellence. It has no chart
But it knows love. Through furies of blown rain
Follow that dubious compass—only know
The heart will bring you where it is you go.[11]

Taken together, the poem and the essay suggest that something basic was happening in Eiseley's life. "Obituary" and "credo" are strong words. The one signals the end of a life—in this case, the end of a certain kind of scientific life. The other indicates a creed—in Eiseley's case, the emergence of basic values, necessarily suppressed for a time, that would prove heretical to the orthodoxies of science.[12]

Before the fall of 1947, Eiseley had been publishing extensively in scientific journals. Of the thirty articles he published between 1935 and 1947, twenty-five were "scientific" by anyone's standards. A few of these were popularizations, but no less scientific for that. Seventeen of the scientific articles came out within a four-year period, 1943-47. Of the five relatively unconventional pieces, *Prairie Schooner* printed two, both personal essays, and in January, 1947, *Harper's* published another, an early version of one of the chapters from *The Immense Journey*. Ten months later, *Harper's* published the "Obituary." There were few poems during these years, only four after 1942. So the record alone shows that in the nine years between receiving his degree and returning to Penn, Eiseley concentrated almost exclusively on science and wrote professional articles almost continuously.

In sharp contrast, he published very little scientific writing after 1947. He wrote a great deal, as much or more than before, but the nature of his prose had altered noticeably. In the next four years, for example, he published nine essays. Six appeared in *Harper's*; they were either early versions of *Immense Journey* chapters ("The Snout" and "The Great Deeps") or other personal essays ("Busby's Petrified Woman," "Places Below," "Fire Apes," and "People Leave Skulls with Me"), three of which he collected in *The Night Country*.

Only one article came out in the *American Anthropologist*, two in *Scientific American*. The difference is as striking as it is obvious.

In *All the Strange Hours*, Eiseley makes this change seem almost casual or accidental; but before he finishes his account, he alludes briefly to its profound and traumatic character. According to him, he turned to the "personal or concealed essay" during an extended episode of deafness that came upon him in the fall of 1948, about a year after he and his wife had moved to Philadelphia, and that lasted through the winter. While Eiseley "floundered in utter silence,"[13] frightened and anxious for his sanity and livelihood, the editor of a scientific magazine presumably reneged on an article he had asked Eiseley to prepare about human evolution. Discouraged by the rejection, Eiseley says that he then "turned aside from the straitly defined scientific article" and started, in effect, to write *The Immense Journey*:

> Sitting alone at the little kitchen table I tried to put into perspective the fears that still welled up frantically from my long ordeal. I had done a lot of work on this article, but since my market was gone, why not attempt a more literary venture? Why not turn it—here I was thinking consciously at last about something I had done unconsciously before—into what I now term the concealed essay, in which personal anecdote was allowed gently to bring under observation thoughts of a more purely scientific nature?[14]

Forced inward by his deafness, broken open by his fears, and skeptical of orthodox science, Eiseley experienced a trauma that initiated a radical change in his life. He was doing nothing less than altering his primary psychological and intellectual commitments. The timing of this transition was not quite as he represents it, for he had published five essays in the new mode before the fall of 1948: "Obituary of a Bone Hunter" itself appeared a year before. But the way Eiseley stages the change dramatizes the mental events and psychological necessity behind his choice. He was once again using a symbolic moment to dramatize the quality of a critical experience.

Eiseley himself refers to his frantic fears, and we need only recall the story of his life to understand the force these fears would have had. Since he had been at Penn for only a year, he worried that because he was deaf he might lose his job and thus his livelihood. This threat evoked all those paralyzing memories of poverty that originated in his childhood and youth and motivated so much of his adult behavior. And of course he thought almost obsessively about his mother and her "tortured, straining features." It was impossible for him to dissociate her madness from her deafness, and he probably remembered as well those vague allusions from the past to the mad Shepards. And so Eiseley naturally began to fear, once more, that he, too, would go mad: "How long," he had to wonder, "before I turned paranoid?"[15]

When Eiseley describes his deafness as a long "winter silence," it assumes a symbolic meaning far surpassing its actuality—traumatic as that was. He gives us only this to go on: "I had lived so long in a winter silence that from then on I would do and think as I chose."[16] Here, "silence" suggests a period of withdrawal and contemplation that led Eiseley to follow his own independent way. But "winter silence" suggests much more. Eiseley had found his professional world—and himself, as well—silent on many things that mattered. In this sense, the previous ten years of his life had been like a long winter, barren in certain ways, though successful and absolutely necessary, but also dormant in critical ways. Moreover, before that decade Eiseley had lived through many "winters" of deprivation and isolation, "silences" in their own way, and as he looked back, he must have realized that he did not fully emerge from those periods of discontent until he found his authentic voice and way of being.

Whether the crisis and subsequent change occurred so dramatically within a relatively short period (a matter of months), as Eiseley reports, or whether it extended over a longer period and involved additional factors, it is clear that Eiseley went through some sort of crisis that made him see himself in a new way. The events brought back much of his troubling past and forced him to find a place for it; they opened up dimensions of feeling and experience that conventional science simply excluded. The crisis reawakened his need and desire to write more comprehensively— extravagantly, in Thoreau's terms; it made him realize, more clearly than before, the relative incompleteness of his work in science; above all, it may have intensified his thinking about death and the fragility and transience of his own life. The way he dramatizes the change brings all these possibilities to mind. Less confusing and enervating than earlier crises, however, this one stimulated Eiseley to act and enabled him to recover a voice that he had laid aside for some time and to transform it into the unique voice of *The Immense Journey*.

In effect, "Obituary of a Bone Hunter" announces all of this. From then on, Loren Eiseley "would do and think as [he] chose"— before, one can imagine his saying, it was too late. Although the essay is indeed a declaration, it is first of all a confession of failure. Eiseley had failed to become an original scientist within the conventions of the profession. He had not succeeded as either a researcher unearthing important new fossils and artifacts or a theoretical anthropologist advancing and supporting new formulations for inadequately explained data. He had participated in field research of some significance; he had a remarkable command of his and related fields of knowledge; he had published a number of important analytical and critical papers; he had developed a great ability for exposing the inadequacy of others' work; he was in fact an outstanding scholar and critic in science; and he had obviously become a very successful academic scientist, as his return to Penn attests. But as for greatness—the life of a big bone hunter— well, only the small and virtually unknown oreodont skull in the Nebraska State Museum carries Eiseley's name. His original genius lay elsewhere.

This obituary also announced Eiseley's inability to go on in a conventional mode. It was not simply a matter of failing to make it big (in an academic sense he had), for even so he might well have chosen his own private way—as he did later, in 1961, when he left the provost's office at Penn and decided not to consider offers of college presidencies. He realized then that by becoming so involved in university administration, he had "starved and betrayed" himself; administrative work had led him to a creative dead end. In 1947, he had reached his first professional dead end. Science no longer served his primary purposes. It did not permit the full expression of his sensibility. To grow and flourish, he required something more. In an important sense, science now failed him, though of course without it he would never have arrived at the threshold of his unique genius.

With this essay, Eiseley also seemed to recognize the limits and possibilities of his particular style of science. Over the course of a decade, his work had become increasingly critical, interpretive, reflective, and speculative—even personal, and finally skeptical.

There were limits to what conventional science could tolerate and recognize, and there were limits to the strict scientific success such a mode could achieve.

As he followed his new direction, he learned repeatedly about those limits. Younger students, and colleagues especially, made Eiseley quite conscious of his heresies. Once when he was trying to illustrate for a class his sense of how species evolve (they figuratively crawl through a chink or an opening in nature and become something else), he told the story of a mouse that crawled into a friend's history seminar and "listened" to the lecture. Immediately after his own lecture, a student objected to his "foolish anthropomorphism." Eiseley tried to explain the point:

> I sighed and reluctantly confessed that perhaps the mouse, since he was obviously a very young mouse recently come from the country, could not have understood every word of the entire lecture. Nevertheless, it was gratifyingly evident to my weary colleague, the great historian, that the mouse had at least tried.
>
> "You see," I explained carefully, "we may have witnessed something like Alice in reverse. The mouse came through a crevice in the wall, a chink in nature. Man in his time has come more than once through similar chinks. I admit that the creatures do not always work out and that the chances seemed rather against this one, but who is to say what may happen when a mouse gets a taste for Byzantium rather beyond that of the average graduate student? It takes time, generations even, for this kind of event to mature."[17]

No matter how he explained (and his account continues for another page), the student simply could not see it. She was too literal-minded and inflexible. Science was science; stories were stories; metaphors were metaphors; and they shouldn't be mixed.

> "This woman is evidently part of a conspiracy to keep things just as they are," I later wrote to my friend. "This is what biologically we may call the living screen, the net that keeps things firmly in place, a place called now.
>
> "It doesn't always work," I added in encouragement. "Things get through. We ourselves are an example. Perhaps a bad one. About the mouse. . . ."[18]

Shortly after *The Immense Journey* was published, a young colleague at Penn told Eiseley that he was wasting his time writing books that expressed personal feelings and opinions, and tried "to correct [his] deviations and to lead [him] back to the proper road of scholarship."[19] This critic probably spoke for many more than himself; the profession did not measure success with one's personal essays.

In *All the Strange Hours*, Eiseley reports a similar incident. This time his antagonist's scientific orthodoxy seemed to be combined with considerable resentment. Apparently this younger man did not like Eiseley's style of science in either its personal (*The Immense Journey*) or its historical (*Darwin's Century*) aspects, and so decided to needle him by urging him to get some practical experience. "'Eiseley,' he said loudly, with seeming solicitude, 'you ought to get a grant. You ought to go out into the sun. Learn what it's like in the heat and dust. It would help your writing. The big spaces would do you good. You need practical experience.'" In the particular context, Eiseley is trying to show that stirring up the dust of old books and crawling through hot libraries can be as fascinating and valuable as "crawling about in tombs and deserts."[20] The experience illustrates, once again, the difficulty narrow scientific minds caused Eiseley.

But these responses were nothing compared to the contempt and disdain directed at Eiseley by some of his "colleagues"—most notably John Buettner-Janusch of Yale. In a review of *The Firmament of Time* (1960), Buettner-Janusch ridiculed the book and its author:

> This slim volume is hailed as an iridescent study, strongly recommended to all who enjoy thinking about fundamental problems by Newsweek magazine and two well known litterateurs. A mere physical anthropologist opened it with trepidation, even awe. This physical anthropologist, unfortunately, after reading it, closed the book with disappointment and a poor impression of the judgement [sic] of Newsweek magazine.
>
> The six chapters of this book are lectures delivered at the University of Cincinnati in 1959. The style, the studied cadences of dramatic emphasis, the plays upon words, the conjuring up of picturesque images, suit the hortatory mode of the semi-popular lecture. . . .
>
> Chapter four—How Man Became Natural—is a very literary interpretation of the record of hominid fossils. Unfortunately, the writing is sentimental and trite, and the apparent ideas do not seem to be in focus. It is not easy, because of the figurative and emotional language, to determine if the interpretations presented are sound.

Chapter five—How Human is Man?—is a series of moral parables on a somewhat higher level than those found in the repertory of a fundamentalist preacher. Their relevance to the discussion of an important part of the history of modern science eludes the reviewer. . . .

As is already obvious, the reviewer is disappointed by this book. It purports to have something to do with the history of science, with the genesis of evolutionary thought. Despite this assertion, we feel this book is a work of obscurantism. Science *is* exciting and absorbing because of what it is, and, even for undergraduates, we need not inject mystery, fevered prose, overblown metaphors, and sentimental twaddle into our subject. It is all the more disappointing when we find a writer of such splendid reputation as Eiseley producing such a book.[21]

His words make the point. Eiseley did pay for his unorthodoxy.

Although his personal version of science prompted some resistance, incomprehension, and occasional contempt within his profession, great possibilities existed for Eiseley just beyond its confining walls. His analytical and scholarly interests would lead him to impressive achievements in the history of science. His interpretive and generalizing capabilities would help him teach science to students and readers alike in a sensitive, eloquent, and humane way. His reflective and speculative impulses would lead him to explore the personal and philosophic dimensions of science. His introspective and creative inclinations would result in some remarkable autobiographical narratives. In the end, his finest work would combine all of these elements into an informative, authoritative, and compelling whole. Looking back, one can easily see that Loren Eiseley *had* to break sharply with his past because his was not quite the orthodox way and because he needed to find a new and more comprehensive version of science—a science "for the uses of life," or, as he also called it, "a natural history of souls."[22]

More than anything else, "Obituary of a Bone Hunter" is a declaration of independence. From this point onward, Eiseley began to press "his hands against the confining walls of scientific method."[23] Eventually, those walls would yield, and he would discover his true vocation. When he said in 1947 that "there will be no further chances," he meant it. However, he was not being fatalistic or giving up. He was deciding that he had other roads to travel. The obituary reports an end; it also announces a rebirth.

NOTES

1. "Obituary of a Bone Hunter," *Harper's*, 195 (Oct., 1947), 325-29.
2. *Night Country*, p. 182.
3. Ibid., p. 183.
4. Ibid., pp. 184-85.
5. Ibid., pp. 186, 187.
6. Ibid., p. 187.
7. Ibid., p. 188.
8. Ibid., p. 190.
9. The version published in *Harper's* reads "Ten years have passed . . ."
10. Ibid., pp. 191, 187.
11. Loren Eiseley, "Credo," *Prairie Schooner*, 18, no. 3 (Fall, 1944), 199.
12. See E. Fred Carlisle, "The Heretical Science of Loren Eiseley," *Centennial Review*, 18, no. 4 (Fall, 1974).
13. *All the Strange Hours*, p. 182.
14. Ibid., p. 182.
15. Ibid., p. 180.
16. Ibid., p. 183.
17. *Unexpected Universe*, pp. 150-51.
18. Ibid., p. 152.
19. Loren Eiseley, *Francis Bacon and the Modern Dilemma* (Lincoln: University of Nebraska Press, 1962), p. 80.
20. *All the Strange Hours*, pp. 186, 187.
21. John Buettner-Janusch, review of Loren Eiseley, *The Firmament of Time*, in *American Anthropologist*, 65 (1963), 693-94.
22. *Francis Bacon and the Modern Dilemma*, pp. 25, 94.
23. *Immense Journey*, p. 13.

10

The Immense Journey

> Forward and backward I have gone, and
> for me it has been an immense journey.

By the time Loren Eiseley wrote the opening chapter of *The Immense Journey*, he understood clearly the direction he had taken, and he warns us that we should not look for "science in the usual sense." Eiseley has done all he could "to avoid errors in fact," and he has told the story of evolution in some detail. But *The Immense Journey* is also the result of many years of silent rebellion "against the confining walls of scientific method."[1] Rather than an impersonal and wholly "objective" account of the history of evolution, this book is a "somewhat unconventional record of the prowlings of one mind which has sought to explore, to understand, and to enjoy the miracles of this world, both in and out of science." Although Eiseley includes a great deal of data and knowledge (it *is* a very informative book), he must admit finally that his book is "a confession of ignorance" and a recognition of all that science does not know. Impatient with walls and clearly defined borders, and looking for meanings and miracles as well as the fossil record, Eiseley was discovering more and more about the world, but he was finding fewer and fewer answers.[2]

When the book first appeared in August, 1957, it carried the name Loren Eiseley on the title page. Until that moment, Eiseley had published everything he had written under his conventional name, Loren C. Eiseley. It was a small but decisive elision, for with it Eiseley publicly—and possibly unknowingly—acknowledged the implications of "Obituary of a Bone Hunter." In a sense, he had fulfilled the declaration—or prophecy—made there and had become a new man. By dropping that *C*, he announced and accepted the fact that now he was primarily a writer, even if his career as a university administrator had not yet reached its peak and would not end for another five years. By leaving out that initial, he also dropped Corey, his mother's maiden name, from his own name, and thereby he seemed to say that he was finally free of that part of his past. He was Eiseley, not Corey. He had fulfilled his father's prophecy ("the boy is a genius, but moody"), not his mother's; and he had taken his father's legacy and made a book out of it, which he dedicated to the memory of Clyde Edwin Eiseley, "who lies in the grass of the prairie frontier but is not forgotten by his son."

Above all, at almost fifty years of age, Eiseley was finally himself. Since names are intrinsically tied up with personality and identity, changing one's name announces, at the least, an intention to be different; or it recognizes that one already is so. Walter Whitman dropped two letters from his name, and along with the first edition of *Leaves of Grass*, that signaled a radical change in his life. Samuel Clemens became Mark Twain, and that, too, indicated a profound change for him. Obviously, Eiseley did not modify his manner or name so completely; he continued to use Loren C. Eiseley, officially, and his widow still does. In one sense the transition was almost invisible—only a middle initial—but it was, nevertheless, profound. With the elimination of the letter *C*, Loren Eiseley seemed to realize that at last he had found his true voice and identity.

Essays from what would become *The Immense Journey* started to appear as early as January, 1947, when Eiseley published "Long Ago Man of the Future" in *Harper's*. Not quite his first personal essay, it was still an early one; and by the time he had included it as the ninth piece in the book, he had modified it considerably, retitling it "Man of the Future." Over the next nine years, Eiseley published essays in *Harper's*, the *American Scholar*, and *Scientific American* that later became chapters in his book. Nine of the thirteen pieces received prior publication:

in *Harper's*
    "Long Ago Man of the Future"   January, 1947
    "The Snout"   September, 1950
    "The Great Deeps"   December, 1951
    "The Secret of Life"   October, 1953

"Was Darwin Wrong about the Human
Brain?" ("The Real Secret of
Piltdown")   November, 1955
"The Bird and the Machine"   January, 1956
in *American Scholar*
"The Flow of the River"   Fall, 1953
"The Judgment of the Birds"   Spring, 1956
in *Scientific American*
"Antiquity of Modern Man"   July, 1948

Most of these articles were included in *The Immense Journey* relatively unchanged, as if from about 1950 on, Eiseley had found the mode he wanted. He obviously did not write the essays in anything like the order in which they finally appear. But the coherence of his voice and vision and, more specifically, the sequential character of the story the essays told made *The Immense Journey* into a unified book. It took a long time, however, for Eiseley to find the right order and title, and in fact it took him several years even to discover the book he wanted to write.[3]

Eiseley was thinking about a volume based on his essays as early as 1948. Initially, he discussed the idea—the tentative title was *Manhunt*—with Harper and Brothers, and for several years he and John Fischer, the Harper editor, tried to work out a plan. At first, the two of them seemed to be thinking about a more conventional scientific book than *The Immense Journey* turned out to be. Although Eiseley signed no contract, the correspondence was quite specific about Harper's interest, what might be included, the order of chapters, and a completion date. In 1950, Fischer was asking Eiseley when the book might be finished.

In 1952, however, Eiseley became aware that *Manhunt* was changing. That presented Eiseley with composition problems and John Fischer with a different book from the one he had in mind. On December 23, Eiseley wrote to explain: "Because of the philosophical twist which the thing has taken, I have found great difficulties in its organization, and this had me badly stumped for a while so that I had to lay aside parts that I had originally written. I do not pretend to have solved all the difficulties yet but, as of this writing, I have a good scheme. It will demand, however, a much different title than our old one. . . . I am inclined to favor . . . 'The Great Deeps.'" It is difficult to tell how uneasy Fischer became with this, but at this point their interests began to diverge.

In early January, Fischer acknowledged the change: "Your book has developed into something quite different from the original project which we were thinking of." He expressed his belief that there was still an excellent market for a popular scientific book about prehistoric man and asked if, later on, Eiseley might wish to return "to that more limited field of subject matter." They continued to correspond, and in July, 1953, Fischer proposed an outline for the book. He didn't insist on this particular order, but he was trying to get Eiseley to decide on *some* arrangement—"*any* arrangement which will present the material in an order which the reader can easily follow." He was also trying to help Eiseley understand the necessity of making a book, not simply a collection of magazine articles: "At all costs we need to avoid any impression that the reader is starting all over again with each new chapter." Although the editor valued the poetic and philosophic content of Eiseley's writing, his outline in no way resembles *The Immense Journey.* At this point, no book came forth—either the one Fischer wanted or the one Eiseley was trying to write.

By 1956, if not earlier, it was clear that Harper had no place on its list for Eiseley's book. In the meantime, Hiram Haydn of Random House and the *American Scholar* had become fascinated with Eiseley's essays, and he proposed, late in 1955, that Eiseley do a book for them. Haydn's enthusiasm—"I have read a marvel," "you are rapidly reducing me to the status of an abject fan," "my fanatical devotion"—naturally interested and flattered Eiseley. Within six months, he was changing publishers. He wrote John Fischer about Haydn's inquiry, and Fischer confirmed Harper's position: "Nobody here believes that we could find a market for a collection of magazine pieces which would be satisfactory either to us or to you." And so on October 11, 1956, Eiseley signed a contract with Random House for a nonfiction book titled *The Crack in the Absolute.* He received an advance of $1,250.

Finding the right chapters, the right order, and, obviously, the right title still presented a problem. Eiseley and Haydn agreed that the book needed more unity than a collection of essays would have. And that required a coherent order and clear transitional links— the same problem Eiseley and John Fischer had discussed at length. When Eiseley wrote Haydn that fall, however, he still did not know the final shape of his book. He talked about placing "The Judgment of the Birds" last (it was in fact published third from last), and he indicated his uncertainty about the placement of the first six chapters.[4] At one point Eiseley evidently became exasperated, causing some friction between him and his new editor, but Haydn handled it and Eiseley well—not, however, with complete aplomb:

> Reverting to your letter: just let me say that I do wish you would stop talking about holding the check and—if I am not content with the new version—calling the whole deal off. Honest to goodness, Loren, how many times do I have to tell you that it's your book, that we were quite ready to take it to start with as a collection of essays and nothing more, that you and I then agreed that it would be useful, if possible, to give the book a greater unity, finally, that I have assured you that as things stand now I'll take whatever you decide is the form you want it published in? Aside from being unable to understand why you continue to say what you have in the face of these assurances, it also upsets me to have you continually referring to the fact that you can give this only so much time and that if not right then it will have to go by the boards. I am perfectly willing to go along with your intent of having it finished by March, but it just isn't rational to say, "Either this—or nothing." Certainly you must be persuaded, as I am, that there is so much good stuff in this that it is going to make a first-rate book and not a book that depends upon a meeting of a deadline. Please calm down, chief, and apply yourself with at least a minimal serenity.

When the discovery came, the book apparently coalesced very fast. Eiseley had hit on the title late in November and wrote Haydn on December 2. "I now think . . . that the title should be THE IMMENSE JOURNEY." There was some kind of manuscript before January, and it was in galleys by April. Just when he did the work that completed the book is not clear. But *what* he did is. He excluded chapters he had intended earlier to include; he wrote his introductory chapter, "The Slit"; he composed two additional chapters ("The Maze" and "The Dream Animal") to complete his account of human brain development, begun with "Was Darwin Wrong about the Human Brain?"; and he found an order that transformed the separate essays into the unified book.

Appropriately enough, *The Immense Journey* took a long time to develop. Ten years passed between "Obituary of a Bone Hunter" and the book's publication—not to speak of the lifelong preparation before that. Eiseley was engaged in his own long journey, his struggle as a writer. There may have been other factors as well. According to many comments by Eiseley himself, he was not a fast worker: "I write slowly, and by hand." He also continued his full-time career in science, teaching, and university administration, and so he had to write at night (sometimes late when he could not sleep), on weekends, during stolen moments, or during the brief periods he was freed from professional duties by something like the Wenner-Gren Foundation grant he received for 1952-53.

Moreover, in the early 1950s, he was asked by Doubleday to do a well-researched book on the Darwinian epoch, and although he did not begin to write it until after he completed most of *The Immense Journey*, the research for *Darwin's Century* absorbed enormous amounts of time. *The Immense Journey* necessarily emerged slowly. But when it did appear, it became a great personal and public success.

That story is almost legend now. The book was reviewed favorably in the *Saturday Review*, the *New York Herald Tribune Books*, the *Christian Science Monitor*, *TLS*, and twice in the *New York Times*. There were no unfavorable reviews in the popular press and only one that was even partly mixed. Although critics were generally enthusiastic, the book was not reviewed very widely. After all, it did not quite fit anyone's conventional categories. Was it science? literature? autobiography?

Besides expressing approval and enthusiasm, several of the early reviews grasped well the general character of Eiseley's achievement:

These highly personal reflections, queries, doubts, and affirmations make up a literary offering by a scientist thinking and feeling about the very fundamentals of life and being.—*Saturday Review*, January 4, 1958.

His style is beautiful, compelling in impact and poetic in its imagery. His subject is one of the epics of natural science. . . . Eiseley may be called unscientific in the laboratory sense . . . because he is looking for something beyond the analysis science is capable of making.—*Christian Science Monitor*, September 5, 1957.

A good book and an exceptionally well written one. . . . When it was published last August, I was sure that I did not want to read it, and this in spite of urgent recommendations from discriminating friends who had my best interests at heart. I was wrong and they were right.—*New York Times*, December 27, 1957.

Two of the reviews were particularly perceptive. One appeared in the August 15, 1958, *TLS*, a year after the book's publication:

> He is the master of an imaginative and swiftly moving prose that grips the reader and bears him willingly into enchanted realms. The appearance of such a book as this is an event, and it is to be hoped that it is a portent. The twentieth century is the age of science, and it might be expected that in science writers and poets, artists and musicians would find such an inspiration as the Renaissance drew from classical studies. We have so far waited in vain, and the gulf between the world of letters and the world of science has remained obstinately wide; but now Dr. Eiseley has written a work of true science which must surely take its place also as great literature.

The other review, written by Joseph Wood Krutch, was the longest and most thoughtful of any.[5] An informed literary critic and nature writer, he saw just a little farther into the book's significance than other popular press reviewers did, and in a sense he was more able than many scientists. He recognized the "unusual eloquence and imagination" with which Eiseley told his story; he readily understood the speculative theme of the book—man's potentially enormous extension of vision; and he also fully comprehended the biology. In questioning the rigidities of Darwin, Eiseley dug deeper and stated the arguments more clearly than any other recent book Krutch knew. Above all, Krutch perceived the irrelevance of the materialism-vitalism issue. It is no longer a question, he pointed out, whether life "may exist as something separate from matter. It has become, instead, whether or not life is, like mass and energy, simply an aspect of matter which under certain circumstances becomes manifest." He understood Eiseley, and without quite knowing it, he saw the new idiom Eiseley was developing to speak about man's evolution.

The professional science and anthropology journals barely noticed *The Immense Journey*, probably because it was *not* science in the usual sense. There were, however, a few reviews. The British journal MAN commented briefly on the book. Its reviewer either felt ambivalent or confused or simply missed one of Eiseley's major points, that life *does* reach out and repeatedly assert itself:

These are poetic essays in prose reflecting on the long drama of life from beginnings that grow into richer mysteries as research progresses right on to man and his formidable machines. And they are coloured throughout by the feeling of the oneness of nature. If a naturalist in the Paleozoic Age had interpreted certain fishes as failures of the sea lingering in the muddy reaches of streams, he would have missed life's persistent reaching-out to new environmental contacts that was to make these fishes the ancestors of land animals. Likewise, the inconspicuous sexual elements of early plants reached out to insects that helped to lift them into flowering plants with seeds, to feed and transform animal, including human, life. The *Challenger* expedition may have failed to find Trilobites living in the ocean depths, but Eiseley might have mentioned the stalked Crinoid. The essays have many references to recent research; they will attract a thoughtful laity to bio-anthropological science, and may stimulate, and sometimes very slightly annoy, an imaginative biologist or anthropologist.[6]

The reviewer for the *Quarterly Review of Biology*, C. P. Swanson, a botanist, read Eiseley's book sympathetically and perceptively. He especially liked "How Flowers Changed the World," the chapter closest to his professional interests:

Parts of this volume appeared in print as early as 1946, and it may well be that the centenary of Darwin's *Origin of Species* has prompted its reprinting, thus making it a companion of other books on Darwinism which have appeared and will continue to do so throughout the year. Be that as it may, I can only be grateful that it has been done, for it is one of the finest accounts extant of the whole panorama of evolution. Simply written, but with a literary elegance attained by few of our contemporary scientists, it possesses that surety of touch and breadth of outlook that is the mark of one who not only knows whereof he speaks, but also knows he has a story worth the telling.

The Immense Journey is the story of the origin of man from Pooh Bah's ancestral "protoplasmal primordial atomic globule" to the man of the future. But it is also more than this, for it is as well a serendipitous journey, full of unexpected delights. As a botanist, I thought the chapter, "How Flowers Changed the World," a rare treat, and my students, skeptical beings though they are, thought so, too. At a time when the reappraisal of Darwinism is the subject of the hour, there will be no more appropriate reaffirmation of its essential truth than that which Loren Eiseley offers in this modest, but compellingly persuasive, book. Would that there were more volumes like it.[7]

Professionals *could* read *The Immense Journey* both as science and as literature—if they had the mind to. Some did. Obviously many did not, although there is no way to know their numbers for sure. I have found none of the contempt and disdain of a Buettner-Janusch expressed publicly about the *Journey*, but it is easy to imagine some scientists thinking or talking privately about "obscurantism," "fevered prose, overblown metaphors, and sentimental twaddle."

Eiseley paid a price for being unusual (he once talked about his "badly chewed" ears), but he also achieved fame and some satisfaction by refusing to stay in his designated category. The book *was* a great success, and since its publication it has gradually become a masterpiece. Over the years, it has sold more than half a million copies;[8] it has been translated into ten languages; essays from it have been widely anthologized in volumes of outstanding English prose; and both science and English classes in college teach Eiseley along with the usual "great writers." Although that last achievement may be as much a curse as a blessing, it at least indicates that some of his own kind take him very seriously.

Because of the unusual nature of *The Immense Journey*—the unique fusion in it of scientific, literary, and personal qualities— readers sometimes overlook its sound scientific base. In fact, the book provides a clear, orderly, informative, and accurate account of the evolution of man as science then knew it. Although some details have changed (with the discovery of new fossils, for example, human antiquity seems somewhat greater now), the basic story has not. When he wrote the book, Eiseley tried to avoid errors in fact; he attempted to explain others' interpretations or theories clearly; and he endeavored to make his own interpretations consistent with scientific data. In short, he made a scientist's effort to say something true about reality. He even tried to ground his speculations in scientific knowledge. He made no leaps. Instead, he extended science and explored meanings, and the paths back to science from his farthest extensions are very clear. But an explanation of that will have to wait. First, it is important to understand the themes and organization of Eiseley's scientific story.

In the opening essay, "The Slit," Eiseley introduces several features of the book—its personal and symbolic nature and its intent to take us on a journey through time. He establishes his relationship with us, his readers, one that is cordial but not intimate. As he describes the day when he came across the Slit, a deep crack in the prairie sandstone, and recounts the drift of his thought while he dug out a skull he had found, Eiseley also manages to tell us where we came from ("we came from the water") and begins to explain how we got here: ". . . through several million years of Paleocene time, the primate order, instead of being confined to trees, was experimenting to some extent with the same grassland burrowing life that the rodents later perfected. The success of these burrowers crowded the primates out of this environment and forced them back into the domain of the branches. As a result, many primates, by that time highly specialized for a ground life, became extinct." Although "The Slit" does not provide a great deal of information, Eiseley makes quite clear by the close of the chapter that he is going to talk about evolution, and to that end he has had to project himself and us across time.[9]

In "The Flow of the River" (chap. 2), Eiseley's story begins. He turns his attention to man's distant origins in water and to a time when in fact man and the catfish may have been only unpredictable, future developments of a common ancestor: "We were both projections out of that timeless ferment and locked as well in some greater unity that lay incalculably beyond us." Both man and catfish emerged through evolution, out of life's basic impulse to reach out and change. Without trying to explain it here, Eiseley indicates that all forms of animal life can be traced to common origins in water and living matter: "Turtle and fish and the pinpoint chirpings of individual frogs are all watery projections, concentrations—as man himself is a concentration—of that indescribable and liquid brew which is compounded in varying proportions of salt and sun and time." At our present stage in evolution, man and catfish—or any two radically different organisms—can live only momentarily, if at all, in the world of the other. But that is the point: eon by eon, life has assumed many shapes and has become almost infinitely various, and organisms have adapted to innumerable environments. In this chapter, Eiseley's main subjects are origins, life, and change.[10]

"The Great Deeps" continues the story, as Eiseley takes up two
historical notions about the origins of life in the oceanic abysses.
The first proposed that life may have begun in those abysses and
then developed and radiated from there. The other supposed that
the ocean depths were populated by living marine fossils from past
geological ages, thus implying that the record of the past could be
found there. Both notions turned out to be mistaken. Life surely
originated in water, but not in the deeps. From its origins in the
shallows, it "has crept upward from the waters," and it has penetrated the abyss. It "crawls in the fields, it penetrates the air," and it
continues to reach out as it has for a billion years.[11]

Eiseley also introduces another basic feature of evolution—the
stability of life or form, the organization of life—manifest fundamentally in the conditions of cellular life. Evolution requires
both the capacity of life to organize and sustain itself and the
ability to reach out and change. At this point, Eiseley's topics are
origins, life, change, and stability.

Near the end of "The Great Deeps" he speaks of the "enormous
extension of vision of which life is capable."[12] In the preceding
chapter, he dramatized a parallel extension of the senses. This
theme of extension does not reach its full scientific meaning until
the last chapters, where Eiseley shows that this "power" is one of
the marvels evolution has produced. So even if "extension" seems
at first like an impressionistic overlay, it will become in Eiseley's
exposition a conclusion based on scientific data.

"The Snout" takes up the development of life on land: "It began
as such things always begin—in the ooze of unnoticed swamps, in
the darkness of eclipsed moons. It began with a strangled gasping
for air." In telling his story, Eiseley concentrates on the Crossopterygian (a group of mostly extinct fishes, possible ancestors of
terrestrial vertebrates), and he talks about the first dim beginnings
of the kind of brain that led, "in three hundred million years," to
the human brain. That new kind of brain required a lot of oxygen
and, eventually, a high degree of metabolism. Eiseley also explains
the difference between the "so-called solid brain" ("the brain of
insects, of the modern fishes, of some reptiles and all birds") and
the mammalian brain, and he remarks on the mystery and unpre-
dictability of the paths evolution takes.[13]

In this essay his subjects are still origins (terrestrial life and the human brain); life (it continues to reach out); change (trapped in marginal environments, some organisms change and adapt); stability (the basic organization that sustains life through change). He has added conditions (environments forcing extinction or survival) and open-endedness (the historic and unreturning nature of time).

About 100 million years ago, before flowering plants, there were very few warm-blooded animals. Conditions could not support the necessary high metabolism. "How Flowers Changed the World" explains the spectacular emergence of the angiosperms that made possible further animal evolution and ultimately the evolution of the human brain. What Eiseley calls a "soundless, violent explosion"[14]—the relatively sudden emergence of flowering plants—occurred in Cretaceous times, shortly before the end of the Age of Reptiles. Mammals had existed for a long time before that, but the reptiles had been the dominant fauna. The explosion helped change this:

> The mammals, too, had survived and were venturing into new domains, staring about perhaps a bit bewildered at their sudden eminence now that the thunder lizards were gone. Many of them, beginning as small browsers upon leaves in the forest, began to venture out upon this new sunlit world of the grass. Grass has a high silica content and demands a new type of very tough and resistant tooth enamel, but the seeds taken incidentally in the cropping of the grass are highly nutritious. A new world had opened out for the warm-blooded mammals. Great herbivores like the mammoths, horses and bisons appeared. Skulking about them had arisen savage flesh-feeding carnivores like the now extinct dire wolves and the saber-toothed tiger.
>
> Flesh eaters though these creatures were, they were being sustained on nutritious grasses one step removed. Their fierce energy was being maintained on a high, effective level, through hot days and frosty nights, by the concentrated energy of the angiosperms. That energy, thirty per cent or more of the weight of the entire plant among some of the cereal grasses, was being accumulated and concentrated in the rich proteins and fats of the enormous game herds of the grasslands.[15]

Under those conditions, the apes would evolve, then man, and eventually humanity: "Apes were to become men, in the inscrutable wisdom of nature, because flowers had produced seeds and fruits in such tremendous quantities that a new and totally different store of energy had become available in concentrated form."[16] Thus Eiseley's story of origins and of the conditions of change continues. To this point, he has sketched evolution from the origins of life in water to man's own origins in terrestrial life, mammals, and apes. Now he is ready to explain, in some detail, the evolution of man's brain and his culture—the critical features that differentiate humankind from other animals.

The next three chapters—"The Real Secret of Piltdown," "The Maze," and "The Dream Animal"—explain the emergence of man's brain and define the way we differ from nature. The answer to Eiseley's question "How did man get his brain?"[17] is still not altogether clear, and it was perhaps less so then. Eiseley was writing shortly after the exposure of the Piltdown fossil as a fraud. There were fewer fossils then to help determine the course of brain evolution. Some recent findings had brought into question the then current estimate about the time involved. The evidence, however, suggested that man's brain evolved very rapidly over a relatively brief period—a million years or less. Recent fossil evidence (the nearly complete skull of *homo erectus* announced by Richard Leakey in 1976) argues for a slightly earlier emergence of the human brain—at least 1.5 million years ago or more. But this modification in no way affects Eiseley's notion of explosive development. Scientists still consider the development spectacular and extraordinarily rapid; in the perspective of geological time, it took little more than a few moments.[18]

Eiseley's chapters outline some of the conditions necessary for man's evolution, and at one point, he cites four fundamental changes that had to occur:

1. His brain had almost to treble in size.
2. This had to be effected, not in the womb, but rapidly, after birth.
3. Childhood had to be lengthened to allow this brain, divested of most of its precise instinctive responses, to receive, store, and learn to utilize what it received from others.
4. The family bonds had to survive seasonal mating and become permanent, if this odd new creature was to be prepared for his adult role.

These factors were critical, of course, but as Eiseley explains, the parallel emergence of man's sociocultural world made the definitive difference: we are totally dependent on human society. While our evolution may resemble natural evolution and once *was* part of that process, once man "escaped out of the eternal present of the animal world into a knowledge of past and future," the character of evolution changed forever. The new evolution depended mainly on culture and much less on nature. Man had moved into "a new world where the old laws no longer totally held."[19]

Even though science knows a lot and can tell a fairly persuasive story about human evolution, Eiseley also recognizes how little it knows, how very difficult it is to determine the truth. The Piltdown hoax, conflicting interpretations, new data, the very limited fossil record—all of which Eiseley mentions—make that difficulty vivid: "It is as though we stood at the heart of a maze and no longer remembered how we had come there."[20]

By this point, the narrative has covered a vast period of time. All the while, Eiseley's focus has been steady, and these three essays about the brain fit in very well. They continue to develop his themes: origins (the biological origins of humanity); life (it goes on reaching out to new worlds and toward new forms); change (all that led to man); stability (the continuity of biological principles through mammals, apes, and man); and conditions (the environmental, biological, and cultural conditions necessary for man's emergence).

The story has arrived at man, and it *has* been an immense journey: "For the first time in four billion years a living creature had contemplated himself and heard with a sudden, unaccountable loneliness, the whisper of the wind in the night reeds."[21] For the rest of the book—the last five essays—Eiseley turns his attention to man's future, to the possibilities of life like ours elsewhere in the universe, to the effects or achievements of evolution, and then to the unanswered (and for Eiseley probably unanswerable) questions about origins and evolution. As he explores each topic, he continues to ground his arguments in his knowledge of evolution.

Besides expressing Eiseley's pessimism about what lies before us, "Man of the Future" reviews several of the biological developments that led to modern man, those associated with pedomorphism and foetalization; then it recounts briefly science's knowledge of the "Boskopoids," an extinct line of humans related in some way to the Kalahari Bushmen. Long ago they manifested ultramodern skull features (a very large cranium and brain, presumably, along with small teeth and jaw—an amazing cranium-to-face ratio, according to Eiseley). Yet they did not survive. The record seems to support Eiseley's conclusion that biological changes like those leading to modern man do not necessarily guarantee a future. He speculates that the biological clock somehow speeded the Boskopoids out of their time, as it may have speeded us. If man is to survive, in Eiseley's view, "the need is not really for more brains, the need is now for a gentler, a more tolerant people than those who won for us against the ice, the tiger, and the bear."[22] Here we are beyond biology and in the realm of the new evolution. And in fact we are beyond even that, for one can only guess about the future.

Even when Eiseley begins to speculate in "Little Men and Flying Saucers" about man-in-the-universe (are there others like us, anywhere?), he stays close to his main themes. His answer—"Of men elsewhere, and beyond, there will be none forever"—is based on biological and evolutionary principles: ". . . once undirected variation and natural selection are introduced as the mechanism controlling the development of plants and animals, the evolution of every world in space becomes a series of unique historical events. The precise accidental duplication of a complex form of life is extremely unlikely to occur in even the same environment, let alone in the different background and atmosphere of a far-off world." In other words, he concludes, "man is a solitary and peculiar development." Although Eiseley is tentative about it, he does seem to think that there may be extraterrestrial intelligence ("There may be wisdom; there may be power"), but nowhere are there beings like us.[23]

By recounting several personal experiences in "The Judgment of the Birds" Eiseley develops another aspect of his themes about life, change, and stability. First, he relates a couple of incidents in which the borders between species momentarily shifted or dissolved. These two epiphanies vividly dramatize the type of change basic to evolution—one species becomes another (although historically the change is never so radical)—and also show how in extraordinary moments man can overcome his isolation from nature and fleetingly return. Second, Eiseley tells about a time when he stood in the badlands, in the midst of desolation, with the ruins of fifty million years beneath him, and watched a flight of birds pass overhead. The flight represented for him life's organization (stability) in the midst of disintegration—an assertion of life against death.

Eiseley thinks of these experiences as "miracles"—natural miracles, to be sure; and with such a word, he seems to leave science far behind. But he is still speaking about the human brain—"a very remarkable thing"[24]—and its power. A result of biological and cultural evolution, the brain enables the scientist to understand his past, and mankind to discover something of its significance. Science and imagination are miracles of the mind, as the mind is a miracle of nature. In this chapter scientific knowledge and Eiseley's way of treating it complement one another: evolution leads to a particular organism with an extraordinary brain, and that brain enables the organism to explore the facts and meaning of its own emergence. Thus, even though Eiseley is far into the realm of speculation, "The Judgment of the Birds" is still part of the straightforward story he has been telling all along about evolution.

The last two chapters continue in this interpretive and speculative mode, but they, too, relate closely to Eiseley's underlying subjects. In "The Bird and the Machine," he once again selects incidents that illustrate the capacity of the brain. The tempo of time is a human illusion, he points out, and he imagines himself, as in "The Slit," sinking back into another tempo. Both human time and the other (reptilean time that he can only dimly sense) result from man's remarkable brain—its capacity to design, remember, and imagine.[25] When Eiseley compares the brain and computers, he decides, "It's life I believe in, not machines,"[26] for it is life's impulse that has brought us this far and will, if anything will, take us further. At the end of the chapter he tells about trying to capture two sparrow hawks, and in so doing extends his use of birds as symbols of life's constant impulse to reach out and assert itself.

In a book that poses as many unanswered questions as answered ones, the last essay, "The Secret of Life," presents the final definitive mystery. "I do not think," Eiseley writes, "if someone finally twists the key successfully in the tiniest and most humble house of life, that many of these questions will be answered, or that the dark forces which create lights in the deep sea and living batteries in the waters of tropical swamps, or the dread cycles of parasites, or the most noble workings of the human brain, will be much if at all revealed."[27] No matter how much we know—and science will, he believes, teach us a great deal—we will never discover that secret. So Eiseley arrives, in the end, neither at final answers to the questions about origins nor at the achievements of science. He comes, instead, to a mystery and to the limitations of science. But he has done so through an orderly exposition and interpretation of scientific knowledge.

Although this account of man's evolution is only the beginning of what Eiseley achieved in *The Immense Journey*, it is a critical dimension of the book—more than just the ground or foundation for his personal experience and imaginative speculations about science. It exists in a critical relationship of complementarity with the other dimensions. And even though we must talk about one dimension at a time, the book is all of its features at once; none is primary or definitive.

When Loren Eiseley warns his readers that they should not look for science in the usual sense, he explains that besides recording the history of evolution in his book, he has also written down "a bit of [his] personal universe," what one researcher thought as he tried to explore, understand, and enjoy the multitudinous "miracles of this world." In effect, *The Immense Journey* provides two records—the events of man's and nature's past and the events of Eiseley's personal world as he explores that past. Both involve difficult journeys into known and unknown realms where the methods and knowledge of science ultimately fail.[28]

When Eiseley talks about exploration and miracles, he does not say "imagination," but it is clear that is what he means. For without imagination, without taking a personal leap beyond known and observable facts, no one can understand the human significance of scientific facts and discoveries and of nature's secrets. Science becomes complete only with imagination.

In this unconventional record, Eiseley sometimes speaks extravagantly about miracles, the magic of water, enormous extensions of vision. He wanders beyond the limits of conventional science to tell one of its epic stories and simultaneously provide an imaginative and artful expression of it. In the end, the two records become one. Loren Eiseley has fused his personal journeys in science and mankind's evolutionary journey into a single history. To explain this, let us look again at several of the essays.

"The Slit"

As he has done in so many other essays and books, Eiseley begins *The Immense Journey* with a personal experience. On one of his numerous field outings in the 1930s, he evidently came across a cut in the prairie, "a narrow crack worn by some descending torrent." He was looking for fossils, but his description of the Slit (and his consistent capitalization of the word) indicates that there is more to the story than excavating a fossil skull: "The Slit was a little sinister—like an open grave, assuming the dead were enabled to take one last look—for over me the sky seemed already as far off as some future century I would never see."[29] Eiseley then returns to his scientific purpose, explaining that the Slit provided a perfect cross-section of the geological strata of the area and speaking briefly about actually excavating the skull. His attention shifts again, and he starts thinking about the kinship between himself and that skull, and for a moment he almost believes that he is a fossil already, caught in the strata a few feet above the skull. Shortly thereafter, he mentions the chemistry of bones and the anatomical relationships of hand, fin, reptilean feet, and furry paw.

The Slit is clearly something more than an actual place into which Eiseley climbed in search of fossils. It is, first, Eiseley's platform for brief lectures and commentaries about the past and evolution. For example, he mentions comparative anatomy and also summarizes the events of the Paleocene. Second, the Slit serves as Eiseley's stage for meditations about time and flux. He proposes, for example, that the evolutionary journey he will describe has no meaning except for the journey itself. Third, the cut provides a base for Eiseley's projection of himself across time. While he literally descends into the past, down through geological strata, he also imaginatively crosses both time and species boundaries as he thinks about himself as a fossil and speculates on what he might have been had evolution turned another way. Finally, the Slit represents time—the "dimension denied to man"[30]—and symbolizes, as well, Eiseley's situation in the world. Trapped in a particular time, he can go back into the past only with effort, knowledge, and imagination (but never actually), and he cannot look toward the future with anything but ignorance. Like so many other places in Eiseley's life, the Slit is at once a place, an occasion, and a metaphor or symbol.

This opening chapter establishes the fundamental rhythm, or movement of attention, in the book, and this helps to identify its multiple dimensions. Besides moving variously from autobiography to science, to metaphor, and to speculation, the narrative also moves from the present into the past, back to the present, and into the future. If one were to trace both of these movements in detail, the result would be quite complex, because Eiseley frequently, and artfully, changes his focus. In doing so, he creates the multiple dimensions of the book—science, autobiography, figuration, and metaphysics; and he shows how they interact or even how one, by a slight transformation, becomes another. Thus one of Eiseley's scientific subjects may turn into a general theme with broad human and existential significance, or a physical site might function simultaneously as an occasion and a metaphor.

There are several such transformations in "The Slit." One develops from Eiseley's notion that a long time ago we were once and for all (figuratively) driven out of the prairie-dog town that he remembers observing on one of his expeditions. When man evolved his human brain, lost most of his instincts, and began to develop culture, he became fundamentally different from every other animal and, in that sense, isolated from nature. In a larger thematic sense, man lost his home, his Eden. In Eiseley's terms, he became a "castaway": "On the world island we are all castaways."[31]

This theme—man's personal and existential loneliness and isolation—emerges from the intertwining of the book's four dimensions. Autobiography provides the specific incident or circumstance—here, the prairie-dog town. This lends both concreteness and vitality to the account, and it also dramatizes Eiseley's scientific point about our separation from nature. Human brain development and the consequent new or cultural evolution are the events that explain the separation. Combined with its scientific explanation and expressed in more general terms, the concrete example then functions symbolically or figuratively to represent man's existential condition—isolation or exile. It is a matter of different modes of discourse, mainly a question of language. Eiseley will speak of the condition in scientific terms ("the primate order . . . was experimenting . . .") and then in more general philosophic or metaphoric words ("we are all castaways"). By changing his terminology—by paying attention in a different way—Eiseley transforms his scientific subject into a general theme.

In this first essay, Eiseley sets the character of *The Immense Journey* and introduces several of its major features. Whether one thinks about the underlying rhythms or movement in "The Slit" or about its several dimensions or about subjects and themes, the chapter indicates, above all, that the book is both a personal and a species history and a work of science and art.

"The Flow of the River"

At the beginning of his second chapter, Eiseley narrates an extraordinary personal experience when his mind sank away "into its beginnings" and he momentarily escaped "the actual confines of the flesh." It happened one day along the Platte River when he was roaming over that territory searching for fossils. Something tempted him to try a new adventure: he was going to float. The idea came to him slowly, as he explains, and it posed some risk, for Eiseley could not swim; but once he lay back and shoved off, he experienced an altogether new sensation: "For an instant, as I bobbed into the main channel, I had the sensation of sliding down the vast tilted face of the continent." During that extraordinary moment, he "*was* water and the unspeakable alchemies that gestate and take shape in water."[32] The young man momentarily projected himself across time and species boundaries.

Eiseley begins autobiographically—a technique that not only makes his scientific narrative interesting and personal, but also makes him—as he warned in "The Slit"—one of the main subjects of the book. As he develops this dimension through later chapters, Eiseley does more than simply combine personal history with our species history. He is saying that our personal selves are implicated in everything we say and do. He especially liked Thoreau's notion that "we commonly do not remember that it is, after all, always the first person that is speaking." For Eiseley, it is simply not possible to separate the personal from the scientific. Nor is it possible for him to fragment or polarize experience in other ways—to oppose intellect and emotion, reason and imagination, objective and subjective, impersonal and personal, or science and literature. They are all of a piece in his world, joined together in the experiences and imaginations of individuals. They are all of a piece in his book, too, joined together by the comprehensiveness of his own imagination and the richness of his language.

The way Eiseley transforms one into the other shows how inseparable personal experience and science are for him. When he lay back and floated on the Platte, he found himself sinking back to his beginnings in water. As he recalls the experience, he thinks of the primordial life forms that developed there, and that brings him to one of the main scientific subjects in this part of his narrative—the origins of life in water. His adventure frightened and endangered him; as he mentions, he had almost drowned once, and still he could not swim. But he took a chance. By relating that personal experience, he comes to his second scientific subject—the impulse of life to reach out and explore or experiment. He drifted on the river, and his mind drifted back, first into the recent past of the pioneers, then deeper through the time of the mammoths, and finally back to his origins in the slimy jellies where he *was* water. By reversing evolutionary change, he takes himself, us, and his story back to the beginning; by describing the way he crosses time and species borders, he comes to his third scientific subject—change.

In the first sentence of "The Flow of the River"—"If there is magic on this planet, it is contained in water"—Eiseley is thinking not only of water's pervasiveness and its power to assume beautiful forms and destroy others, but also of other general meanings. First, he is talking about the magic that originally produced forms of living matter. Life quite literally began in water, and it emerged, he suggests, because of the "mysterious principle known as 'organization'"—the alchemy of water: "Water has merely leapt out of vapor and thin nothingness in the night sky to array itself in form." Second, he has in mind the "extension of the senses" that he experienced as he floated. He calls it "some kind of clairvoyant extension"—what we might think of as an imaginative or intuitive expansion of consciousness. But in terms of this chapter, it is a *magical* extension, related rather directly to the magic of water. Starting with the first primordial forms and after eons of evolution, the human brain emerged with its capacity to organize and imagine, and that enabled man to make sense of his world and to project himself across time and even into other lives. The principle of organization links the two. Nature organizes matter into *living* forms, and the mind (a natural phenomenon) organizes physical and mental phenomena into *meaningful* forms.[33]

Eiseley has chosen his words carefully. None but "magic" and "mystery," or elsewhere "miracle," "marvel," and "revelation," could convey for him the wonder and magnificence of nature or its inexplicableness. He wants to communicate *that* at the same time he is explaining the natural history of mankind. These are obviously dangerous words for a scientist, or a naturalist. No doubt Eiseley wants the emotional force and intellectual implications of the alchemical and religious meanings of the terms, but he is using them metaphorically, and not literally in any traditional sense. That is why the qualification "natural" with "magic," "miracle," or "revelation" is so important and significant. Otherwise, such words might evoke religious associations or suggest supernatural forces that Eiseley does not mean. He is trying to explain evolution, and simultaneously he wants to show that "there is no logical reason for the existence of a snowflake any more than there is for evolution."[34] Both evolution and the unknown are cause for wonder. To make his point, Eiseley searches for a language that can bridge the gap between materialistic and idealistic accounts, that somehow hovers between the known and the unknown, that transcends science, yet still retains scientific explanation as part of it. It is a difficult and delicate balance he seeks, but one absolutely necessary to tell his whole story.

At this level of thought, we are well into the figurative as well as the metaphysical dimensions of the book. Just as Eiseley made the Slit an important image and symbol, he has developed water into a major symbol. It evokes the organizing power of nature, the common substance of all life, and the physical unknown. It is also mysterious and magical in these senses. But water implies meanings even beyond these, for Eiseley gives it psychological, religious, and alchemical associations that make it shimmer with suggestions about origins, renewal, transformation, and ultimate mystery.

This chapter is the first to develop Eiseley's main scientific subjects. It continues to show the close connection in his mind between personal experience and the evolutionary history of mankind. And like the book as a whole, it extends scientific subjects into the general themes and other major dimensions of the book.

Extension is the key. Eiseley's method, his own imagination, and his understanding of evolution speak to it. In "The Flow of the River" he dramatizes an extraordinary extension of the senses, and in the next chapter he speaks of "the most enormous extension of vision of which life is capable: the projection of itself into other lives." This "lonely, magnificent power" stands at the center of *The Immense Journey.*[35]

"The Snout"

By looking closely at several of the essays in *The Immense Journey*, I wish to show how Eiseley extends and transforms his scientific story into a narrative of great thematic and artistic complexity and of wide human significance. What he does in each chapter fairly typifies the way the book as a whole achieves its personal, scientific, figurative, and metaphysical purposes. Each is rich with possibilities and surely open to more detailed literary analysis than this very selective treatment. But given the purpose—to describe the book by explaining the main features developed in several chapters—more detailed criticism would be inappropriate. The account is already intricate and involved enough. A look at one more chapter, therefore, should suffice to make the point. And rather than comment on it in any detail, I will simply focus on two important features: the movement of the narrative through time and from personal experience to evolutionary history, and the use of specific metaphors to make connections across time.

In the first part of the essay, Eiseley indicates that evolution is unfinished; nature is still busy with experiments. That knowledge gives him "a feeling of confidence,"[36] but as his report of a conversation with a friend shows, it worries his wife and quite frightens his friend: "'I don't know why, . . . I just mean they make you feel that way, is all. A fish belongs in the water. It ought to stay there—just as we live on land in houses. Things ought to know their place and stay in it, but those fish have got a way of sidling off. As though they had mental reservations and weren't keeping any contracts.'"[37] The story begins in the present, with a personal experience that leads Eiseley directly to his subject—the distant origin of human life and the transition of vertebrate life from land to water.

In the second part of the chapter, Eiseley shifts his attention to the conditions of life in the Paleozoic, 300 million years ago; it was a time of great change. The narrative here describes what might have happened as the Snout—a freshwater Crossopterygian living in swamps and tide flats—penetrated the land and somehow managed to survive. At this point Eiseley has journeyed far back into the geological past to describe the evolution of a Devonian fish—our ancestor. He dramatizes this movement of attention and the relationship between past and present by radically juxtaposing Snout and men:

> At times the slowly contracting circle of the water left little windrows of minnows who skittered desperately to escape the sun, but who died, nevertheless, in the fat, warm mud. It was a place of low life. In it the human brain began. . . .[38]

> It was a monstrous penetration of a forbidden element, and the Snout kept his face from the light. It was just as well, though the face should not be mocked. In three hundred million years it would be our own.[39]

These extraordinary images compress millions of years into human terms and enable Eiseley to possess time imaginatively, as well as to know and understand it.

In the third part of the essay, he speculates briefly about "what sort of creatures we, the remote descendents of the Snout, might be, except for that green quagmire." He is once again thinking in the present; but now he is considering humanity and not events in his personal life. He then turns directly back to the Devonian period and explains the way the Snout's brain evolved. Here he makes one of the most radical and startling juxtapositions in the entire book: "Out of the choked Devonian waters emerged sight and sound and the music that rolls invisible through the composer's brain." After that he brings us quickly back to the present, pointing out that "in the mangrove swamps by the Niger, fish climb trees and ogle uneasy naturalists who try unsuccessfully to chase them back to the water." Back in the present, Eiseley is attending to science and natural phenomena and not, for now, to autobiography.[40]

In the fourth part, he talks about the virtual impossibility of going back into the past: "No man can return across that threshhold." He also observes that the advance from sea to shore "was made by the failures of the sea":

> Some creatures have slipped through the invisible chemical barrier between salt and fresh water into the tidal rivers, and later come ashore; some have crept upward from the salt. In all cases, however, the first adventure into the dreaded atmosphere seems to have been largely determined by the inexorable crowding of enemies and by the retreat further and further into marginal situations where the oxygen supply was depleted. Finally, in the ruthless selection of the swamp margins, or in the scramble for food on the tide flats, the land becomes home.

The focus here is on current explanations of past events. Then Eiseley shifts his attention more explicitly back to the Paleozoic— "If we had been making zoological observations in the Paleozoic Age . . .," and with that he imagines what we might have seen and thought. Thus he does not simply talk about the past; he takes us, once again, back into it.[41]

In the last part of "The Snout," Eiseley returns to the present, to his own reading, conversations, personal discoveries, and beliefs, and, finally, to the meaning of nature's continuing experiments: "Perpetually, now, we search and bicker and disagree. The eternal form eludes us—the shape we conceive as ours. Perhaps the old road through the marsh should tell us. We are one of many appearances of the thing called Life; we are not its perfect image, for it has no image except Life, and life is multitudinous and emergent in the stream of time."[42] When the essay appeared originally in *Harper's* in 1950, there were two additional paragraphs at the end that described an experience he had "yesterday at the zoo." They brought the article back even more firmly into Eiseley's personal world.

In a rather complicated way, "The Snout" intertwines the past with the present; personal experience, observation, and commentary with scientific knowledge and interpretation; and a narrative and dramatic style with scientific explanation. Such movement of attention and alternating technique is typical, and in this chapter, the order of events and explanation is particularly expressive. It perfectly illustrates Eiseley's own description of his journey: "Forward and backward I have gone, and for me it has been an immense journey." His mind and imagination traveled over immense periods of time and through many worlds as he pursued both his own and his species' histories. By intertwining past and present and radically juxtaposing moments of time 300 million years apart, Eiseley suspends time and dramatizes the wholeness of his world and the remote past.

The Immense Journey is truly a rich and complex personal record of a long, unfinished journey through science and through the evolutionary history of mankind and of life on earth. The personal dimension is there in the autobiographical incidents, many of them drawn from Eiseley's experiences as a young fieldworker in Nebraska. It comes through in the sound of his voice as he tells his scientific story. It is revealed in his meditative, interpretive manner and in the extensions of scientific subjects into broad human themes. This personal dimension also emerges in the figurative and symbolic character of the book. Finally, it is there in the comprehensive imagination that fuses all of this into a seamless whole. Yet beyond these things, there exists a still deeper autobiographical dimension—the role science played in Eiseley's lifelong quest for personal wholeness. The book also reports that aspect of his life.

The quest began in a divided household and in the mind of an anxious and lonely child. It continued into an emotionally and economically deprived—and still lonely—youth. Running and hiding—either within himself or in nearby places—the boy began searching for what he never had had, struggling to define and preserve his very identity. As he grew, young Eiseley became more visibly unsettled, the journey more aimless and confused. He left high school at least once; he began riding trains cross-country; his father died; he could not finish college on time; he continued to feel anxious, depressed, threatened, confused, and alone. His poetry became part of his flight and quest. Through poetry, he not only tried to find his true voice and an acceptable vision of his own life and life in the Midlands; he was also looking for stability, a role, and a future—something that would reduce the fragmentation and confusion of his life.

The journey led Eiseley into the prairies and uplands of western Nebraska in search of fossils, and from there it took him on to science, where he discovered the "ideology" that reordered his life and gave him his past. Loren Eiseley's scientific journey was as much a search for his lost home as were his poetry, his aimless wandering across the country, or his childhood fantasies. By extending his sense of place deep into prehistory, by learning about man's origins in the far fields of his home territory, and by discovering the correspondences between his own personal history and the evolutionary history of mankind, Eiseley was beginning at last to find his home and himself. While his marriage remains the hidden factor in all of this, the commitments he made there and the love he expressed suggest a greater degree of self-possession than he had known before. When he declares, in "Obituary of a Bone Hunter," his independence even of orthodox science, Eiseley seems to recognize and accept his solitude. And on that he begins building his true voice and identity.

In *The Immense Journey*, Loren Eiseley portrays himself as a solitary scientist searching for his and our human origins. He dramatizes himself as an isolated and lonely man wandering through the world in search of his lost home. This mythic character and the psychological themes in Eiseley's autobiographical and poetic work express a common impulse. Frequently, for example, he cast himself as an orphan or as a changeling who was trying to restore his primordial relationship with nature or with his mother. This theme has obvious roots in his childhood, and even though Eiseley understood and accepted his homelessness, he nevertheless felt powerful longings for the home and mother he had never had.

This impulse to some extent directed his scientific attention and shaped his interpretation of the evolutionary record. In the book, for example, Eiseley explains that mankind's evolution has cut him off forever from his beginnings. In a sense we are all orphans. Eiseley experienced this in part as a great loss. This "fact"—man's isolation—is a fundamental feature of the current, synthetic theory of evolution, but it isn't necessary to interpret it precisely as Eiseley does. When he speaks in "The Slit" about the prairie-dog town and observes that we "were driven out of it once" and "can never go back,"[43] he is speaking as much about his own past as about mankind. He was deprived of an effective mother and a secure home, and as a result he always felt a sense of personal loss. Here the psychological themes and the scientific subject come together and lead to a version of evolution that expresses Loren Eiseley's personality.

The parallel between Eiseley's sense of his own psychic survival and his explanation of the Snout's place in evolution provides another example of the way psychological and scientific factors converge. Starting in a marginal childhood environment, Eiseley struggled out of one dead end after another to survive and actually flourish. One could describe his journey as "a stealthy advance made in suffocation and terror, amidst the leaching bite of [emotional] discomfort"—which *is* the way he described the Snout. In the marginal environments that the Snout endured, "the living suffer great extremes" and out of desperation make new starts. That also could describe Eiseley's life. In that same chapter, he speaks about the fish as a water-failure, and he suggests that its very failure enabled it to survive in a new element—partly by accident. Eiseley talked about himself similarly; he had a strong sense of the accidental character of his success.[44]

The science Eiseley learned helped him to understand his own life; where he implicitly sees himself in terms of the Snout or of evolutionary imagery in general, science is providing the metaphor or analogy. But the reverse holds true as well. Where he sees the Snout in terms of his own life, the psychological themes are determining the particular quality of the scientific subjects or interpretations. In a review of *The Unexpected Universe*, Theodosius Dobzhansky questioned Eiseley's notion that it is always the failures who survive. Dobzhansky may have misunderstood Eiseley; nevertheless, his disagreement suggests that Eiseley's assertion ("it was the failures who had always won") is at least partly an interpretation deriving from his own experience and way of being in the world.[45]

At the end of his essay about extraterrestrial life, "Little Men in Flying Saucers," Eiseley speculates that while intelligence may exist elsewhere in the universe, no beings like us exist anywhere: "There may be wisdom; there may be power; somewhere across space great instruments, handled by strange, manipulative organs, may stare vainly at our floating cloud wrack, their owners yearning as we yearn. Nevertheless, in the nature of life and in the principles of evolution we have had our answer. Of men elsewhere, and beyond, there will be none forever."[46] His conclusion is consistent with the principles of biological evolution that *The Immense Journey* explains.

When Eiseley speaks of intelligent life elsewhere, he says "may be" in his typically guarded, ambiguous way. The manner is characteristic, but the state of knowledge in the 1950s probably also required it. Now, however, a scientist like Carl Sagan can argue quite boldly, from statistical probability and current knowledge, that extraterrestrial intelligence, superior to ours, must exist. Although Eiseley and Sagan more or less agree on the principle, they differ significantly in their styles as well as in what they have come to know. The differences are instructive.

Besides writing about the virtual impossibility of evolutionary processes producing beings like us anywhere else, Eiseley writes about man's inconceivable loneliness. For him, the absence of "men elsewhere, and beyond" underscores man's isolation and intensifies his own parallel feelings. The last several paragraphs have considerable expressive force precisely because, rather than explore the possibility of intelligent life elsewhere, Eiseley has chosen instead to concentrate on loneliness. When Sagan writes about the possibilities of extraterrestrial intelligence, however, he does not propose that *men* exist elsewhere; but he does write about contact and implicitly about kinship, and not about loneliness. Perhaps only a deeply lonely man, with a past similar to Eiseley's, would read the record as Eiseley did. Once again, no matter how scientifically sound his conclusion may be, he interprets the evidence in his own psychological terms. That is perfectly consistent with his theory of science.

These convergences of psychological themes and scientific interpretations reflect fundamental psychological and perceptual correspondences. They are not simply examples of metaphor, analogy, or intellectual parallel. In fact, the themes and interpretations mutually determine and explain one another, though just how seems ultimately impossible to say, for cause, effect, priority, and sequences are obscured by the intricate and complex wholeness of Eiseley's life.

The Immense Journey completed a critical phase of Loren Eiseley's quest, for in it he found a way to intertwine all the strands of his life into a coherent personal and professional vision and into a strong new voice. By weaving together a comprehensive version of evolutionary history with his own personal universe, Eiseley publicly announced the outcome of the psychological and intellectual processes that had been at work for years. The ideology and the idiom were now complete, but by their very nature they would remain forever problematic.

NOTES

1. *Immense Journey*, p. 13.
2. Ibid., pp. 12-13.
3. The relevant correspondence cited in this chapter is in the Penn Archives.
4. The Penn Archives has a manuscript page of unknown date with two outlines for the book listing at least five chapters that Eiseley did not include at all in his final version. They were published fourteen years later in *The Night Country*.
5. *New York Herald Tribune Books*, Aug. 25, 1957.
6. H. J. Fleure, *MAN*, Nos. 316-20 (Nov., 1959), p. 201.
7. *Quarterly Review of Biology*, 34 (Sept., 1959), 237.
8. Obituary, *Philadelphia Inquirer*, July 11, 1977.
9. *Immense Journey*, pp. 6, 9-10.
10. Ibid., pp. 24, 20.
11. Ibid., p. 42.
12. Ibid., p. 46.
13. Ibid., pp. 49, 51, 53.
14. Ibid., p. 63.
15. Ibid., pp. 73-74.
16. Ibid., p. 75.
17. Ibid., p. 79.
18. Eiseley's account of the human brain is the part of *The Immense Journey* most out of date. In "The Dream Animal," at the end of a long discussion, he concludes: "It would appear, then, that within the very brief period between about five hundred thousand to one hundred fifty thousand years ago, man acquired the essential features of a modern brain. Admittedly the outlines of this process are dim, but all the evidence at our command points to this process as being surprisingly rapid" (p. 118). The evolution of the human brain was indeed rapid, but not so rapid as Eiseley proposed. Earlier dates for the emergence of man and somewhat later dates for continuing rapid evolution lengthen the time span during which brain evolution occurred. See, e.g., Karl W. Butzer, "Environment, Culture, and Human Evolution," *American Scientist*, 65 (Sept.-Oct., 1977), 572-84. I am grateful to Miles Richardson for the reference.
19. *Immense Journey*, pp. 122-23, 120, 124.
20. Ibid., p. 106.
21. Ibid., p. 125.
22. Ibid., p. 140.

23. Ibid., pp. 162, 158, 158, 162.
24. Ibid., p. 178.
25. There is an interesting scientific dimension to this, also. The theory of the triune brain suggests that Eiseley may not have just been imagining another tempo of time; he may in fact have found a way to let the R-complex of his mind dimly express itself. He may have been "sinking" down into a more primitive, reptilean part of his brain and then using his imagination to find words for it. Cf. Carl Sagan, "The Brain and the Chariot," in *The Dragons of Eden* (New York: Ballantine, 1977), pp. 51-79.
26. *Immense Journey*, p. 181.
27. Ibid., p. 210.
28. Ibid., pp. 13, 12.
29. Ibid., pp. 3, 4.
30. Ibid., p. 11.
31. Ibid., p. 14.
32. Ibid., pp. 16, 19.
33. Ibid., pp. 15, 26, 27, 17, 16.
34. Ibid., p. 27.
35. Ibid., p. 46.
36. Ibid., p. 47.
37. Ibid., p. 48.
38. Ibid., pp. 49-50.
39. Ibid., p. 51.
40. Ibid., pp. 52, 54.
41. Ibid., pp. 54-55, 56.
42. Ibid., p. 59.
43. Ibid., p. 7.
44. Ibid., pp. 54, 51.
45. Theodosius Dobzhansky, review of Loren Eiseley, *Unexpected Universe*, in *American Anthropologist*, 73 (1971), 305-6.
46. *Immense Journey*, p. 162.

11

The New Idiom

For the uses of life.

When Loren Eiseley said that he had "made no great discoveries. . . . There will be no further chances," he meant, of course, that he had made no great scientific discoveries, and for all of his professional achievement, evidently that was true. But he did make a remarkable discovery in the new idiom he achieved and in the personality he finally created. His acknowledgment of "failure" in one sense enabled him to identify and realize his true and original genius in another.

As a young poet Eiseley developed considerable control, complexity, and subtlety in his work and achieved a level of sensitivity and maturity that extended the significance of his poetry beyond the experience of a particular young man and region. He wrote well in the mid-1930s. Nevertheless, his work created no new poetic idiom, nor did it discover any new perspectives. The images, forms, and themes were all rather conventional. The evolution in his style reflected to some extent his increasing personal confidence and stability, but Eiseley did not discover in poetry a way of moving beyond certain emotional and psychic resolutions.

In science he seemed to find the order, system, and ideology he needed to insulate himself from the turmoil of his life. There he discovered control and explanations that confirmed his experience, gave it wider significance, and enabled him to escape the relative isolation of a lyric poet. As a member of a professional community, he developed a style appropriate to the impersonal and analytic conventions of science. But that style soon gave way to a more personal and fluent language. Eiseley was apparently trying to recover certain qualities of expression, feeling, and insight that he had developed as a poet but subdued as a scientist, and was trying also to expand the potential meanings of his prose. He was making the critical turn toward a language of continuity, of wholeness.

Kenneth Burke once proposed that "all terminologies [all discourses, let's say] must implicitly or explicitly embody choices between the principle of continuity and the principle of discontinuity."[1] These are basic themes or visions embedded in the discourse itself. Analytical discourses, like those in science and most other intellectual disciplines, typically develop terminologies that divide and separate and are thus discontinuous. Although science was his profession—at least his visible profession—Eiseley began to develop a language of continuity or wholeness to counter the discontinuities and fragmentation that he found in science and scientific discourse, as well as in himself.

For Eiseley, extension was the key, as I have already suggested. In "The Flow of the River" he speaks, for example, of an extraordinary extension of the senses that enables him to project himself across space ("It was then that I felt the cold needles of the alpine springs at my fingertips, and the warmth of the Gulf pulling me southward"), to range through time ("I was streaming over ancient sea beds thrust aloft where giant reptiles had once sported"), and to escape momentarily his own biological boundaries ("I *was* water and the unspeakable alchemies that gestate and take shape in water"). In "The Great Deeps" he writes about an "enormous extension of vision"—the ability of life to project itself into other lives. This quality of mind, one that keeps imagining itself across conventional and existential boundaries, enabled Eiseley to develop his unique voice and vision.

His new idiom can be characterized through the layers or dimensions he has so artistically intertwined in *The Immense Journey*: science, autobiography, figuration, and metaphysics. The layer of science is very clear. It is realized in the story of evolution that Eiseley tells—a direct, informed account that gives the book its narrative structure.

The autobiographical aspects are equally as clear. From the first chapter on, Eiseley is telling two stories—one about evolution, the species history, and one about himself from his personal experiences as a fieldworker to his discoveries of significance and relationship. Autobiography constitutes part of what he calls the "unconventional record" of the book.

Figuration or metaphor is, first, the dimension that gives interest, texture, and impact to Eiseley's style. Such dramatic metaphors as "out of the choked Devonian waters emerged sight and sound and the music that rolls invisible through the composer's brain" compress time and radically connect different species in a powerful and meaningful way. Through them, Eiseley helps us see *our* place in the story—not just as its end but as we are still connected to its origins. The metaphoric dimension also enables him to relate the two histories. The Slit in chapter 1 is but the first example. Actual place, occasion for explanation and speculation, and metaphor for time and for Eiseley's situation in time, the Slit helps intertwine all of the dimensions.

The metaphysical or speculative layer is associated most closely with the enormous extension of vision Eiseley speaks about. Although the later chapters seem more speculative than earlier ones, this layer is present throughout, beginning with Eiseley's thoughts about himself and time in "The Slit."

Eiseley has made explicit and functional aspects of discourse and of experience that are at best implicit or invisible, and often absent, in the writing of most scientists or poets. This alone suggests that he is not simply a scientist who writes well about science or about human values; nor is he simply a popularizer (if he is one at all) who explains science to others; nor is he just a writer who makes "poetry" out of science, thereby changing it into something else. His achievement of a new idiom is more considerable. The thematic and structural rhythms he created in *The Immense Journey* also help demonstrate that.

These rhythms reflect the movement of Eiseley's attention—the movement, in effect, of his mind—and thus define the underlying rhythms of his prose. They are, by way of summary:

1. The rhythm of the self, personal experience, and species experience in relation to scientific theory and knowledge. This is evident in "The Snout," where Eiseley reports a conversation with a friend and describes conditions of life in the Paleozoic. It also informs "The Slit," where Eiseley sets a specific personal experience in relation to observations about the Paleocene.

2. The rhythm of inward and outward movement. This is particularly evident in "The Flow of the River," where Eiseley writes about a specific place (he did walk along the banks of the Platte)

and then recounts his (magical) inward journey through time and space—all to make a particular point about origins. The essay seeks to explain that all life begins in water, and to make the point, as a scientific *and* a personal point, Eiseley narrates his own imaginative experience of those origins.

3. The rhythm of present, past, and (sometimes) future. This is evident in "The Slit," where we traced the narrative from the present into the past, back to the present, then into the future, and also in "The Snout," in which the movement of attention through time is even more complex.

4. The rhythm of intensiveness and extensiveness. This is manifest in the chapters on the brain in which Eiseley provides details of human brain development and also writes about man the dream animal. It functions in "The Snout," where Eiseley identifies a critical development in the brain of the Crossopterygian and also dramatizes the Snout's move from sea to land as "a monstrous penetration of a forbidden element" that in 300 million years would lead to the music in the composer's brain.

5. The rhythm of form and stability in relation to process and change. "The Great Deeps" illustrates this. Here, change and process (life reaching out) are the main themes, but they alternate with the concept of "the stability of the interior environment." We see balanced change and continuity, difference and similarity.

6. The rhythm of scientific "fact" and ethical or mythic significance. In "The Slit," for example, Eiseley explains the difference the brain made in isolating us from the rest of nature, then interprets that to mean that we are all castaways or orphans.

These rhythms are features of Eiseley's special idiom. Through them, he is able to intertwine the layers of his discourse, achieve the transformation of one into another, realize extensions of his senses and vision, and constitute a more comprehensive idiom and self than he had heretofore developed.

With the publication of *The Immense Journey*, Loren Eiseley was finally himself in name and in words, as well as in person. For at least thirty years, he had been trying to fit together a language and an identity. Although his achievement was still exploratory, he had in fact arrived at a certain complex equilibrium, represented by his professional accomplishments, the apparent stability of his personal life, and the new idiom he had created. Words had become not just a happy feature but a critical part of his life. Without them, Loren Eiseley would have been someone altogether different.

Earlier, Heinz Lichtenstein helped us understand the dynamics of Eiseley's problematic personality development. His theory of identity is relevant here, too, for Lichtenstein also understands the critical relationship between language and identity. Without words, one would be lost in silence, isolation, and ignorance. Moreover, his sense of identity, as indeterminant, open-ended, and tentative, is even more significant. While every person may indeed have an underlying and unchanging identity theme, beyond that there are almost unlimited possibilities for variation. Like art—or a style or an idiom—identity is an act of human creativity.

As the symbol-using animal, in Kenneth Burke's phrase, man builds up much of his reality through symbol systems. We have ascended from the realm of motion and matter to action and consciousness through symbols. We perceive and learn through them (they function as screens that both filter and project versions of reality); we act with symbols in effective and meaningful ways (as actions, words can have as much or more impact than physical acts); and in fact, we live in worlds constituted largely by symbols. To a great extent, therefore, we become what our words or discourses—our worlds—enable us to become.

In Eiseley's case this seems especially true. He was a man-of-words—and not just in a casual or simple vocational sense. He was a man-*of*-words, a person created by and through words in the most significant psychological and social senses. Like everyone else, Eiseley depended on language (and other symbolic systems) to organize his inner and outer worlds and identify their interdependence. But not everyone is so dependent on words as the writer—especially the writer who from youth onward was a confessional poet and an autobiographer, as well as an essayist and scientist. Not only did Eiseley achieve a language and an identity together, he realized each through the other. Idiom and identity were inseparably interwoven.

As a child Eiseley lived in virtual silence and solitude, and the "moment" when his father helped break that silence with words—eloquent and moving words, as Eiseley reports it—he began to grow. This was a prototypical experience in his life. Over and over, in one form or another, he experienced the rhythms of silence and sound, solitude and society, distance and relationship. In silence and solitude there is no possibility of human identity. In speech and society there obviously is.

Through words Loren Eiseley achieved a critical and always problematic balance between solitude and society, thereby satisfying, in one basic act, his own deepest needs for concealment and protection and his equally powerful needs for human contact. In his books and essays, he created a world that placed a barrier between himself and others and yet enabled him to speak and reveal himself at the same time. The world of words was a space where he could define himself and control his relationships. He could talk with others in a relatively intimate way but still stand at a distance or even be *absent* from these conversations. That was the trick—to simultaneously reveal and conceal, to stand at once at a distance and in relationship.

I realize now that in some way I threatened that delicate balance and violated that carefully created and controlled space. Eiseley told me as much when he quoted one of his reviewers because, as he said, "it has a bearing on the relationship between us": "Dr. Eiseley [the reviewer had written] is a man of closely-guarded passionate intensities and sensitivities, paradoxically and skilfully veiled even when he is revealing them."[2]

By trying to strike through the mask, I was attempting, in effect, to divide the man-of-words from the man behind them. That was not possible, for the one was realized only in the other. And without his written words, the man behind could and would say very little, and he understood that, too. "I have become my own 'fox at the woods edge,'" he warned in a letter, "looking on at humanity with curiosity, but always ready to vanish into a bush when the hunt comes in my direction. In other words, to a discerning eye, I am there in my books, more articulate and less limping than I would be in any personal interview."[3]

When Eiseley wrote the foreword to *Not Man Apart*, he identified what he called the paradox of Robinson Jeffers's demon— "to escape and not to love; to love and not escape." This was Eiseley's demon and agony, too. As a man-of-words, a man of his particular words and language, he could both love *and* escape, and thereby control his demon and lessen his agony.

In the end Loren Eiseley wrote, I believe, to avoid a fatal turn inward—inward into silence and loss of identity. Once he wrote movingly about two brilliant men who after considerable achievement lost their capacities to write. Of the first he says, "Only the pen was denied to him and so he passed toward his end, leaving behind the quick streak of a falling star that slips from sight. A genius in personal relationships, he was voiceless—somewhere a door had been softly, courteously, but inexorably closed within his brain. It would never open again within his lifetime."[4] Of the second, who eventually could not even answer letters, he says much the same thing: "Somewhere behind that door was a landscape we were never permitted to enter."[5] For Eiseley, their isolation and inarticulateness were virtually fatal.

A few pages later, he speaks of a fictional character who "'could not gain the art of letters and . . . had lost the art of humanity.' He was turning fatally inward as surely as those men whose stories I have recounted."[6] Although there were many times in his own life when he might have turned inward and away, Eiseley obviously never did. Each time, he managed somehow to speak and write, and as a writer, he achieved both the art of letters and the art of humanity.

NOTES

1. Kenneth Burke, *Language as Symbolic Action* (Berkeley and Los Angeles: University of California Press, 1968), p. 50.
2. Eiseley to Carlisle, Jan. 21, 1976.
3. Eiseley to Carlisle, Mar. 23, 1974.
4. *Night Country*, p. 205.
5. Ibid.
6. Ibid., p. 208.

Checklist

The following checklist includes all of Loren Eiseley's signed work I consulted up to *The Immense Journey*—poems, personal essays and stories, reviews and features, and scientific articles.

Many of Eiseley's early poems were recently collected in *All the Night Wings* (New York: Times Books, 1979), making them available to general readers. *All the Night Wings* also prints a number of unpublished poems as well, apparently made available to the editor by Mrs. Eiseley. My checklist includes over twenty poems not reprinted in *All the Night Wings*.

When I wrote chapter 4, none of Eiseley's early poems had been collected, and he would hardly acknowledge their existence—saying he didn't bother to keep track of his juvenilia. However, when I sent him the texts of over sixty of the poems, he thanked me and pointed out three or four that I had overlooked.

Most of Eiseley's early poems, essays, and reviews appeared in little magazines like *Prairie Schooner*, the *Midland*, *Voices*, and *Poetry*. Thanks to the Kraus Reprint Company, *Prairie Schooner* is available in many libraries. The *Midland* is available in large university libraries, especially in the Middle West. *Voices*, however, is very difficult to find. Only a few major repositories, such as the New York Public Library, have it. *Poetry* was a more national publication and is, therefore, fairly common in university libraries. Since most of Eiseley's scientific publications appeared in major professional journals, they are rather easy to find.

Poems

"Spiders," *Prairie Schooner*, 2, no. 2 (Spring, 1928), 92. Reprinted in *All the Night Wings*, p. 3.
"The Last Gold Penny," *Prairie Schooner*, 2, no. 4 (Fall, 1928), 242.
"The Quainter Dust," *Prairie Schooner*, 3, no. 2 (Spring, 1929), 160. Reprinted in *All the Night Wings*, p. 5.

"Waste," *Bozart*, 2, no. 4 (Mar.-Apr., 1929), 12.

"Poison Oak," *Prairie Schooner*, 3, no. 4 (Fall, 1929), p. 247. Reprinted in *All the Night Wings*, p. 6.

"The Deserted Homestead," *Poetry*, 35, no. 3 (Dec., 1929), 142-43.

"Warning to Lovers," *New York Herald-Tribune Books*, Jan. 26, 1930, p. 6. Reprinted in *All the Night Wings*, p. 9.

"Dusk Interval," *New York Herald-Tribune Books*, Apr. 13, 1930, p. 8.

"Bleak Upland" ("Against Lineage," "Upland Harvest," "Words to the Stoic," and "Be Glad, You Worshippers"), *Voices*, No. 55 (1930), pp. 158-60.

"One Remembering the Marshes," *Prairie Schooner*, 4, no. 2 (Spring, 1930), 78-80.

"Sonnet for Age," *New York Herald-Tribune Books*, June 15, 1930, p. 6. Reprinted in *All the Night Wings*, p. 15.

"The Poet Surveys His Garden," *Midland*, 16, no. 3 (May-June, 1930), 159. Reprinted in *All the Night Wings*, p. 10.

"Tasker's Farm," *Midland*, 16, no. 4 (July-Aug., 1930), 182-84. Reprinted in *All the Night Wings*, p. 11.

"Against Cities," *Prairie Schooner*, 4, no. 4 (Fall, 1930), 252.

"For a Lost Home," *Prairie Schooner*, 5, no. 2 (Spring, 1931), 157-58. Reprinted in *All the Night Wings*, p. 18.

"Toward Winter," *Voices*, Winter, 1931, p. 274. Reprinted in *All the Night Wings*, p. 17.

"Earthward," *Midland*, 18, no. 2 (June, 1931), 54. Reprinted in *All the Night Wings*, p. 21.

"Death Song for Two," *Prairie Schooner*, 5, no. 4 (Fall, 1931), 253.

"Branch of Stone," *Midland*, 19, no. 2 (Mar.-Apr., 1932), 34. Reprinted in *All the Night Wings*, p. 23.

"Coyote Country," *Midland*, 19, no. 2 (Mar.-Apr., 1932), 49. Reprinted in *All the Night Wings*, p. 22.

"Two Poems" ("Brief Song" and "Night Wakening"), *Voices*, Apr., 1932, p. 240. Reprinted in *All the Night Wings*, pp. 25-26.

"Whisper behind a Guide at the Cliff House," *Midland*, 19, no. 4 (July-Aug., 1932), 85. Reprinted in *All the Night Wings*, p. 27.

"Spring in This Town," *Midland*, 20, no. 2-3 (Mar.-Apr., May-June, 1933), 42.

"Fire in the Wind" ("If He Hears No Sound," "Sonnets for a Second Death" [4 sonnets], "Note at Midnight," and "Taste of Salt"), *Voices*, No. 69 (Apr.-May, 1933), pp. 16-20. Reprinted in *All the Night Wings*, pp. 35-39.

"Song for the Wolf's Coat," *Voices*, No. 71 (Aug.-Sept., 1933), p. 26. Reprinted in *All the Night Wings*, p. 40.

"Nocturne for Autumn's Ending," *Prairie Schooner*, 7, no. 4 (Fall, 1933), 165. Reprinted in *All the Night Wings*, p. 41.

"Fabric for the Moth" ("Fox Curse," "Word for the Frost," "Letter of Parting," "For the Tongueless," and "Portrait"), *Voices*, No. 74 (Feb.-Mar., 1934), 13-15. Reprinted in *All the Night Wings*, pp. 42-46. "Fox Curse" was reprinted in the *Literary Digest*, May 19, 1934, p. 35.

"Four Poems" ("Words for Forgetting," "Return to White Mountain," "Poem to Accompany a Poem," and "Incident in the Zoo"), *Prairie Schooner*, 8, no. 3 (Summer, 1934), 118-20. Reprinted in *All the Night Wings*, pp. 48-51. "Incident in the Zoo" was reprinted in the *Literary Digest*, Nov. 10, 1934, p. 32.

"Nocturne in Silver," *American Poetry Journal*, Mar., 1935, p. 15.

"Six Poems" ("Last Wing," "Things Will Go," "Now the Singing Is Done," "On the Pecos Dunes," "So with the Heart," and "Song without Logic"), *Voices*, No. 81 (Apr.-May, 1935), pp. 16-19. Reprinted in *All the Night Wings*, pp. 53-58. "Last Wing" was reprinted in the *Literary Digest*, June 22, 1935.

"Words on a Spring Road," *Prairie Schooner*, 9, no. 3 (Summer, 1935), 186. Reprinted in *All the Night Wings*, p. 52.

"Sonnet," *Prairie Schooner*, 9, no. 4 (Fall, 1935), 242. Reprinted in *All the Night Wings*, p. 59.

"Now in This Drowsy Moment," *Prairie Schooner*, 10, no. 4 (Winter, 1936), 251. Reprinted in *All the Night Wings*, p. 66.

"Five Poems" ("Hill Orchard in Spring," "Last Headland," "Out of This Crystal," "Compound," and "Masked Dance: Night Club"), *Voices*, No. 85 (Spring, 1936), pp. 30-32. Reprinted in *All the Night Wings*, pp. 60-64.

"Leaving September," *American Mercury*, 39, no. 153 (Sept., 1936), 90.

"Fox Way," *General Magazine and Historical Chronicle* (University of Pennsylvania), 39 (Jan., 1937), 191.

"These Are the Stars," *Prairie Schooner*, 12, no. 1 (Spring, 1938), 17. Reprinted in *All the Night Wings*, p. 67.

"Two Poems" ("Tasting the Mountain Spring" and "The Spider"), *Poetry*, 54, no. 6 (Sept., 1939), 316-17.

"Three Poems" ("Prairie Spring," "Never like Deer," and "Fishers"), *Prairie Schooner*, 15, no. 1 (Spring, 1941), 30-31. Reprinted in *All the Night Wings*, pp. 70-72.

"October Has the Heart," *Prairie Schooner*, 15, no. 3 (Fall, 1941), 151.

"Say It Is Thus with the Heart," *Prairie Schooner*, 16, no. 1 (Spring, 1942), 23.

"Winter Sign," *Prairie Schooner*, 17, no. 3 (Fall, 1943), 163.

"Winter Visitant," *Prairie Schooner*, 17, no. 4 (Winter, 1943), 218. Reprinted in *All the Night Wings*, p. 74.

"Credo," *Prairie Schooner*, 18, no. 3 (Fall, 1944), 199.

"The Trout," *Prairie Schooner*, 19, no. 4 (Winter, 1945), 323.

Personal Essays and Stories

"Autumn—A Memory," *Prairie Schooner*, 1, no. 4 (Oct., 1927), 238-39.

"Riding the Peddlers," *Prairie Schooner*, 7, no. 1 (Winter, 1933), 45-50.

"The Mop to K. C.," *Prairie Schooner*, 9, no. 1 (Winter, 1935), 33-39.

"Apes Almost Men," *Prairie Schooner*, 18, no. 3 (Fall, 1944), 170-76.

"There *Were* Giants," *Prairie Schooner*, 19, no. 3 (Fall, 1945), 189-93.

"Long Ago Man of the Future," *Harper's*, 194 (Jan., 1947), 93-96. An early version of "Man of the Future," *The Immense Journey*, pp. 127-41.

"Obituary of a Bone Hunter," *Harper's*, 195 (Oct., 1947), 325-29. Later published in *The Night Country*, pp. 181-91.

"Places Below," *Harper's*, 196 (June, 1948), 547-52. In *The Night Country* ("The Places Below"), pp. 15-27.

"Buzby's Petrified Woman," *Harper's*, 197 (Nov., 1948), 76-79. Included in "The Relic Men" in *The Night Country*, pp. 107-23.

"Fire Apes," *Harper's*, 199 (Sept., 1949), 47-55.

"Snout," *Harper's*, 201 (Sept., 1950), 88-92. In *The Immense Journey*, pp. 47-59.

"People Leave Skulls with Me," *Harper's*, 202 (May, 1951), 43-49. In *The Night Country* ("Barbed Wire and Brown Skulls"), pp. 91-104.

"Great Deeps," *Harper's*, 203 (Dec., 1951), 71-76. In *The Immense Journey* ("The Great Deeps"), pp. 29-46.

"The Flow of the River," *American Scholar*, 22 (1953), 451-58. In *The Immense Journey*, pp. 15-27.

"Secret of Life," *Harper's*, 207 (Oct., 1953), 64-68. In *The Immense Journey*, pp. 195-210.

"Was Darwin Wrong about the Human Brain?," *Harper's*, 211 (Nov., 1955), 66-70. In *The Immense Journey* ("The Real Secret of Piltdown"), pp. 79-94.

"Bird and the Machine," *Harper's*, 212 (Jan., 1956), 69-73. In *The Immense Journey*, pp. 179-93.

"The Judgment of the Birds," *American Scholar*, 25 (Spring, 1956), 151-60. In *The Immense Journey*, pp. 163-78.

Reviews and Features

"Crossroads," *Prairie Schooner*. A regular feature of the *Schooner* from Winter, 1929, through Spring, 1938.

"Wings in the Wilderness," *Voices*, Feb., 1932, pp. 153-54. Review of *Wings against the Moon* by Lew Sarett.

Review of *Mead & Mangel-Wurzel* by Grace Stone Coates. *Prairie Schooner*, 6, no. 2 (Spring, 1932), 175.

Review of *Hymn to Chaos* by Harold Vinal. *Prairie Schooner*, 6, no. 2 (Spring, 1932), 175-76.

"Music of the Mountain," *Voices*, No. 67 (Dec.-Jan., 1932-33), pp. 42-47. Review article about Robinson Jeffers.

"Stature against the Earth," *Voices*, No. 75 (Apr.-May, 1934), pp. 53-56. Review of *Give Your Heart to the Hawks* by Robinson Jeffers.

"Bard of the Rustic Art," *Voices*, No. 81 (Apr.-May, 1935), pp. 44-46. Review of *Man with a Bull-Tongue Plow* by Jesse Stuart.

Review of *Hurricane* by Harold Vinal. *Prairie Schooner*, 10, no. 2 (Summer, 1936), 165.

Review of *The Olive Field* by Ralph Bates. *Prairie Schooner*, 10, no. 4 (Winter, 1936), 315-16.

Review of *The Deer Come Down* by Edward Weismiller. *Prairie Schooner*, 11, no. 1 (Spring, 1937), 86.

Scientific Articles

"Paleontological Evidence for the Antiquity of the Scottsbluff Bison Quarry and Its Associated Artifacts" (with C. B. Schultz), *American Anthropologist*, 37, no. 2 (Apr.-June, 1935), 306-19.

"An Added Note on the Scottsbluff Quarry," *American Anthropologist*, 38, no. 3 (July-Sept., 1936), 521-24.

"Index Mollusca and Their Bearing on Certain Problems of Prehistory: A Critique," in *Twenty-fifth Anniversary Studies of the Philadelphia Anthropological Society*, ed. D. S. Davidson (Philadelphia: University of Pennsylvania Press, 1937), pp. 77-93.

"Significance of Hunting Territory Systems of the Algonkian in Social Theory" (with F. G. Speck), *American Anthropologist*, 41, no. 2 (Apr.-June, 1939), 269-80.

"Pollen Analysis and Its Bearing upon American Prehistory: A Critique," *American Antiquity*, 5, no. 2 (Oct., 1939), 115-40.

"Post-Glacial Climatic Amelioration and the Extinction of *Bison taylori*," *Science*, 95, no. 2478 (June 26, 1942), 646-47.

"The Folsom Mystery," *Scientific American*, 167, no. 6 (Dec., 1942), 260-61.

"Archaeological Observations on the Problem of Post-Glacial Extinctions," *American Antiquity*, 8, no. 3 (Jan., 1943), 209-17.

"Pseudo-fossil Man," *Scientific American*, 168, no. 3 (Mar., 1943), 118-19.

"Who Were Our Ancestors?," *Scientific American*, 168, no. 5 (May, 1943), 212-13.

"Some Paleontological Inferences as to the Life-Habits of the Australopithicine," *Science*, 98, no. 2533 (July 16, 1943), 61-62.

"A Neglected Anatomical Feature of the Foxhall Jaw," *Transactions of the Kansas Academy of Science*, 46 (1943), 57-59.

"Racial and Phylogenetic Distinctions in the Intertemporal Interangular Index," *Transactions of the Kansas Academy of Science*, 46 (1943), 60-65.

"Did Folsom Bison Survive in Canada?," *Scientific Monthly*, 56 (1943), 468-72.

"What Price Glory? The Counterplaint of an Anthropologist," *American Sociological Review*, 8, no. 6 (Dec., 1943), 635-37.

"An Extreme Case of Scaphocephaly from a Mound Burial near Troy, Kansas" (with C. Willet Alsing), *Transactions of the Kansas Academy of Science*, 47, no. 2 (Dec., 1944), 241-55.

"Indian Mythology and Extinct Fossil Vertebrates," *American Anthropologist*, 47, no. 2 (Apr.-June, 1945), 318-20.

"The Mastodon and Early Man in America," *Science*, 102, no. 2640 (Aug. 3, 1945), 108-10.

"Myth and Mammoth in Archaeology," *American Antiquity*, 11, no. 2 (Oct., 1945), 84-87.

"The Fire Drive and the Extinction of the Terminal Pleistocene Fauna," *American Anthropologist*, 48, no. 1 (Jan.-Mar., 1946), 54-59.

"Men, Mastodons, and Myth," *Scientific Monthly*, 62 (1946), 517-24.

"The Fire and the Fauna," *American Anthropologist*, 49, no. 4 (Oct.-Dec., 1947), 678-80.

"Land Tenure in the Northeast," *American Anthropologist*, 49, no. 4 (Oct.-Dec., 1947), 680-81.

"Early Man in South and East Africa," *American Anthropologist*, 50, no. 1 (Jan.-Mar., 1948), 11-17.

"Antiquity of Modern Man," *Scientific American*, 179, no. 1 (July, 1948), 16-19.

"Fossil Man: A Personal Credo," *American Journal of Physical Anthropology*, 10, no. 1 (Mar., 1952), 1-6.

"Program on the Darwin Collection . . . ," *Proceedings of the American Philosophical Society*, 98, no. 6 (Dec., 1954), 449-52.

"The Reception of the First Missing Links," *Proceedings of the American*

Philosophical Society, 98, no. 6 (Dec., 1954), 453-65.

"The Paleo-Indians: Their Survival and Diffusion," in *New Interpretations of Aboriginal American Culture History* (Washington: Anthropological Society of Washington, 1955), pp. 1-11.

Index

Relationships of members of the Eiseley family to Loren Eiseley are shown in parentheses after their names.

"Against Lineage," 59-60
Aiken, Conrad, 59
Aldrich, Bess Streeter, 51, 52
All the Strange Hours, 3, 7, 25, 26, 30, 89-90, 100-101, 121, 143, 147
Alsing, C. Willet, 125
American Anthropologist, 123, 129, 134, 143
American Mercury, 58, 122
American Museum of Natural History, 119
American Poetry Journal, 58
American Scholar, 152
Anthropology: Eiseley's knowledge of, 104-9; function for Eiseley, 88; significance to Eiseley, 109-10
"Antiquity of Modern Man," 152
"Apes Almost Man," 131-33
Atlantic Monthly, 54
Auden, W. H., 108-9
Austin, Mary, 58, 97
Autobiography, 168-69, 182
"Autumn—A Memory," 44-45, 57, 62, 79

"Be Glad, You Worshippers," 60-63, 67
Best Poems of 1942, 59
"The Bird and the Machine," 84, 152, 165
"Bleak Upland," 59-62, 67-68
Blue, Emery, 82, 89
Boas, Franz, 99

Boy and Girl Tramps of America, 31
Bozart, 45
Brinnin, John Malcolm, 58
Buettner-Janusch, John, 147-48, 158
Burke, Kenneth, xii, 182, 185
"Busby's Petrified Woman," 142
Bynner, Witter, 58

Cather, Willa, 13, 52
Christian Science Monitor, 155
Clark, Carroll D., 118, 119
Clemens, Samuel, 151
"Coyote Country," 18, 68, 87
The Crack in the Absolute, 153. *See also The Immense Journey*
"Credo," 141-42
"Crossroads," 43, 45-49

Darwin's Century, 147, 155
"Death in Autumn," 44
de la Mare, Walter, 59
Depression (economic): impact on Nebraska, 18; and Eiseley's personal depression, 36
"The Deserted Homestead," 18, 58, 61-62
The Dial, 57
"Did Folsom Bison Survive in Canada?," 127
Dobzhansky, Theodosius, 177
"The Double," 78-79
"The Dream Animal," 154-62
Duke. *See* Tachibana, Francis
Dyersville, Iowa, 4

"Earthward," 63-64, 67-68

Eberhart, Richard, 59
Eiseley, Charles Frederick (grandfather), 12, 14
Eiseley, Clyde Edwin (father), 6, 135;
  relationship with Daisy Eiseley, 2;
  Loren's affection for, 3, 5, 151;
  legacies to Loren, 5, 6, 9; as actor, 6;
  economic difficulties, 6, 8, 18; death,
  7, 24-25, 73
Eiseley, Daisy Corey (mother), 144;
  physical and emotional problems,
  3-4, 96; Loren's feelings toward, 3, 23
Eiseley, Loren Corey: early years, 1-9;
  family heritage, 6, 11; changes name,
  150-51; personal history summarized,
  175-76
—relationships: with author, ix-xi, xiii,
  186; with parents, 2; with mother, 3-4,
  23, 144; with father, 3, 5, 21-23, 66,
  151; with grandmother Corey, 22, 23;
  with wife, 116-17, 120
—roles: as man-of-words, xii, 184-87;
  as regionalist, 9, 13-14, 62; as poet,
  26, 46-49, 62, 75-76, 144-45; as writer,
  62, 127, 129, 142-44, 155, 158, 167-68,
  176-78, 182-84; as anthropologist, 88,
  119, 135; as orphan, 112, 176
—states of mind: loneliness, 1, 2, 7, 8,
  86, 101, 176-79; internal conflicts,
  29-30, 37, 79, 113; dislocation, 36;
  depression, 36, 67; melancholy, 46-
  47; sense of mortality, 46-47; pain, 67;
  reflected in poetry, 67, 72-74
—needs: for flight or escape, 2, 4, 7, 18,
  20, 21, 25, 29, 36, 37, 63, 81, 113; for
  love, 9; for money, 134; for home and
  security, 135
—education: childhood ownership of
  books, 6; college, 25-26, 40; master's
  thesis, 105-6; dissertation, 106-8
—crises, 21-38, 138, 143-45
—physical problems, 22-25, 96, 143-44
—fears: of dying, 24, 25, 29; of illness,
  96; of poverty, 143; of deafness, 143-
  44
—achievements: as scientist, 145; as
  writer, 175, 178-79, 181-82; as person,
  184-87
See also Fieldwork; Identity; Language;
  Place; Science; Style; Time; and titles
  of individual works

Eiseley, Mabel Langdon (wife), 98, 121;
  relationship with Loren Eiseley, x,
  120; prepares "Crossroads," 45;
  marries Loren Eiseley, 116
Erikson, Erik, xii
Extension, 170-72, 182
"An Extreme Case of Scaphocephaly
  from a Mound Burial near Troy,
  Kansas," 125
Evolution, 158-66, 179n18

"The Face of the Lion," 1, 3
Faust, Richard A. ("Ricky"), 95, 97, 99
Fieldwork, 72, 80-91
Figuration, 168, 182-83
"Fire Apes," 142
"Fire in the Wind," 65-68
The Firmament of Time, 110, 147-48
Fischer, John, 152-53
Fletcher, John Gould, 58
"The Flow of the River," 152, 159,
  162-72, 182
"The Folsom Mystery," 125
Forum, 54
"Fox Curse," 65
Frederick, John T., 57
Frontier (Nebraska), 51-52
Frontier (magazine), 45, 53-54
Frost, Robert, 48

Garland, Hamlin, 52
"Graveyard Studies," 44
"The Great Deeps," 142, 151, 152, 160,
  182

Harper's, 54, 134, 142
Haydn, Hiram, 153-54
Hoffman, Frederick J., 57
"How Flowers Changed the World,"
  157, 161-62

Identity: maintenance of, in early years,
  19; crisis, 42-43; as theme, 42-43; role
  of science in, 111-13; wholeness of,
  175-79; and achievement of language,
  176, 184-87. See also Language;
  Lichtenstein, Heinz
The Immense Journey, 110, 131, 143,
  146, 147; style, 134, 158, 169-72,
  175-78, 182-83; discussed, 150-79; as
  unconventional record, 150, 166-75;

history of composition, 151-55; reviews, 155-58; convergence of qualities and themes, 158, 169-72, 176-78; personal dimension, 158, 175-78; story of evolution, 158-66
"Incident in the Zoo," 65
"Index Mollusca and Their Bearing on Certain Problems of Prehistory: A Critique," 107
"The Innocent Fox," 65

Jeffers, Robinson, 49-50, 92, 118, 186
"The Judgment of the Birds," 152, 154, 164

Kansas, University of, 74, 116, 118-29
Kinkaiders, 17, 51
Konecky, Eugene, 54
Korn, Lou, 95
Kramer, Tom, 33
Krutch, Joseph Wood, 156

Langdon, Mabel. See Eiseley, Mabel
Language: functions of, for Eiseley, xii, 9, 184-87; gift of, from father, 6, 185; and identity, 176, 184-87. See also New idiom; Style
"The Last Gold Penny," 26
Leakey, Richard, 162
Leaves of Grass, 151
"Leaving September," 58, 69
Lichtenstein, Heinz, xii; on identity, 19, 185
Lincoln, Nebraska, 21, 73; growth of, 15; influence of, on Eiseley, 15, 16
Literary Digest, 58, 65
"Little Men in Flying Saucers," 164, 177
The Little Review, 57
"Long Ago Man of the Future," 151
"Lost Nature Notebooks of Loren Eiseley," xi-xii
Love: in Eiseley's poems, 69-75; and science, 116-17

MAN, 156-57
Manhunt, 152. See also The Immense Journey
"Man of the Future," 151, 163
Man-of-words, xii, 185-86. See also Identity; Language
"The Maze," 154, 162

Mencken, H. L., 58
Metaphor, 167-68
Metaphysics, 168, 182
Midland, 26, 45, 53-54, 57, 58
Missouri Pacific Railroad, 34, 35
"The Mist on the Mountain," 2
Monroe, Harriet, 58
"The Mop to K. C.," 27-30
Morrill, Charles H., 81
Morrill Paleontological Expedition, 80, 88
"The Most Perfect Day in the World," 26
Moult, Thomas, 59
"Myth and Mammoth in Archaeology," 129

Names: significance of form, 150-51
Nebraska, 27, 38, 79, 80; influence of, on Eiseley, 14, 16, 17, 55; Kinkaiders, 17; as last frontier, 51-52; life unchanged from 1850s, 62; and fossil hunting, 81
Nebraska, University of, 21, 73
Nebraska Federal Writers' Project, 73, 98
Nebraska State Museum, 16, 27, 38, 79, 80
Nebraska Territory, 9, 12-14, 18
New idiom, 72; and identity, 176, 184-87; complete, 179; analyzed, 181-87; components, 182-83; rhythms, 183-84. See also Language
New Mexico Quarterly Review, 57
New York Herald-Tribune Books, 58, 155
New York Times, 155-56
The Night Country, 3, 138, 142
"Note at Midnight," 66-67, 87
Not Man Apart, 186
"Now the Singing Is Done," 70-72

Oberlin College, 122, 123, 130-31, 135
"Obituary of a Bone Hunter," 138-41, 145, 148, 154, 176
O'Brien, Edward J., 53-54
"October Has a Heart," 59
"On the Pecos Dunes," 72, 110
"Other Dimensions," 78-79

"Paleontological Evidence...," 104-5

Paleontology, 104-10
Panic of 1873, 13
Parnassus, 45
Pennsylvania, University of, 38, 73, 120;
    Eiseley as student, 94-98, 99-100, 103-
    4; Eiseley as chair of anthropology
    department, 99, 135; master's thesis,
    105-6; dissertation, 106-8
"People Leave Skulls with Me," 142
Philadelphia, 73
Place: influence on Eiseley, 13-19
    passim, 55, 90-92; as inner landscape,
    16, 17, 90; Eiseley's sense of, 49,
    108-9; and time, 108-9. *See also*
    Nebraska
"Places Below," 142
Poetry, 26, 58
"Pollen Analysis and Its Bearing upon
    American Prehistory: A Critique,"
    107
Prairie Schooner, 38, 122, 138; Eiseley
    joins staff, 26; "Crossroads," 43, 45-
    49; early years, 43-55; Eiseley's
    reviews in, 48-49; Eiseley's attitude
    toward, 50; as regional magazine, 50-
    52, 54, 57
Prescott, Russell T., 51
Price, Grace (aunt), 89
Price, William Buchanan ("Buck")
    (uncle), 88-89, 102-3, 113

Quarterly Review of Biology, 157-58

The Rat (friend), 8, 15
"The Real Secret of Piltdown," 152,
    154, 162
Regionalism: and *Prairie Schooner*, 50,
    54; limits of, 54
"The Relic Man," 84
"Review of Paleontological
    Evidence...," 105-6
Rhythm: in Eiseley's writing, 183-84
Ricky. *See* Faust, Richard A.
Riding the rails, 30-36

Sagan, Carl, 178
Sandburg, Carl, 52
Sandoz, Mari, 51, 52
Saturday Review, 155

"Say It Is Thus with the Heart," 74, 76,
    110
Schultz, C. Bertrand, 79, 81, 82, 84, 85,
    89, 98, 125; on Eiseley's papers, xi;
    influence of, on Eiseley, 80; and
    Nebraska State Museum, 80; co-
    author with Eiseley, 104-5
Schultz, Marian, 82, 84-85
Science: role of, in Eiseley's develop-
    ment, 69, 109-13, 114, 175-76;
    Eiseley's attitude toward, 102, 112-
    13, 134, 141, 145-46, 167; Eiseley's
    concept of, 102, 138, 146-48, 167,
    176-79; Eiseley's achievements in,
    109, 145; as complement to love, 117;
    and Eiseley's style, 129, 181; Eiseley's
    failures in, 138-41; as heresy, 146-47;
    professional response to Eiseley, 146-
    48
Science (journal), 123
Scientific American, 123, 125, 126, 131,
    143, 152
Scientific Monthly, 123, 127, 131
Sears, Paul B., 107
"The Secret of Life," 151, 165
Shepard family (relatives), 96, 120, 144
"Significance of Hunting Territory
    Systems in Social Theory," 103
Silence, 144, 185-87. *See also* Voice
"The Slit," 154, 159, 167-68, 176
Smith, H. T. U., 119
Smithsonian Institution, 73
"The Snout," 142, 151, 160, 172-75
Social Science Research Council:
    awards grant to Eiseley, 119
"Song for the Wolf's Coat," 64
"Song without Logic," 73
"Sonnets for a Second Death," 66-67
South Party, 27, 79-80, 82-86, 89
Southwest Review, 57
Speck, Frank, 113, 114, 119, 122, 135;
    life and career, 95, 99-103; relation-
    ship with Eiseley, 96, 99, 100-103
Spender, Stephen, 59
"Spiders," 57
"Spring in This Town," 87
"The Starthrower," 69, 111
Style, 106, 125-26, 129, 131-34, 144-45,
    152, 181, 182

Suckow, Ruth, 52
Swanson, C. P., 157
Symbol systems, 185

Tachi. *See* Tachibana, Francis A.
Tachibana, Francis A. ("Duke,"
  "Tachi"), 97-99
"There *Were* Giants," 131, 133-34
"Three Indices of Quaternary Time: A
  Critique," 104, 106-8
Tillotson, Geoffrey, 59
"Timberline," 40-42
Time: and space, 90-92; Eiseley's sense
  of, 108-9; significance of, for Eiseley,
  109-11
TLS, 155, 156
"Toads and Men," 26
Tracy, Henry, 122
Trains, 27-36, 73
*Transactions of the Kansas Academy of
  Science*, 123-25, 126, 129
"The Trap," 26
Twain, Mark, 151

The Unexpected Universe, 7, 65, 69, 99,
  110, 111, 177
"Upland Harvest," 60

Vinal, Harold, 48, 58, 97
Voice, 144-45, 152, 178. *See also* Silence
Voices, 26, 45, 57, 58, 65, 122; Eiseley's
  reviews in, 49-50

Waiting for Nothing, 33, 35
"Was Darwin Wrong about the Human
  Brain?," 152, 154
Weismiller, Edward, 48
Wescott, Glenway, 58
Whitman, Walter, 151
Williams, William Carlos, 58
Wimberly, Lowry C., 43, 46, 51, 53, 86,
  95, 97, 98, 102
"Winter Sign," 74-75, 76
Wittke, Carl, 130, 131
"Word for the Frost," 68, 69
"Words for Forgetting," 69

A Note on the Author

E. Fred Carlisle, born in Delaware, Ohio, on March 20, 1935, studied English and American literature at Ohio Wesleyan University (B.A., 1956), the Ohio State University (M.A., 1957), and Indiana University (Ph.D., 1963). Formerly professor of English and chairman of the department at Michigan State University, he is presently serving there as assistant to the president of the university. In addition to the first two critical articles about Loren Eiseley, Carlisle is the author of *The Uncertain Self: Whitman's Drama of Identity* and other articles on American literature, and co-editor of the anthology *American Prose and Poetry*.

INDEXED IN

MLA